Female Spectators

QUESTIONS FOR FEMINISM

Edited by Michèle Barrett, Annette Kuhn, Anne Phillips and Ann Rosalind Jones, this socialist feminist series aims to address, in a lively way and on an international basis, the wide range of political and theoretical questions facing contemporary feminism.

Other Titles in the Series

UNEQUAL WORK by Veronica Beechey

THE WEARY SONS OF FREUD by Cathérine Clément

THE POLITICS OF DIVERSITY: FEMINISM, MARXISM AND NATIONALISM edited by Roberta Hamilton and Michèle Barrett

FEMALE SEXUALIZATION: A COLLECTIVE WORK OF MEMORY by Frigga Haug and others

SEA CHANGES: CULTURE AND FEMINISM by Cora Kaplan

CONSUMING FICTION by Terry Lovell

ABORTION AND WOMAN'S CHOICE: THE STATE, SEXUALITY AND REPRODUCTIVE FREEDOM by Rosalind Pollack Petchesky

READING THE ROMANCE: WOMEN, PATRIARCHY AND POPULAR LITERATURE by Janice A. Radway

THE PIRATE'S FIANCÉE: FEMINISM, READING, POSTMODERNISM by Meaghan Morris

GRAFTS: FEMINIST CULTURAL CRITICISM edited by Susan Sheridan

Female Spectactors

Looking At Film and Television

◆

Edited by

E. DEIDRE PRIBRAM

VERSO

London · New York

First published by Verso 1988
Second impression 1990
Third impression 1992
This collection © 1988 E. Deidre Pribram
Individual contribution © the authors

Verso
UK: 6 Meard Street, London W1V 3HR
USA: 29 West 35th Street, New York, NY 10001-2291

Verso is the imprint of New Left Books

British Library Cataloguing in Publication Data

Female spectators : looking at film and
    television. — (Questions for feminism).
    1. Cinema films — Feminist viewpoints
    I. Pribram, E. Deidre II. Series
    791.43

    ISBN 0-86091-922-6

US Library of Congress Cataloging in Publication Data

Female spectators : looking at film and television / edited by E.
    Deidre Pribram.
        p.   cm. — (Questions for feminism)

    Bibliography: p.
    1. Feminism and motion pictures 2. Motion picture audiences.
    3. Women in motion pictures. 4. Television and women.
    5. Television viewers. 6. Women in television. I. Pribram, E.
    Deidre. II. Series.
    PN1995.9.W6F45 1988
    791.4′088042—dc19

Typeset by Leaper & Gard Ltd, Bristol
Printed in Great Britain by Dotesios Ltd, Trowbridge, Wiltshire

Contents

Acknowledgements

Permission to reprint Teresa de Lauretis's essay, 'Aesthetic and Feminist Theory: Rethinking Women's Cinema', was kindly given by *New German Critique* where it first appeared in no. 34 (1985). An expanded version of Ann Kaplan's essay, 'Whose Imaginary? The Television Apparatus, the Female Body and Textual Strategies in Select Rock Videos on MTV', can be found in *Rocking Around the Clock: Postmodernism and Consumer Culture in Music Television,* London and New York: Methuen, 1987. An earlier version of Jacqueline Bobo's essay, '*The Color Purple*: Black Women as Cultural Readers', appeared in *Jump Cut* no. 33 (1988).

I wish to thank First Run Features for the still from Lizzie Borden's *Born in Flames,* and Madonna and Warner Brothers Records for use of stills from 'Material Girl'.

My appreciation goes to all the volume's contributors for their hard work, co-operation and sustained enthusiasm. I also wish to extend my thanks to the editoral board of Questions for Feminism. Finally, thank you to Timothy Corrigan for initial faith, ongoing support and access to an infinite source of good advice.

E. Deidre Pribram
May 1988

Introduction

E. Deidre Pribram

How have we come to perceive all forms of filmic gaze as male when women have always taken up their proportionate share of seats in the cinema? How have we come to understand cinematic pleasure (narrative, erotic, and so on) as pleasurable to the male viewer, but not the female? Why have we failed to see our own presence in the audience when women have always watched – and loved – film? Questions of pleasure and spectatorship, as they relate to women, arise out of recent work in feminist film theory. Or rather, they arise as omissions in these theoretical analyses. All too frequently, women's participation in the 'cinematic experience' has been neglected or entirely overlooked.

In the early and mid-1970s, many feminist film-makers and film theorists began to discuss women's historical and cultural position as one of absence from, or marginalization to, dominant cultural forms. Using psychoanalytic and semiotic models,[1] they theorized that women have been defined in masculine culture as lack and as Other. Woman is not a subject in her own right but the object by which the patriarchal subject can define himself. Mainstream cinema's contradictory/complementary representations of women as either idealized objects of desire or as threatening forces to be 'tamed' are not attempts to establish female subjectivity but rather reflect the search for male self-definition.[2] Popular forms of filmic discourse, therefore, are said to 'belong' to the patriarchy; women are silent, without language or voice. Filmic gaze, in terms of both gender representation and gender address, also 'belongs' to the male, leaving the female audience to identify with either the male-as-subject or the female-as-object. In this analysis women are left with no active spectatorial position at all. Any pleasure the female spectator

1

derives from classic realist cinema is false because it is based on woman as object of someone else's desire.

In the 1970s and into the early 1980s, feminist film-makers and theorists, seeking to create new forms outside and beyond those historically known to us, worked towards denying traditional pleasure in film. The resulting work was an attempt to create an alternative cinema in which women were engendered as subjects, and which thus made possible a female spectatorial position. While still indebted to the work of this feminist avant-garde, however, more recent feminist analysis and production have found that these earlier models pose considerable problems.

Freudian and Lacanian psychoanalytic theories have been central to cinema studies in recent years because they have helped forge a link between cultural forms of representation, such as film, and the acquisition of subject identity in social beings.[3] Feminist appropriations of these psychoanalytic models, which connect dominant ideology with bourgeois patriarchy – the individualized male subject formed and re-affirmed through the playing out of the Oedipal drama – have aided our understanding of the existing cultural order. However, they have proven less helpful in subverting, or creating alternatives to, that order. One weakness lies in the fact that many versions of psychoanalysis hypothesize a development pattern for language and subject identity which occurs across all time and across all cultural groups, a pattern established initially in infancy within the nuclear family unit. That is to say, 'self image' is regarded as acquired in uniform manner for members of each gender based upon their respective roles in the Oedipal struggle. Thus while psychoanalytic theories may succeed in recognizing gender as a primary cause of subject formation and social division, they simultaneously fail to address the formation and operation of other variables or differences amongst individuals, such as race and class.

In addition, the transhistorical nature of psychoanalytic models – the presumption that they apply equally across all time and instances – leaves them open to justifiable charges of inaccuracy and inflexibility. When psychoanalysis is applied to film, the potential for theorizing alternative readings or interpretations within any given text is inhibited by a denial of viewing *contexts*: no place is allowed for shifts in textual meaning related to shifts in viewing situation. As a result, varying social groups – white women or women of colour, lower, middle or upper-class women – are readily assumed to have the same viewing experience. At the same time, audiences of differing historical periods and circumstances – a contemporary audience viewing a contemporary work, a contemporary audience viewing a past work, a past audience viewing a work of its own time – are all assumed to be positioned by, and therefore to interpret, a text in the same manner.

Following the psychoanalytic–semiotic argument, then, classic realist cinema – by addressing woman as non-subject – eliminates the possibility of an 'authentic' female spectator. And further, by repressing the fact that women are historically and socially constituted (and therefore differing) subjects, the argument also precludes the possibility of diversity *among* women as female spectators.

Feminist appropriations of psychoanalytic models are useful, however, to the extent that their application is in keeping with the goals of a feminist agenda. In a society which has formalized, as its centre-piece, the white bourgeois male, feminist efforts have focused on the need to open up socio-cultural spaces to include previously excluded or marginalized subgroups. The concept of sexual difference which describes a binary structure of subject/object, in which object function produces subject validation, has seemed an accurate model of what is – for those excluded from it – a dysfunctional system. And it has also pointed the way to the necessity for a more flexible system in which a multiplicity of subjects can operate in a simultaneous and mutually satis-factory manner. But while the concept of sexual difference seems to account for what has appeared to be, throughout historical memory, the systematic exclusion of women (amongst others) from the political, economic and cultural life of Western society, the theories within which the concept is formulated restrict the means to envision alternatives. For if, as some psychoanalytic theories appear to suggest, social subjects are determined, through family relations and language acquisition, *prior* to the introduction of other considerations, including race, class, personal background or historical moment, the social construct thus described is a closed system unamenable to other subject formations. And indeed, feminist applications of psychoanalytic theory have described the ideology of bourgeois patriarchy as not only dominant, but 'monolithic'. A notion of ideology which implies dominance to, and therefore co-existence with, other ideologies leaves open the possibility of inroads by alternative or minority groups: but the concept of monolithic ideology suggests a unified and unyielding structure. The meanings of a filmic text, which can be said to reflect/remake the ideologies of the culture from which it springs, are also seen as closed, fixed in the playing out of the Oedipal drama over all time and in all instances, unavailable to alternative, variable or multiple readings.

While feminist theory generally accepted the notion of a 'monolithic' ideology, no distinction was made between the social constructs described by the theory and the theoretical constructs which were doing the describing; and doing so in such a way as to preclude the possibility of cultural debate or change. Psychoanalysis, which seemed able to explain existing social – or at least psychic – structures, could do so only in terms that implied their very inevitability. No matter what the specifics, women are relegated to playing out 'the same old story', living out the same gender relations.

This may have been a factor in the decision by many feminist film-makers not to participate in dominant cultural forms. The closed system/closed text formulated by theoretical arguments based in psychoanalytic theory left few points of entry for alternative represent-ations of women. The ability to critique was not met by an equal ability to create. The logical extension of arguments surrounding women's exclusion from popular cinema was that filmic gaze, discourse and pleasure belonged inevitably to the male. The only answer was to establish an alternative to this patriarchal cinema.

But women's participation in popular culture on the basis of these theoretical arguments embodies an impossible contradiction. For instance, women have long critiqued our exclusion from the centres of cultural production. Except in rare instances, women have not been involved as directors, producers, technicians, or in any other capacity of significant decision-making in the production of mainstream film. To define popular cultural activity as belonging to the patriarchy is to suggest therefore that women who do participate in mainstream produc-tion are being co-opted by dominant ideology. Yet, if women do not seek to be included at the centre of cultural production, we only reinforce our exclusion from it, in opposition to many of feminism's political aims.

Theoretical work of recent years has emphasized the crucial role played by cultural texts in subject formation: subjectivity is produced and affirmed, and ideology disseminated, through spectatorial identifi-cation with characters, narrative meaning and supporting aesthetic codes. The function of a text is to position the spectator to receive certain favoured – and restricted – meanings which the text 'manages' for the viewing subject in keeping with dominant ideology. In this model the spectator is not an active part of the production of textual meaning but the passive side of a unidirectional relationship in which the text disperses meanings while the spectator-subject receives them. The spec-tator can only interpret (be interpreted by) a text in terms preformulated by gender difference. There is no possibility of a mutually informing relationship between spectator and text, and therefore no accumulative building of textual meaning. As a result, psychoanalytic–semiotic theories do not distinguish the subject formulated by the text from the spectator-subject viewing the text. The intention of the text and the reception of textual meaning are defined as one and the same.

The assumption that the text positions the spectator to receive its intended meanings has led to a foregrounding of textual analysis as a methodology for the study of film, since the text is regarded as both container and disseminater of ideology. Ideology, in turn, is mediated through a medium's aesthetic and technical codes. These codes, through repetition in time, cultural familiarity, context of use, and so on, are themselves presumed to be infused with ideology. If this is so, the question remains: how does one utilize the formal aspects of film to convey alternative ideologies without, in the process, conveying dominant ideology as well? For many feminist film-makers this has seemed an irreconcilable position, and has resulted in a rejection of aesthetic and technical practices associated with mainstream cinema. But again, this view needs to be measured against feminism's political agenda, its intent to alter public consciousness about gender roles and relations. Spectatorship in this sense also involves a consideration of film's widespread appeal and influence: its accessibility, and its availability, to large audiences. The aesthetic and technical codes of mainstream cinema have served traditionally as a common language and meeting ground between those who make and those who watch films. In an analysis which presumes that a text imposes ideology on a fixed spectatorship in a fixed manner, the aesthetic and technical codes of dominant ideology can impose only dominant ideology. But a method of analysis which argues that the viewing process includes the active participation of spectators means that film's codes can be implemented, by both producer and consumer, to allow for alternative usage.

An examination of female spectatorship involves three avenues: the individual female spectator, shaped by the psychic and social processes of subject formation; female spectators as historically and socially constituted groups; and female audiences, participants in film's (and television's) broad popular base. The nine contributors to this volume employ differing perspectives and methodologies, are concerned with differing issues and, finally, offer differing opinions. But they share a concern to examine the issues surrounding female spectatorship and to emphasize women's presence in, rather than absence from, the 'cinematic experience'. Each essay involves a rereading of women's cultural positioning, as well as a reworking of the theoretical approaches by which we read. The contributors' intentions are to expand the possibilities available for women in film and television, in narrative forms, and in feminist theory.

Linda Williams examines a much debated Hollywood classic, *Mildred Pierce*, from the position of the audience which viewed it at the historical moment of its release. Her essay works towards reconciling the too often opposed strategies of psychoanalytic/semiotic and sociological approaches. She argues that psychoanalysis and semiotics provide a method of analysis which explains a text's role in the formation and maintenance of ideology, but that they neglect historical considerations to the extent that they attribute the ideological function of a text solely to the 'eternal repression of the feminine'. A sociological approach, on the other hand, accounts for the specifics of history but is unable to explain how a text mediates or manages history in the service of ideology.

Williams contends that an analysis open to both methodologies – a kind of contextualizing of textual analysis – can account for specific, and changing, forms of feminine repression in response to specific and changing historical moments. This framework would acknowledge dominant ideology and women's marginalized position in relation to it, without characterizing that ideology as imposing itself in a unified, consistent manner. Rather, suggests Williams, it is an ideology which is imposed repeatedly, in response to particular historical occurrences and changing spectatorial concerns. As such, it can be understood more accurately as a *series* of varying strategies which attempt to keep dominant ideology dominant but must do so in response to continual challenges.

Jeanne Allen, in an alternate approach to Linda Williams's examination of historical spectatorship, looks at Alfred Hitchcock's recently re-released 1954 film, *Rear Window*, as it is likely to be viewed by a present-day feminist spectator. How does recently acquired feminist knowledge affect women's cultural positioning and, consequently, textual readings? Allen finds that the contemporary spectator, informed by both the theoretical work and the political awareness of the last years, is able to read *Rear Window* differently from its original audience; and moreover to find in the film's discussion of heterosexual romance much of contemporary concern. A feminist analysis, based upon an examination of narrative structure and formal codes, reveals that the film is in fact 'about' the inadequacies of stereotyped gender roles – what Allen describes as the 'traps and lures of heterosexual romance'.

But while Hitchcock might have critiqued gender relations, his cultural positioning left him unable to offer alternative solutions. It is precisely the feminist spectator's informed position outside of dominant culture which allows her the possibility of envisioning what Hitchcock and this text cannot: 'a way out of the maze,' to relationships based on more satisfying criteria for both genders. Allen's analysis also suggests that the relationship between spectator and text is not fixed, but rather mutually effecting. In offering an alternative reading to that of the film's original audience, a feminist spectator in turn alters textual meaning. This is so because a text is amenable to more than a single reading: alternative interpretations are not imposed upon, but rather apparent within, a text such as *Rear Window*.

Michelle Citron, writing from her point of view as a film-maker, explores the question of women's entry into the production of mainstream cinema. Feminist film makers and theorists, concerned with issues of female representation and spectatorship, have examined the ways in which films *by* women affect the images and viewing experiences *of* women. How can women's inclusion in the film-making process alter that process? When the feminist avant-garde posed this question in relation to mainstream narrative, popular genres and their accompanying aesthetic and technical codes, they found these forms too embedded in partriarchal ideology to serve the needs of women. Citron – part of that avant-garde – raises this question again, and now finds herself responding differently. Her analysis pinpoints the complex interrelations between film-makers, audiences and means of production, a vast network of mutually determining factors from which textual meaning cannot be disassociated. For instance, the move to mainstream production by film-makers like Citron is made in response to changing social and political contexts. As the political climate of feminism has altered, so has a film-maker's ability to reach her audiences. In this sense, 'going mainstream' can be seen as an effort to recuperate a more generally shared filmic language. This involves a 'shifting relationship' to the tenets of the avant-garde in an effort to wrest back cinematic forms (narrative, genres, aesthetic codes) previously defined as belonging to the patriarchy. The move towards popular culture carries with it the possibility that dominant cultural forms will speak for, and to, ever broadening audiences of women.

Christine Gledhill suggests, in place of current theories, a model of 'negotiation' as a more accurate and useful description of cultural production. In this model, meaning is constructed through the meeting of producers (institutional and individual), texts and audiences. The socio-historical constitution of audiences, as well as the production process, become integral elements in the dispersion of textual meaning. As such, female subjectivity is partially informed by, but not identical with, the textual subject of patriarchal ideology, because socio-cultural factors – 'women's history and lived experiences' – also play their part in the configuration of female subject. Textual subject and social subject are thus reconciled as concurrently determining aspects of female spectatorship, while language and the unconscious are retained as significant (but not singular) means of ideological dissemination. The fixed character of psychoanalytic–semiotic theories, which Gledhill calls their 'once and for all' securing of ideology, is replaced by a process in which ideology has continually to be negotiated and renegotiated. The concept of negotiation meets the fundamental requirements of feminism as a political movement by foregrounding the contradictions – the potential points of intervention – inherent in cultural production. Textual study can now be placed within a context which includes the activity of spectators as well as producers, all interacting under the 'umbrella' of negotiation – a system which describes relationships in process, not fixed entities.

Jacqueline Bobo examines the diverse reactions *The Color Purple* has provoked within the Black community and, in particular, the favourable responses the film has elicited from Black women, who both identify with and defend Steven Spielberg's version of the Alice Walker novel. This reaction on the part of Black women cannot be explained, Bobo finds, by a textual analysis of the film – which reveals racist stereotyping and negative portrayals of Black people. In order to understand how Black women have engaged positively with the film Bobo turns instead to recent theories in media audience analysis and to an examination of this specific audience of viewers.

Black women, as members of a marginalized social group and in face of a 'demeaning cinematic heritage', view Hollywood films from an oppositional stance, a stance which could easily have led to outright rejection of the film. That in the instance of *The Color Purple* it did not reflects a particular consciousness on the part of its community of viewers rather than any difference within the text itself. The establishment of a 'writerly community' of Black women, composed of creative producers as well as receptive viewers/readers, has enabled audience members to bring their personal lives and collective history to bear on films which represent them. It is upon the basis of this self-identified ('self'-conscious) community that Black women have constructed alternative, and favourable, readings from *The Color Purple*. Using theories of cultural competency and articulation, Bobo distinguishes social subjects from textual subject, and explains how social subjects can bring meaning to, or construct it from, a given text. Her analysis suggests that alternative ideologies are not necessarily embedded within cultural products but are equally embodied in cultural readings.

Jackie Byars's essay, 'Gazes/Voices/Power' questions the theoretical assumptions which describe women as silent, both in classic realism cinema and in popular television programmes. Her analysis of female-oriented Hollywood films results in the conclusion that a feminine discourse is operative in mainstream cinema at both narrative and enunciative levels. Although this discourse occupies a minority position, and more often than not is repressed in favour of dominant male discourse, it none the less represents an authentic female presence.

Byars's distinction is an important one: acknowledging that women are repressed does not mean to say that they are therefore without language or voice. The contradiction between on the one hand a clearly identifiable female discourse in mainstream film and on the other theories which presuppose that such a discourse is impossible leads Byars to examine the psychoanalytic constructs feminist analysis has employed. Byars maintains that certain psychoanalytic avenues, such as the object relations theory of Carol Gilligan and Nancy Chodorow, while acknowledging women as different from men, are more interested in defining the nature of those differences than in accepting women's position as 'aberrance' from a masculine norm. Her analysis of female-oriented films of the 1950s indicates that while these frequently work towards a repression of the feminine, their terms of communication are women's, identifiable as such by female spectators both then and now. Furthermore, her examination of 1980s television programmes shows that these feminine discourses remain operative today, and in some instances have notably informed male discourse and genres.

Ann Kaplan, looking at Music Television, analyses the 'televisual apparatus' – the ways in which popular television functions as a medium as distinct from the classic realist film. Kaplan finds in television, rather than the monolithic gaze of film, a wide range of gazes and forms of address. The result is that television spectators – male and female – may make multiple identifications both within and across gender lines. The means by which the cinematic apparatus conveys ideology, then, is not equally applicable to television and its differing 'narrative' forms. The problem Kaplan raises is the extent to which these other positions can be considered viable alternatives for feminist purposes. Film addresses a (male) spectator through prolonged narrative identification; the television text's episodic framework positions a 'decentred' spectator. The mapping out of a new subject-to-image relationship holds obvious appeal for feminism, but Kaplan warns against judging by appearances. For while the televisual apparatus blurs polarities such as gender difference and establishes a new relationship between spectator and text, it does so by reducing the subject/image polarity to mere image. The 'sweeping aside' of sexual difference is achieved through the reduction of all, not just women's, bodies to the 'look'. Since gender polarities have provided the basis for a feminist social critique, to the extent that the television screen–viewer relationship and the televisual apparatus eliminate the humanist subject, Kaplan argues, they also eliminate the current basis of feminism's political stance.

Alile Sharon Larkin, writing from her perspective as a Black woman and as a film-maker, examines women of colour's relationship to the film and television media, history, dominant culture and feminism. Her arguments establish that women's experiences are not identical and therefore not amenable to a universalizing theory. Are we running the danger of replicating between women the very problem of marginalization which patriarchal domination has created between women and men? The acceptance of a theory based on totalizing assumptions, and originally used to critique *all* women's exclusion from a patriarchal system, appears unable to avoid the continued exclusion of *some* women's experiences. The task facing feminist film theory is not simply to acknowledge historical and socio-cultural differences, but to formulate theories which genuinely account for differences between women. As Larkin points out, issues of race and gender are complexly interwoven and ultimately inseparable for women of colour, who face the double – too often the triple – oppressions of race, sex and class. Women of colour, as Larkin notes, cannot 'pick and choose' their oppression. Has the notion of gender difference imposed a subject–object world-view in which the female can be defined only in relation to the male? We must examine the degree to which the apparent unity of women's position within masculine culture has led to divisiveness amongst women. The perception of social relations and power structures in polarized, binary terms has done a disservice to all women by its inability to account for the diverse experiences of many women.

Teresa de Lauretis, taking up this point, argues that female spectators are currently being addressed not solely upon the basis of sexual difference, but upon a more extensive, developing feminist aesthetic. In order to understand and formulate that aesthetic, 'a shift in the terms of the question' must be effected. A feminine aesthetic defined in comparison to, or in conjunction with, a masculine or dominant aesthetic will not prove helpful to women, just as defining women in terms of a binary concept of sexual difference only locks us into the orbit of the feminine in relation to the masculine. Women need to be understood upon the basis of their own heterogeneity, the differences of women from the concept of Woman, and the differences amongst women. For women's cinema, a shift in the terms of the question entails a move away from the dominance of the text towards an 'aesthetic of reception' in which the primary concern becomes women as diversified individuals. Spectators are no longer captured by a text in order to be formulated in relation to a male model, but rather are distinguished from it as social subjects, especially as they have been conceived by feminism. Films which address women as social subjects, in what de Lauretis describes as their 'heterogeneity and otherness from the text', can be said to address spectators as female. It is this address to the spectator as female which makes possible the conception of a feminist aesthetic.

Together, the essays in this volume redress a previous theoretical hesitancy to accept the 'unproven' assumption that female spectators exist as subjects: unproven except in so far as women go to film and watch television in overwhelming numbers, and do so without suspending all sight, thought and feeling. As the work here shows, cultural analysis from a feminist perspective yields greater benefits for women when we attempt to reconcile women's lived experiences with their 'cinematic experiences'.

Feminist film theory has accepted certain theoretical models in order to understand an excluding and objectifying cultural positioning of women – theoretical models which themselves have sometimes helped reinforce that cultural positioning. In the process of understanding women's exclusion from the centre of dominant culture we have accepted a definition of ourselves as sexual difference. The problem confronting feminist film theory is not to compete within, or be measured against, criteria which fail to take women into account in the first place, but rather to contextualize and question the assumptions of social relations and power structures in which women, as well as other social groups, fail to 'fit'.

Difference can indeed be otherness, what is left over when we subtract what man is. But it can also be diversity and disagreement in a world in which the most basic of differences – economic, political, racial, issues of family, of violence – still need to be addressed and redressed. In the midst of an already existing female spectatorship, the issue is not to establish her/our presence or to imagine feminist cultural production in some far distant future, but to ask what constitutes a feminist film and feminist filmic moments. What constitutes our differences as spectators?

Notes

1. These theories are too complex to be provided for in a brief summary. For an in-depth examination, see E. Ann Kaplan, *Women and Film: Both Sides of the Camera*, London and New York: Methuen, 1983; and Annette Kuhn, *Women's Pictures: Feminism and Cinema*, Boston and London: Routledge and Kegan Paul, 1982.

2. For an early and influential argument along these lines, see Laura Mulvey, 'Visual Pleasure and Narrative Cinema', *Screen*, vol. 16, no. 3 (1975).

3. While references here are specifically to psychoanalytic theories, their application is inseparable from a semiotic methodology of textual analysis.

1

Feminist Film Theory: *Mildred Pierce* and the Second World War

Linda Williams

Feminist film theory, working along the lines of psychoanalytic cate-gories of spectatorial pleasure and perversion, has produced a remark-able body of work that attempts to explain the many ways in which women spectators have been denied access to traditionally male viewing pleasures, the many ways 'woman as woman' – as subject in her own right – has not been reflected on the movie screens of the world.[1] The feminist theorist working in this tradition most often reads the women characters who appear in dominant cinema as absence, lack or ground to an entire system of visual representation that negates an unspoken subjectivity of women. A key concept in the analysis of this only appar-ent representation of women has been *repression*: the often devious ways in which texts that supposedly represent women actually repress them.

Working parallel to this tradition is a longer history of feminist socio-logy and history of the 'image' of women in popular culture, including, but not specifically focused on, film. This tradition attempts to establish connections between a given female image – say working women in films of the 1940s – and the historical moment that produces such an image. Here, the key concept of analysis is not the inevitable distortion of repression but the accurate or inaccurate *reflection* of historical and cultural 'reality'.[2]

These two traditions have often shown great contempt for one another. Psychoanalytically and semiotically oriented feminists charge that sociologists and historians don't know how to read the textuality of film texts, while sociologists and historians charge that feminist film theorists don't know how to read the dynamics, or even the facts, of history in these texts. Both charges have, at times, been all too correct.

There is consequently a great need for feminists working in both traditions to discuss their very different aims and methods with one another.
One goal of the present essay is to offer a comparative study of these
different aims and methods in the belief that each has something to learn
from the other.

A second goal is somewhat more complex. Here I am interested in
how each of these traditions has constructed a method of analysis
employing its own feminist hindsight to read either the *repression* or the
reflection of woman. My concern is that in reading films in the context
of current feminist enlightenment we sometimes ignore the more difficult task of reading the contradictory situation of the historical female
spectator. The text I choose to examine – Michael Curtiz's *Mildred
Pierce* (Warner Brothers, 1945) – is one that speaks to the above issue
precisely because its contradictions are so apparent on the very surface
of the work. Almost every critic who has written about this film has had
something to say about the contradictions within the text – especially the
visual contrast between the extended evenly lit past-tense sequences
narrated by Mildred and the dark, *film noir* quality of the present-tense
episodes depicting the more sinister and seemingly criminal aspects of
her life.[3] In the evenly lit past-tense episodes, Mildred (Joan Crawford)
sympathetically tells the story of her abandonment by her husband, her
love for her daughters and her rise to success in the restaurant business.
In the *film noir* present-tense episodes we see a very different Mildred –
we see, for example, her attempt to set up a male friend as suspect for
the murder of her second husband, her apparent involvement in that
murder and the many lies she tells to the detective investigating the
crime.

For many critics, the fascination of *Mildred Pierce* has rested in the
extreme contrast and conflict of two gender-inflected forms of discourse
that powerfully mark the film text: the day-time woman's filmic
discourse of Mildred's own story and the *noir* male discourse of a
dangerous, nocturnal underworld.[4] Albert LaValley's interesting investigation into the film's production history could be said to substantiate the
gendered nature of this discursive conflict. LaValley reports that the
first two versions of the screenplay – relatively faithful adaptations of the
original novel by James M. Cain in the style of the 1930s woman's film –
were written by a woman, Catherine Turney. But Turney's original
screenplays were so much reworked in the direction of *film noir* by later
male screenwriters – including the author of the final version, Ranald
MacDougal – that she eventually removed her name from the credits.[5]

Thus, it would be possible to treat what many feminist critics consider
the triumph of the film's male style as the direct result of the male
screenwriter's imposition of crime-related, *film noir* masculine concerns

upon the narrative of the novel and original screenplay, that of mother love.[6] In a related vein it would even be tempting to see the erasure of Turney's name from the final credits as analogous to the effacement of Mildred's name and story within the film. For in the flashback versus present-tense form imposed upon both the novel and Turney's script by its male authors, it is precisely the possibility of female authorship that is apparently undercut; Mildred tries to tell her story, but the film image conspires to turn her words against her. Even the very name of that story is not Mildred's *own* name – if a woman can be said to have her own name – but the name of her first husband, the one to whom she is *not* married as the present-tense story begins.

It would be tempting, then, to pursue the finer points of the repression of the feminine in this most fascinating and contradictory of 1940s 'women's films.' But to do so would be simply to offer additional grim proof of the monolithic nature of the repression of the feminine in film. In my judgement, this is a task that many feminist film critics have become almost too adept at performing. We have long been in need of ways of saying more about a film text's historical moment of reception – of the possible use contemporary female spectators might have made of a film. The problem, then, is how to go about recovering more of the contradictory moment of the film's first emergence without letting feminist hindsight read too much into that moment.

All criticisms of *Mildred Pierce* – not only feminist – have attempted to read the film in some relation to its release date, 20 October 1945, a date which coincided with the return of thousands of American soldiers following victory over Japan. The autumn of 1945 was thus that most contradictory of transitional moments: the end of war, the beginning of peace, the return of the GIs and the end of unprecedented employment for American women. But even though many of these readings point to this historical moment as the primary determination of the text's reflection and/or repression of woman, they do so with very little appreciation of the historical female viewer's experience of the contradictions of history.

One work that might seem to appreciate these contradictions is Andrea Walsh's *Women's Film and Female Experience: 1940–1950.*[7] Walsh is a sociologist who examines a great many women's films of the 1940s in order to understand the complex changes experienced by women during this period. Like many feminists, she considers the wartime decade of new opportunities for women crucial to the emergence of an explicit feminist consciousness in the later 1960s and 1970s. Walsh writes,

We can view recurrent patterns within popular 1940s women's films as threads running through the lives of women in American culture. In the 1940s women in the United States did not connect the feminist threads of their 'common sense' to weave a coherent feminist ideology. Yet, that fact alone neither obliterates the existence of these threads nor denies their historical importance. Analyzing popular women's films of the 1940s compels us to recognize the nascent feminism of wartime female consciousness.[8]

Walsh's impulses are typical of a whole generation of feminist daughters who seek to discover the nascent feminism of their mother's generation in the popular films of the 1940s. Walsh proposes, with well-intentioned feminist hindsight, to read her mother's 'common sense' as an emerging form of feminist ideology and part of the reason for the film's popular success. *Mildred Pierce* was certainly a success, with its Oscar-winning comeback performance by Joan Crawford and its sensationalist advertising campaign based on the enigmatic slogan, 'Mildred Pierce – don't ever tell anyone what she did'.[9] But it is arguable whether its narrative of a noble mother caught in the snares of a villainous daughter can be called 'nascent feminism'.

Walsh takes up a discussion of *Mildred Pierce* at the end of a chapter entitled 'The Evolution of the Maternal Melodrama'. She characterizes the film as a bleak, atypical maternal drama, but a maternal drama none the less: 'Between the suspicion of the first segment and the tragedy and resignation of the last is a tale of female success and supportive female bonding.' She also claims that although Mildred is tragic, she is nevertheless 'a winner and a survivor'.[10] In addition, Walsh argues that despite the film's apparent ideological function, which was to justify the move of women from the workplace back into the home, it actually values female success and bonding as more important. Walsh's decision to read the ending – in which Mildred and her first husband Bert Pierce are reunited – as unconvincing is thus clearly a decision to give the middle of the narrative more weight than the beginning and ending, which are about 'tragedy and resignation'.[11] Walsh then reads the film's middle segment from a feminist perspective as an instance of an emergent group's struggle with patriarchal hegemony.

From the perspective of feminist psychoanalytic critics there are two immediately apparent problems with Walsh's selective reading. The first is that it ignores some parts of the film in favour of those that correspond with the revisionist scenario of 'nascent feminism'. The second problem relates to the film's form. In her attempt to read a 'nascent feminism' in as dark a maternal melodrama as *Mildred Pierce*, Walsh assumes that the fundamental form of the maternal drama has simply been carried over from the 1930s, speaking to female audiences in the same way it always had about the nobility of maternal courage and sacrifice. Thus, although Walsh's goal is to read the changes in female experience during the war years, she seems to regard the form of the maternal drama as relatively static.

In her recent book on the woman's film, Mary Ann Doane argues, to the contrary, that relatively few films of the 1940s activate the classic figures of the maternal melodrama as they had been portrayed in the 1930s. By the war years, Doane argues, the reorganization of sexual roles had introduced such a degree of ambivalence about mothering that 'the maternal becomes a fractured concept in the 40s, necessitating its dispersal in different [film] genres'.[12] For Doane, then, the contradictions in the maternal as experienced during the war years created a new and 'fractured' form, whose discontinuity from previous maternal forms is significant. Thus Doane argues for a basic 'incoherency' in the manifestations of the genre during the 1940s; these forms of interference do not permit a simple mining of the film for examples of female experience.

In *Mildred Pierce*, the iconography of *film noir* has been read by feminist critics using psychoanalytic and semiotic methods of analysis as the mark of that incoherence. In contrast to Walsh's reading of an empowering 'female consciousness', these feminist critics resolve the film's contradictions in quite the opposite direction, emphasizing the triumphant subversion of Mildred's story of female consciousness by the *noir* crime drama that casts suspicion on everything Mildred says. The most influential of these readings is undoubtedly that of British feminist Pam Cook, whose 1978 article, 'Duplicity in *Mildred Pierce*', elaborated upon the structure of warring male and female discourses identified in Joyce Nelson's earlier article. Cook contrasts the present-tense investigations into the murder of Monte Beragon at the beginning of the film, which are marked by extreme *film noir* lighting, with the extended past-tense flashbacks narrated by Mildred, which constitute the bulk of the film's narratives and which are marked by the more evenly lit world characteristic of woman's film melodrama.[13]

Cook notes that the *noir* style of the 'male discourse' is associated with a host of flashback-structured film narrative of criminal confession or investigation. The pervasive atmosphere of mystery and suspicion compels the viewer to follow the detective's line of reasoning in pursuit of the singular answer to the narrative's enigma: 'Who killed Monte Beragon?' The need for this truth-seeking discourse is overdetermined both by the *noir* style and by a 'snare' in the film's opening scene in which Monte's murder is shown, but not the murderer. We see Monte's reflection in a full-length mirror as his body is riddled with bullets, followed by a close-up of his dying face as he utters his last word, 'Mildred'. Instead of the expected reverse shot of who holds the gun, an abrupt cut to the Santa Monica pier reveals Mildred walking in a suicidal state of despair. We learn later that these two events do not follow one another in time, but that a great deal has happened between the murder and Mildred's walk on the pier. But for most of the film's duration we are led by the implied logic of these two successive shots – what Joyce Nelson has called their 'false suture' – to suspect that Mildred is the murderer.[14]

Mildred's story, told in flashback and introduced by her voice-over in three separate sections, attempts to explain not only the events surrounding the crime but the entire story of her life beginning on the day she and Bert separated and she found herself the sole support of two children. This 'female discourse' has as its subject Mildred's love of her children, her struggle for success and her final betrayal by both her daughter and her male business partners. Pam Cook argues, however, that Mildred's attempt to tell her own *story* – the chronological sequence of events – is undercut and invalidated by the structure of the film's *plot* – the order in which the film arranges these events – which casts a literal shadow of suspicion over all that she says. For example, her first flash-back, told in answer to the detective's question, 'Why did you divorce Bert Pierce?', begins as Mildred's effort to clear Bert but ends on an event that only implicates him further. Similarly, the events recounted in the second flashback, including the high point of Mildred's financial success in a classic 'success montage', are undercut by the fact that Mildred has herself just confessed to the crime.[15]

Finally, Cook argues that Mildred's presumed responsibility for the murder colours the viewer's perception of her non-criminal, though misguided, upbringing of her daughter Veda. It leads us to judge harshly Mildred's indulgence of her daughter's snobbish arrogance. Thus, even though we do not know that Veda is the real criminal until the detective orchestrates Veda's surprise entrance and confession just before the third flashback, we nevertheless read the exclusive mother–daughter bond as inherently dangerous. According to Cook, the viewer cannot help but be relieved when the representative of the law solves the crime, dispels duplicity, separates the dangerous matriarchy, and literally lets in the light of day by opening the blinds of the interrogation room. The film's final shot then reiterates the patriarchal significance of Mildred and Bert's reunion as they head off into the new dawn of the post-war economy with everyone back in their 'proper' place, including two women scrubbing the steps of the Los Angeles Hall of Justice in the background of the final shot who, in Joyce Nelson's words, are 'back on their knees, keeping the façade clean' (Fig. 1).[16]

Both Walsh and Cook acknowledge the significance of the film's release date, 1945, as a pivotal moment of women's history – the moment men returned from the war and women were put back in their 'proper' place in the home. Neither critic doubts that the film's primary message to female audiences was that the male world of business and work could no longer accommodate women. Both take for granted that the film reflects the ideology of the American government regarding the place of women: that they must give up their new-found power and make room for the returning men. Walsh, however, stresses the film's ability to reflect what, after all, was women's real guilt and confusion regarding conflicting roles as mothers and workers. Even the vilification of Veda, she argues, offers a point of identification for working mothers who feared the harmful effects of their employment on their children.[17]

Cook, on the other hand, begins with the ostensible identification of women viewers with the woman's film discourse. But she then proceeds to show how that identification is undercut through its positioning within the male, juridical discourse that locates the criminal in the person of Mildred's daughter. Cook's point is that filmic enunciation establishes a subordination of female discourse to that of the male. No matter how much sympathy Mildred generates in telling her story, the simple *enounced* of that story – its narrative of mother-love – is literally overshadowed by its filmic *enunciation* – the specific manner in which that story gets told.[18]

To summarize: Walsh's sociological-historical reading of the film's *enounced* stresses its reflection of an ambiguous but emerging female consciousness, while Cook's psychoanalytic emphasis on filmic *enunciation* stresses the repression of female consciousness. Reflection and repression are the key, and mutually exclusive, terms of each reading. Walsh's theory allows that a film's 'symbol and metaphor' may mediate between reality and fantasy, but she is wary of psychoanalytic concepts of manifest and latent meanings, and so subsumes the need for such concepts under Gramsci's and Raymond Williams's notions of dominant, residual and emergent hegemonies. Thus, although her theory stresses textual mediation, her reading simply isolates the text's static reflection of a political and historical referent: emerging female consciousness created by new wartime opportunities for women. Even when Walsh asserts the film's reflection of women's own ambiguous atttitudes towards those opportunities, she does so without acknowledging the film's active 'management'[19] of the elements of that historical referent.

Cook, however, emphasizes textual repression to such an extent that she ultimately defers any discussion of the film's relation to history. While acknowledging that the end of the war is a factor in the film's final shape, she shifts her attention away from these historical specifics to the larger, and I think ultimately evasive, problem of the origins of patriarchy itself as theorized by the Hegelian historian J.J. Bachofen. The passage in which Cook makes this move is worth quoting in full. Isolating the 'repression of female sexuality' as the primary ideological work of the film, Cook writes that she would like to avoid

the idea that the film simply reflects the historical needs of post-war America. The drama of the institution of the patriarchal order, the familiar Oedipal story, is enacted and re-enacted throughout history in many and various forms; in the context of the transition to a post-war economy, and impaired masculine population, the disintegration of the family unit and the increased economic and sexual independence of women, the Oedipal structure is threatened: the system which gives men and women their place in society must be reconstructed by a more explicit work of repression, and the necessity for this repression must be established unequivocally, by resolving equivocation. The ideological work of the film then is the way in which it articulates its project, encouraging certain subject positions rather than others, signifying a problem which is not only specific to *Mildred Pierce* itself, and the conditions in which it was produced, but also general in so far as the institution of patriarchy is an historical problem.[20]

Cook then goes on to summarize Bachofen's theory of the patriarchal revolution that overthrew an original 'mother right' and to see *Mildred Pierce* as a re-telling of this same story. Although the recourse to Bachofen is unique to Cook, the theoretical move away from a specific history and towards a more 'universal' Oedipal one is typical of the way many feminist film critics have, in fact, avoided the difficulties of dealing with a more bounded history. For Cook, *Mildred Pierce* is significant for its repetition of the institution of Oedipal law. Representation becomes a re-presentation that eternally represses the feminine.

Where Bachofen's Hegelian study was an attempt to pinpoint the (ultimately unattainable) historical moment when matriarchal rule gave way to patriarchy, Cook's study operates to deny whatever may be new in the historical moment of 1945 by assimilating it to the theories of Bachofen and Freud. Woman as historical subject gets lost in the process. Thus, even though the notion of a dialectical conflict between two discursive structures is enormously suggestive to the reading of the film, this reading ultimately assimilates Mildred's body, like the 'body' of the film, to an originary structure founded in lack, absence and castration which the symbolic 'truth' of the detective asserts.

Both readings suffer from a form of debilitating one-dimensionality. Walsh's emphasis on the text's *reflection* of easily isolated political and historical referents, such as new wartime opportunities for women or the contradictory referent of the closing down of those opportunities, fails to account for the complex ways in which a text mediates, rather than simply reflects, history. Although her theory stresses such mediation,

Walsh's analyses of actual films rely upon a cataloguing of contradictory images: Mildred as strong and successful versus Mildred as suspect or tragic. On the other hand, Pam Cook's emphasis on the text's *repression* of an original 'mother right', though it does a better job of reading the way the text positions the reader, nevertheless defers establishing that reader's relationship to the historical referent of the text.

If the feminist sociologist optimistically reads an emergent feminism in even the bleakest of women's films, the psychoanalytically influenced feminist film critic pessimistically reads the power of patriarchy as eternally and monolithically repressive. Reflection theory appears to underestimate, and repression theory to overestimate, the power of patriarchy.[21]

These erroneous estimations of patriarchal power derive from an equally erroneous estimation of the power of a present feminism to reinterpret the past as a clear conflict between male and female forms of power. My point is that this kind of feminist hindsight may oversimplify the contradictions experienced by the historical female viewer. This is not to say that Walsh and Cook employ their hindsight in the same way. Walsh stresses the continuity between her present feminism and the 'nascent feminism' of her mother's generation, with Mildred's broad-shouldered strength serving as role-model for her own generation's more explicit feminist ideology. Cook, on the other hand, stresses the discontinuity between today's empowered feminist in possession of the psychoanalytic and semiotic tools with which to understand the patriarchal mechanisms of oppression and the more gullible historical female spectator who was presumably taken in by the film's duplicity. But in both cases the feminist critic sees a dominant male ideology at war with either an emergent or a repressed female consciousness. In addition, in both cases the analysis of this gender struggle radically simplifies the ideological complexity of the film *and* the historical situation of its female viewers.

Clearly we need feminist readings that can be more sensitive to specificities of the historical moment of film production and the situation of its original audience. We also need to be able to read the film's historical referents without becoming trapped in simplistic realistic notions of reflection; similarly, we need to be able to read the unconscious repressions of the text without universalizing them and hence cutting them off from their historical determinations. This means that in *Mildred Pierce* we must put aside a priori notions of the dominance of either repression or reflection in order first to determine the way these interact. For me, a useful model of this interaction is Fredric Jameson's formulation of the 'political Unconscious'.[22] Jameson stresses the importance of history as the ultimate cause of textuality, but, following

Althusser, insists that it is an absent cause, apprehendable only through narratives. For Jameson, then, one important way of reading a text is to look at how, specifically, it represses history – to perform a symptomatic analysis not on the repression of the desires of its individual characters, but on its collective denial of historical contradictions. It is this denial which Jameson calls the political Unconscious. What is ultimately repressed in the political Unconscious is the revolution that would have to occur if repression did not take place; the text registers the strain of keeping it repressed. But the text is also a form of Utopian compensation for that repression; in Jameson's terms, it 'manages' the Real of history, draws it into its own texture, submits it to a transformation of form.[23]

So rather than looking, as Walsh does, for the immediate reflection of an emergent women's consciousness in *Mildred Pierce*, or, as Cook does, for the repression of an ancient 'mother-right', we might look instead at the way the film reflects *and* represses the contradictions of its historical moment. The immediate problem in doing so, however, is that *Mildred Pierce* turns out to be most evasive about that historical moment. Like a great many films made during the Second World War, both in the United States and elsewhere, its contemporary present-tense sequences project specific images – of dress, cars, home furnishings – which depict mid-1940s life, without anchoring those images to specific political-historical references. Thus, in each of the three major time frames of the film – the brief period at the beginning of Mildred's first flashback when Mildred and Bert are still living together as man and wife; the extended period of Mildred's independence, struggle and rise to economic success; and the brief present-tense period of the crime, its investigation and Mildred's and Bert's reunion – there are conflicting clues as to the temporal location of these events. For example, we might surmise that Mildred and Bert could have split up some time towards the end of the Depression. Bert *is* out of work and discouraged. Yet there is no reference to the economic hard times that have caused his discouragement and apathy. Bert at first seems simply unwilling to work. In wartime he would be termed a slacker; during a depression he would simply be a victim of hard times. The film remains open to both interpretations.

In the second time-frame, Mildred gains economic success during a period clearly corresponding to the war years. However, we are not encouraged to read her new-found independence in the context of a collective national experience of wartime. Mildred must make it on her own because her husband left her with no money. Bert never goes off to war. Mildred and her business partner Ida (Eve Arden) are thus presented as ambitious entrepreneurs who, in the absence of husbands

(Ida is the wisecracking, brittle career woman Eve Arden made famous), and with a little help from some unscrupulous male investors, make it big in the restaurant business. Yet the film does encourage us to read the events of female bonding and economic independence against a *non-specific* context of a never-mentioned war. The war becomes the real, but hidden, explanation of why Mildred and every other significant female character in the film – Ida, and Bert's strangely maternal and matronly sometime lover, Mrs Biederhoff – are women alone. It also explains why the men who remain in the picture after Bert leaves – Wally, the lowlife unscrupulous realtor (Jack Carson), and Monte, the aristocratic but equally unscrupulous playboy (Zachary Scott) – are such sleazy no-counts. It is as if the 'real' men, the men who do not need to feed off women, are elsewhere. Other oblique references to war include: Monte's remark upon seeing Mildred's legs that he is glad 'stockings are out for the duration'; the presence of two sailors in the audience watching Veda's night-club act; and finally Ida's cynical remark upon hearing that Bert has finally found work 'in a defence plant' that the 'manpower shortage must be worse than we think'.

Finally, the third time-frame of the film – the present-tense sequences of the crime and its solution climaxing in Bert's reunion with Mildred outside the Los Angeles Hall of Justice – appears, most obliquely of all, to allude to the return of the fathers at the end of the war.

The question, then, is why does *Mildred Pierce* constantly allude to, yet refrain from specific reference to, the Second World War? One obvious explanation rests with the original time-frame of the James M. Cain novel on which the film is based. The novel spans the period of the early Depression through 1941. It is thus possible to explain the absence of specific historical references in the film simply as a form of superficial updating that vaguely alludes to more recent times but does not entirely rethink the narrative in these newer historical terms. This is a frequent phenomenon of the movies, especially in films based on novels or on earlier films; and it certainly contributes to a quality of free-floating temporal vagueness that characterizes many films.

But in the case of *Mildred Pierce* there are other reasons for these extreme temporal obfuscations. Dana Polan has written that many films made during the war years found it difficult to reconcile the dominant ideology of wartime writing with the more individualized concerns of classic narratives of romance or success. Given these difficulties, a great many films of the war period preferred to locate their narratives in spaces outside the official parameters of the struggle – exotic places, like *Casablanca* (1942), filled with gangsters, eccentrics and romantics, where the narrative of wartime unity was not all-determining, though it certainly remained a determinant.[24]

Mildred Pierce is perhaps another example of a solution to that problem. It erases *specific* temporal-historical markers in order to facilitate an individualist story that could not be told within the parameters of wartime collectivism. If this is so, then we might ask, following Jameson and revising both Walsh and Cook, what the absence of direct reference to the war and to the demobilization that followed permits the text both to *reflect* and to *repress* about women's experience during that timeframe.

How, for example, does the absence of reference to the war permit the historical female spectator to interpret Bert Pierce's abdication of paternal authority at the beginning of the film and his accession to it at the end? I would suggest that the film invites us to read both in terms of the absent referent of the war but that this referent must remain absent in order for the woman's story to emerge at all. Thus the repression of specific reference to the war as the reason American men first left and then returned to their families permits the film both to reflect more of the very real upset in gender relations caused by the war and, at the same time, to 'manage' or repress the experience of this upset through the displacement of its real issues on to narratively resolvable ones.

A comparison with a film that does directly inscribe the war into a comparable women's film text of female bonding might be useful. Selznick's *Since You Went Away* (1944) is also about mother–daughter bonding, matriarchal power and self-reliance, and it offers an ostensibly more 'positive' image of home-front matriarchy. But unlike *Mildred Pierce* with its monstrous daughter and its collection of three weak, even morally deficient, male characters none of whom seem centrally important to Mildred's life, *Since You Went Away* – as its title suggests – revolves around the noble sacrifices of the absent patriarch. Mother and daughters carry on all life in his name. And if mother and daughters do grow and change in his absence, it is always understood that this new-found strength will never challenge that of the war hero they revere. The story of wartime unity is too strong for that.

Mildred Pierce's oblique suggestion of highly selected aspects of wartime reality – in particular, the absence of paternal authority – permits a more substantial *reflection* of the new opportunities for women in a wartime economy. It permits that reflection because Mildred and Ida succeed financially for their *own* sakes and not in the name of a heroic but absent patriarch. The absence of direct reference to the war allows the film initially to reflect more of the exhilaration of female independence, of being genuinely on one's own. This exhilaration was undoubtedly experienced by many women during the war but was unacceptable to the dominant ideology of national unity.[25] In these representations women's work was portrayed as a heroic and noble sacrifice – of material goods, time, even of femininity – and was inevitably compared to the much greater sacrifice of GIs.

But if the lack of direct reference to the war permits an initial *reflection* of the otherwise unrepresentable exhilarations of matriarchal power, it also makes necessary a much more massive *repression* of that power. Here, Cook is entirely correct in her argument that the film solves the problem of an excess of female power by casting so much suspicion upon that power that it seems perverse and harmful. But she misses the opportunity to explore the specific situation of the 1945 female spectator when she conflates repression of the female with repression of the Oedipus. For the more interesting question is not whether the feminine gets repressed, or even how that repression operates in terms of cinematic discourse, but how the specific forms of that repression are made to work for female spectators at a particular historical moment. In other words, how does *Mildred Pierce* effect a trade-off of reflection and repression for its historical female spectator, and how can we understand and appreciate the cinematic pleasure of that spectator even as we might regret the ways in which it has manipulated her?

Here, a useful comparison might be made with another film genre which flourished during the war and post-war period. In 'gothic' films we find an analogous avoidance of specific reference to contemporary history, yet there is a peculiar sense in which these films are able to be 'about' that history in ways that more obviously contemporary films could not be. In an interesting article on gothic films produced between 1940 and 1948, Diane Waldman notes that the films undergo a shift between the 1940–41 period and the wartime and post-war films. In the early wave of gothics typified by Hitchcock's *Rebecca* (1940) and *Suspicion* (1941), the following formula emerges: a young, inexperienced woman meets and marries a mysterious man and returns to an ancestral mansion to experience bizarre incidents revolving around her fears that he may be a murderer. Waldman notes that in the early wave of gothics the woman turns out to be paranoid: her fears are unfounded; her husband loves her. However, the resolution of her doubts is purchased at the cost of the invalidation of her independent judgement.[26]

In the later wartime and post-war gothics, the woman's original suspicions are usually validated: the husband *is* a murderer in *Gaslight* (1944), *Experiment Perilous* (1944), *Dragonwyck* (1946), *Sleep My Love* (1948), and in many other films as well. Waldman's point is that both forms of the gothic work out female anxieties about women's confinement and isolation within the home, but that the later films affirm the woman's worst fears about the dangers of such confinement.

This shift occurs because greater wartime mobility outside the home finally permitted women to see the debilitating effects of their former confinement.

For our purpose, however, the significant point of Waldman's analysis is that, as in *Mildred Pierce*, some of the most important issues raised by the war are not reflected in the films about the war. It is as if only those films that could both reflect *and* repress could also *manage* these issues so important to women's new wartime experience. The late gothics, for example, reflect women's newly realized experience of the past abuses of patriarchal power only in a narrative that has the potential of resolving those problems by replacing the patriarchal tyrant with a more gentle and democratic type. Waldman calls this the 'wrong man' solution: the only thing wrong with the heroine's former situation of confinement is that she fell victim to the 'wrong man'. The 'right man' will correct the problem. The problems of women's confinement within the house and the abuse of patriarchal authority are thus raised more insistently in the latter part of the decade when the war had offered women other options. But if the problem could be raised it then had to be managed by a narrative resolution that ultimately manoeuvres women right back into the home.[27]

Like the wartime and post-war gothics, *Mildred Pierce* is better able to reflect the problems encountered by women under patriarchal rule precisely because it does not reflect the specific historical conditions that made this criticism possible in the first place. In the gothics, the wartime female consciousness that could never be permitted in a film that directly inscribed the war in its text shows up in the form of the tyrannical 'wrong man'. In *Mildred Pierce*, however, the absent referent of the war necessitates a more complicated judgement as to who is the 'right' and who is the 'wrong' man. There is of course the obvious sense in which Monte Beragon's playboy aristocrat must be judged – in the light of the demands of wartime democracy and unity – as the wrong man. But there is also the less obvious sense in which Bert too, at least in his early manifestation as Mildred's do-nothing husband, is also wrong. Yet as we saw earlier, Bert's initial historical placement is so ambiguous that his inactivity can be read in two ways: he might be passive and inactive as the result of a discouraging Depression economy, or because he is a lazy slacker, unwilling to work for his country. The film can have it both ways because it is so vague about which temporal referents operate. In this sense we might say that Bert Pierce functions as a 'wrong man' rehabilitated through patient suffering into the 'right man': in narrative terms, he finally redeems himself by finding work in a defence plant and by allowing Mildred to divorce him. As the rehabilitated right man, Bert eventually earns the right to criticize Mildred's indulgence of their daughter Veda's materialism. So although we might agree with Walsh that Mildred's ambiguous reunion with Bert offers a 'parallel to that of the war wife and her GI mate',[28] the more important point is that the film is actively *managing,* not merely *reflecting,* the dilemmas encountered by women in the immediate post-war era. One of the positive aspects of this management is that it permits a chastening and rehabilitation of the returning husband which could never occur in the war story or the post-war story proper, where the man's direct association with the sacrifices of war are automatically ennobling.

One of the negative aspects of this management, however, is the excessive vilification of Mildred's daughter, Veda, and the related submergence of the class issues that were so important in the original novel. Here, as we have seen, the indirect evocation of wartime ideology operates to judge Veda's – and by extension Mildred's – materialism harshly. In the original novel, Mildred's materialism encounters no such censure because it arises directly out of her experience of want and social humiliation during the Depression. Similary in the novel, Mildred's excessive mother love and spoiling of Veda appears misguided, but it leads to no crime. It leads, rather, to the emergence of Veda as a talented coloratura soprano, permitting Mildred some brief moments of genuine maternal pride at her daughter's advancement before Veda finally goes too far by sleeping with, and then running off with, Monte. Both novel and film end with Mildred and Bert reunited and Mildred and Veda separated. But the moods are radically different. Instead of the film's upbeat march into the light of a new day, in the novel a now plump and worn Mildred finally says good riddance to Veda and settles down to 'get stinko' with Bert.[29]

The demands of wartime unity could thus be said to repress the original class motives for Mildred's quest for success, motives important both in Cain's novel and in women's films of the 1930s. In the novel, Mildred's working-class origins are a constant source of embarrassment to her. She experiences her early waitressing as a genuine stigma, while in the film it is presented as proof of her democratic mettle, the sort of thing all good Americans did to 'pull together' for the war effort. Similarly, in the novel, her hair really does smell of bacon grease: in one scene she furiously washes it before a romantic tryst with the aristocratic Monte. In the film, however, the 'smell of grease' becomes a metaphor that does not so much reflect upon Mildred – we never for a moment suspect that Joan Crawford's hair could smell of grease – as it negatively reflects upon Monte's and Veda's villainous aristocratic disdain for those who work.

Thus if the absence of direct reference to the war permits the film to chasten and rehabilitate the patriarch, the war's indirect shadowy presence nevertheless forbids it to raise issues of class which were enormously important to women and mothers during a period of unprecedented social mobility. Mildred's concern for Veda's social advancement thus gets read against the shadow-referent of the war as materialistic spoiling that leads, ultimately, to the daughter's transgressive passion, the criminal result of an excess of mother love.

While Pam Cook's view of this solution as repressive of mother-rule is accurate, it cannot be entirely attributed to an eternal Oedipal repression. I have suggested instead that the very reason mother-rule can become a problem of this sort is that historical conditions momentarily displaced the rule of the father at a time when women really did make substantial advances into the public sphere.

The problem with Cook's reading, then, is that it ignores the historical conjuncture of the 1945 woman viewer. It is certainly important for feminist critics to associate *film noir* with a public 'male' discourse suspicious of the duplicitous woman, and it is certainly equally important to associate the woman's film with a more personal woman's discourse. It is also useful to note that these two discourses are at war with one another in *Mildred Pierce*. But it does no good at all to conclude that one discourse triumphs over the other and then to interpret this victory in terms of an ahistorical original and mythic victory of Oedipal or Apollonian law over Demetrian mother rule. To do so is to divorce male and female conflict from their real social-historical contexts. It is also to forget that these discourses themselves have particular historical associations and origins. The woman's film is most purely evident in the 1930s and is associated in its maternal sub-types with long-suffering mothers who, unlike Mildred, never enter the public sphere, while *film noir* is associated with post-war male disillusionment and disequilibrum. Neither can be regarded as warring forms of male and female power. In other words, we can no more regard *noir* discourse as a straightforward source of patriarchal (Apollonian) power than we can regard Mildred's and Veda's bond as the woman's film expression of matriarchal power.

If we try to grasp *Mildred Pierce* as an example of *film noir* triumphant, we encounter the problem that *film noir* is itself an inherently off-balance and un-triumphant genre. The detective as agent of the law may defeat Mildred in the name of that law, but he is not a character with whom anyone, male or female, has been asked to identify throughout the course of the film. We come back, then, to the situation of the historical post-war female viewer and her multiple and often contradictory identifications with Mildred as Depression-era wife, wartime mother, businesswoman and post-war *femme fatale*. None of these roles should be read apart from the social and historical contexts that produce it, in spite of the film's own constant attempts to do so. I have tried to argue that the female viewer of 1945 was much more likely to be aware of these contexts than Cook allows, but that she was also less likely to be aware of them as part of an emerging feminist 'common sense' than Walsh allows.

Thus the lesson of *Mildred Pierce* is neither the eternal repression of the feminine nor its realistic reflection, but very specific, and historically changing, forms of repression and reflection that operate hand in hand. This is not to say that repression does not operate in the text. As we have seen, it does so in many ways, in the most fundamental repression of the specificity of the Second World War and in all the subsequent reflections and further repressions that this original repression permits. But it *is* to say that current feminist hindsight can often get in the way of seeing the real ideological conflicts experienced by the historical viewer and managed by the text. This is perhaps primarily to say, with Jameson, that the most important repression in the text is that of history. But if so, it is also to say, this time perhaps not with Jameson, that one of the most important of historical repressions has been that of women. For as we have seen, while the text's initial repression of history permits other reflections of female experience and history in disguised forms, it also calls forth new forms of repression. The most important point, however, is for feminists to see how their own well-intentioned hindsight, whether psychoanalytic and semiotic or sociological and historical, may blind them to the historical conflicts managed by the film for the historical viewer.

Thus while many feminists have been quick to point out the metaphoric significance of the position of women on their knees 'back in their proper places' in the final shot of *Mildred Pierce*,[30] I would point out a somewhat more literal reading: what the shot actually shows is a well-dressed middle-class couple in a state of momentary and uneasy equilibrium – each chastened in their respective maternal and paternal roles – and two decidedly working-class women 'in their place' on their knees. These working-class women are oppressed in ways that are very different from Mildred, and this film is not their story. They should not be made to stand, monolithically, for the repression of the feminine throughout history. The text of history is not quite as simple as that.

The above thoughts are not intended as an exhaustive analysis of *Mildred Pierce*. They are simply a sketch of new possibilities and directions for future readings. As I have suggested in an earlier article on a much more straightforward generic example of the maternal melodrama, the 1937 film, *Stella Dallas*, the most important task of feminist film criticism now seems to be that of locating the variety of different subject positions constructed by the text of the woman's film.[31] The notion of the repression of the feminine, although it certainly occurs in these films, seems too crude to deal with the variety of contradictory social roles at play in them.

This is not to say that there is *no* repression of the feminine in these films, but only that we should not underestimate the complexity of the female spectator's recognition of the contradictory particularities of her situation. Nor should we assume that these films seduce their *specifically* gendered viewers into a naive belief in their fate of self-sacrifice, suffering and loss. In *Stella Dallas* I have argued that the viewer experiences conflicting divisions in her identifications that make her at least somewhat resistant to the fate of the character she views. In *Mildred Pierce* different historical circumstances produce even greater divisions and conflicts in the roles of woman, wife, mother and worker. Feminist film criticism has reached the point where it must begin to analyse the complexities of these contradictions.

Notes

This article began as part of a panel organized by Sumiko Higashi for the 1985 Convention of the Organization of American Historians. The panel was entitled 'Social Scientists versus Film Theorists on Women's Films of the Forties'. I was the 'film theorist' and Andrea Walsh was the 'social scientist'. *Mildred Pierce* was our bone of contention. I hope that the present version of this article has sufficiently erased the 'versus' from the original panel topic in order to engage the deeper concerns that feminists share in the project of reading our past. I am indebted to both Sumiko Higashi and Andrea Walsh for the original opportunity to explore these issues and to Constance Penley for the opportunity to explore them further on a panel at the University of Illinois Urbana's Humanities Colloquium Series. I would also like to thank Judith Gardiner and Karen Hollenger for helpful comments.

1. Two early key formulations of this approach are Claire Johnston's 'Women's Cinema as Counter Cinema', *Notes on Women's Cinema*, Screen Pamphlet no. 2, 1973, and Laura Mulvey's 'Visual Pleasure and Narrative Cinema', *Screen*, vol. 16, no. 3 (1975), pp. 6–18. Later, more extended, explorations of these issues include Annette Kuhn's *Women's Pictures: Feminism and Cinema*, Boston and London: Routledge and Kegan Paul, 1982, E. Ann Kaplan's *Women and Film: Both Sides of the Camera*, New York: Methuen, 1983, and Teresa de Lauretis's *Alice Doesn't: Feminism, Semiotics, Cinema*, Bloomington: Indiana University Press, 1984.

2. See, for example, Sharon Smith's early article, 'The Image of Women in Film: Some Suggestions for Future Research', *Women and Film*, no. 1 (1972), pp. 2–15; Marjorie Rosen, *Popcorn Venus: Women, Movies and the American Dream*, New York: Avon, 1973; Sumiko Higashi's *Virgins, Vamps and Flappers: The Silent American Movie Heroine*, St Albans: Eden Press, 1978.

3. The list includes: Joyce Nelson, '*Mildred Pierce* Reconsidered', *Film Reader*, no. 2, Patricia Erens and Bill Horrigan (eds.), Film Division of Northwestern University, 1977, pp. 65–70; Pam Cook, 'Duplicity in *Mildred Pierce*', *Women in Film Noir*, E. Ann Kaplan, ed. London: British Film Institute, 1978, pp. 68–82; Janet Walker, 'Feminist Critical Practice: Female Discourse in *Mildred Pierce*', *Film Reader* no. 5, Film Division of Northwestern University, 1982, pp. 164–172; Albert J. LaValley's introduction to the published screenplay, *Mildred Pierce*, Madison: University of Wisconsin Press, 1980, pp. 9–53.

4. See especially Nelson and Cook.

5. LaValley, pp. 21–30.

6. LaValley reports that Paramount released *Double Indemnity* in 1944 just as *Mildred Pierce* was moving from the status of property to project at Warner's. The enormous popularity of Billy Wilder's sordid *film noir* crime drama, narrated in flashback by the guilty and dying insurance agent had an enormous influence on *Mildred Pierce*'s producer Jerry Wald, who ordered Catherine Turney's original script rewritten many times over – one version is even by William Faulkner. LaValley, pp. 22–46.

7. Andrea Walsh, *Women's Film and Female Experience, 1940–1950*, New York: Praeger, 1984.

8. Walsh, pp. 4–5.

9. LaValley, p. 52.

10. Walsh, p. 131.

11. Walsh, p. 131.

12. Doane, *The Desire to Desire*, Bloomington: Indiana University Press, 1987.

13. Cook, pp. 75–8.

14. Nelson, p. 65.

15. Cook, pp. 78–9.

16. Nelson, p. 70.

17. Walsh, p. 131.

18. Cook, p. 69.

19. The term is from Fredric Jameson's 'Reification and Utopia in Mass Culture', *Social Text*, vol. 1, no. 1 (1979), p. 141.

20. Cook, p. 61.

21. Both are thus guilty of what Judith Newton has called an over-simplification that reduces woman's sense of historical agency. Of this overestimation of the power of patriarchy Newton writes, 'Insofar as our constructions of history see gender relations as discrete or disconnected from other relations of power and as universally the same, they simplify what we are up against .... Insofar as our constructions of history suggest a monolithic male hegemony, they rob women of a sense of agency and quite simply give men too much "credit".' 'Making – and Remaking – History: Another Look at "Patriarchy"', *Tulsa Studies in Women's Literature*, vol. 3, no. 1/2 (1984), p. 126.

22. *The Political Unconscious: Narrative as a Socially Symbolic Act*, Ithaca, New York: Cornell University Press, 1981, p. 18.

23. Jameson, p. 81.

24. Polan, *Power and Paranoia: History, Ideology and the American Cinema*, New York: Columbia University Press, 1986, p. 155.

25. See, for example, Connie Fields's film documentary *The Life and Times of Rosie the Riveter* (1980).

26. Waldman, '"At Last I Can Tell It to Someone!": Feminine Point of View and Subjectivity in the Gothic Romance Film of the 1940s,' *Cinema Journal*, vol. 23, no. 2 (1984), pp. 29–40.

27. Waldman, p. 38.

28. Walsh, p. 131.

29. James M. Cain, *Mildred Pierce*, New York: Vintage Books, 1978, p. 238.

30. Nelson, p. 70.

31. Linda Williams, '"Something Else Besides a Mother": *Stella Dallas* and the Maternal Melodrama', *Cinema Journal*, vol. 24, no. 1 (1984), pp. 2–27.

2

Looking Through 'Rear Window': Hitchcock's Traps and Lures of Heterosexual Romance

Jeanne Allen

On the verge of solving the mystery of a neighbour's disappearance, you watch your lover risk her life, climbing a fire escape and entering the window of the neighbour's apartment. She finds an abandoned wedding ring that will confirm that the 'absent' wife was murdered by her husband. As she leaves the bedroom, you see the husband-murderer returning, trapping your lover in the apartment. Helpless in a wheelchair you watch, calling to her urgently but unheard, as the wife-murderer finds her, struggles with and hits her. You watch riveted, moaning helplessly and dreading her death before your eyes. The police arrive, and as she speaks to them, she signals to you, hands behind her back, that the ring you both wanted (but for different reasons) is safely on her finger. Just as relief settles over your body, the murderer notices her signal and follows the eyeline from her hands across the open courtyard to your window. As he stares blankly into your unlighted apartment, you slide your wheelchair backwards. The police and your lover leave together as the murderer continues to stare stonily.

This vivid moment belongs to our popular memory of Alfred Hitchcock's *Rear Window*. The recent re-release of this 1954 film affords the critic the opportunity to consider the position of one of Hitchcock's most carefully constructed explorations of dependency in a relationship. The thirty years or so that have elapsed since the film first appeared have been marked by the emergence of the feminist movement as a part of the civil rights movements, affording a framework through which the implications of the film can be seen anew. The strain of polarized gender roles, the rising rates of women's employment and the growth of women head-of-household families have intensified in economic and political terms our perception of Hitchcock's darkly humorous version of the 'battle of the sexes', rendering it more profound for the intervening decades. These years have taught us to take both him and films seriously. And, as in the post-war decades, the various reactions to the feminist movement leave us with the realization that while sexism may be sexy (creating desire from lack as psychoanalytic criticism suggests), it nevertheless deforms us through a dependency and an incompatibility for which we pay dearly.

Re-released commercially in the 1980s (Fig. 2), *Rear Window* now addresses an audience which includes those participating in and influenced by the women's movement of recent decades. It is the experience of this audience, of feminists in particular, that I wish to examine, though also assuming an audience made familiar with film as a constructed medium of artistic representation. I am not interested in characterizing the experience of a general audience, but rather a particular reading community which is feminist and sophisticated about films and which engages in film viewing both for 'entertainment'[1] and for insight into the relation of representation and 'reality'.

In a recent article,[2] Robin Wood, whose book, *Hitchcock's Films*, written in 1960, affirmed Hitchcock as the *auteur* that French critics had already perceived him to be, claims that if he were re-writing his book today, his central question would not be 'Should we take Hitchcock seriously?' but rather, 'Can Hitchcock be saved for feminism?' While some feminists might question why Hitchcock must be 'saved for feminism', I do agree with Wood's reading of these films as containing the beginnings of a critique of heterosexual dependency and 'gamesmanship', arising from Hitchcock's well-crafted representation of adolescent fears and fantasies.

First, it is necessary to deal with auteurist references to one of the leading figures in film history. Hitchcock has held the interest of academics since the journal *Cahiers du Cinéma* took up the 'cause' of serious consideration of a popular director in the late 1940s; Hitchcock criticism continues unabated today. While a number of prominent writers and essayists have taken up the post-structuralist problems of treating the individual subject as the primary textual determinant,[3] the popular orientation to auteurism as the dominant aesthetic in our culture persists. In addition, the operation of a highly refined machinery of persona construction, which began for Hitchcock in the 1930s as a means to a measure of control over studio-based film production, is another reason why Hitchcock figures as a factor in the spectator's experience of films made under his imprimatur. Such components of this experience as Hitchcock's brief appearances in his films, his playful publicity which addresses the spectator as the object of his suspense technique, and an array of stylistic markings which popular critics have cited as constituting his signature, engage that contemporary film spectator on a variety of levels, constructing the 'cat and mouse game' between director and spectator at which Hitchcock excels. The presence of 'Hitchcock' as a cultural institution must obviously be taken into account.

While there is perhaps no doctrine essential to feminism but rather a meta-communicative style of negotiating strategies to deal with particular historical conditions, I would argue that reciprocity – an insistence upon egalitarian distribution of power informed by empathic understanding in social and sexual relationships – is a fundamental goal of this social philosophy and political movement. The feminist viewer finds in *Rear Window* a carefully constructed maze of incompatible desire, a power struggle of dependency between characters without narrative resolution. That maze can be explored with a variety of critical tools which can similarly be applied to the reconstruction of relationships along more feminist lines, both between persons, and between spectators and films. Because the characters in *Rear Window* lack the resources to engage in a meta-communication in which they negotiate and compromise in meeting their needs and gratifying their desires, the spectator is encouraged, particularly in a film which draws attention to its own narration, to construct another film in her reading that imagines and realizes a version of this goal. In *Rear Window* the feminist spectator finds a directorial persona, a series of characters, as well as herself and other spectators pacing the maze. Having analysed its dynamic system, she is pushed to the task of designing and realizing the possibilities of reciprocity.

I will argue that the position of the female spectator, myself included, for *Rear Window* affords the pleasure of critically engaging the analysis of the traps and lures of heterosexual romance as presented by the constructed persona (not the historical person) 'Hitchcock'. The feminist spectator may view this film as an impetus for converting and transforming meaning in the discursive cinematic realm of the feminist critic. Having assessed the terms, the traps and lures in gender-based power struggle which *Rear Window* articulates, she may transform these terms into negotiation and convert a zero-sum proposition into an empathic compromise.

Rear Window presents protagonist L.B. Jefferies (James Stewart), a photographer and adventurer who tours the world snapping pictures. Crippled for six weeks by an accident during a car race he was assigned to photograph, he is 'wooed' by his socialite-model fiancée Lisa Fremont (Grace Kelly) to marry and 'stay put'. But Jefferies resists her blandishments, absorbed in watching his projections played out on the rear windows he viewed from his two-room apartment (Fig. 3). Only by entering his obsession, submitting to the role he has cast for her, does

Lisa arouse and engage his attention. As his neighbour, Thorwald (Raymond Burr) acts out Jefferies's fears and desires, Jefferies confronts that darker part of himself which Thorwald mirrors. Jefferies is nearly murdered by his own intuited reality/projection fantasy, falls into infantile surrender, and is crippled so that he will 'stay put' a while longer. But Lisa, taking power by learning his obsession and casting herself in it as his moll (though manipulating its outcome), succeeds in domesticating him while maintaining a submissive appearance.

Recent methods of film analysis, such as formalism and structuralism, can help us understand how various kinds of pleasure are produced for the spectator in the film by the tightness and symmetry of *Rear Window*'s narrative form. In this case it is pleasure produced by a highly controlled 'imagined world' representing the chaos of psychic and physical violence and disorder. An examination of its linear connections along two levels (Barthes called them proeiretic and hermeneutic[4]) reveals the well-constructed 'Hitchcock' narrative of the incompatibility of stereotyped gender roles.

Rear Window opens with L.B. Jefferies asleep with his back to an open window, his leg in a cast from hip to heel. The camera tracks and pans left to reveal the explanatory visual details of who he is and how he came to have his leg in a cast. The film closes with a similar *mise-en-scène* of Jefferies, who now has both legs in hip-to-heel casts, but this time the camera pans right to Lisa Fremont's beautifully sculpted legs. Across her reclining body, the camera frames the magazine she is reading: *Beyond the Himalayas*. When she notices that Jefferies is asleep, she pulls *Harper's Bazaar* from behind the *Himalayas* and continues to read with a satisfied smile. Such a symmetrical framing device invites reflection: what are the relevant details to explain this change from the story's opening to its close?

The explanatory steps of 'Hitchcock' are presented in scenes, punctuated with fades, for the entire film is in one visually contiguous space: a two-room apartment, a shared courtyard and the spaces visible to the apartment. Having set the task of making a movie, which surely loves to move, in a fixed space from the point of view of a man in a wheelchair, Hitchcock uses these fades to mark temporal ellipses in a five-day sequence. As in most of his films, the story has two interrelated lines of development: the solving of a crime and a relationship between a man and a woman.

Vittorio Giacci claims[5] this combination is not incidental but mutually reinforcing; crime seduces and its solution gives pleasure. The couple and the spectator experience the risks and the mystery of uncovering the 'crime' in a manner that disturbingly parallels the criminal's arousal. The film spectator's enmeshment parallels the romantic enmeshment of the sleuths. Sexual arousal and risk-taking are fundamentally linked in *Rear*

Window. The lines between the crime's uncovering and the couple's enmeshment continually crisscross, most concretely during the climactic scene when Jefferies's fiancée wins her ring, both necessary evidence of murder and symbol of female security in a patriarchal society. Her apparent success is the moment of his demise. Signalling to him across the courtyard, hands behind her back, she betrays his presence to the murderer as he follows the eyeline of her finger to Jefferies's unseen gaze. The tightness of *Rear Window*'s narrative is evident in the way developments that advance the crime's solution also advance the romantic psychic involvement. During the film's opening scenes, the two threads move somewhat separately, but by the final scenes (eleven to fourteen of fifteen scenes), the same action advances both lines, accounting for the intensity of its dramatic resolution.

In the itemization of scenes below, the romance thread is in plain text, the detective mystery in italics and the actions which combine the two are underlined. This enumeration of the film's scenes abstracts a shape from interpreted details that suggest: a) that the film's hero is professionally frustrated at the film's opening; b) that Jefferies's fears of intimacy and responsibility and his desires for mystery and transgression are both projected on to and enacted by his neighbours; and c) that by allowing herself to be cast as the heroine of this adventure, his fiancée produces a situation in which Jefferies will have to confront his own fantasy incarnate, be frightened almost to death and accede to his infantilized state with blissful self-abandonment and delusion, his professional (male-defining) ambition still in abeyance.

1. Jefferies describes his boredom at his invalid predicament contemplating marriage on the phone while *he watches Thorwald from his window.*
2. His nurse Stella discusses Lisa and marriage.
3. Lisa makes dinner during which *Jefferies sees a confrontation between Thorwald and his wife.*
4. Lisa and Jefferies reach a stalemate in their argument about marriage.
5. *Wakened by a scream, Jefferies observes Thorwald carrying his sample case out of the apartment.*
6. After his conversations with Stella and Lisa about marriage *Jefferies uses a telephoto lens to glimpse the knives and saws in Thorwald's case of sales samples.*
7. Unable to seduce him, *Lisa becomes his moll and enters his story.*
8. *Jefferies explains his detective work to Tom Doyle.*
9. *Doyle and Jefferies watch a neighbour's dog dig in Thorwald's flowerbed.*

10. *Doyle refuses to search Thorwald's apartment, saying witnesses have confirmed seeing Mrs. Thorwald leave the apartment on her own.*
11. *While Thorwald packs his bag,* Lisa arrives with her overnight bag to help Jefferies, who makes his first sexual advance towards her.
12. After Doyle leaves, assuming a sexual liaison between Jefferies and Lisa, Lisa models her nightgown while *Jefferies reasons that Thorwald is the murderer of the dog and his own wife.*
13. *Jefferies's slides of the courtyard confirm his suspicion that someone has been digging in the flowerbed before the dog;* Lisa delivers Jefferies's message: 'What have you done with her?'
14. Lisa finds Mrs Thorwald's wedding ring left behind and is rescued just in time by the police while she shows Jefferies the ring and, inadvertently, shows Thorwald that someone is watching her. Jefferies is attacked by Thorwald, falls from his window but is rescued by the police and Lisa.
15. Jefferies sleeps while Lisa watches over him.

At the level of the narrative and its characters, this structural outline allows us to tease out the exploration 'Hitchcock' makes of curiosity, sexuality, dependency and marriage. Jefferies deals with his psychic anxieties at one step removed, projecting them onto his neighbours where they are fortuitously appropriate. He is able to bond his lover, Lisa, only when he has distanced her by projecting himself on to her body. She assumes the role of his surrogate (a simultaneously narcissistic and objectified position) who then absents herself in a moment of crisis, leaving him to confront his own vulnerability. This shift and absenting tells us about the degree to which relationships become struggles between the partners' projections of an inner landscape which the other must learn, act in and manipulate – breaking the other's 'love code'. It is a struggle engaged in by people with varying degrees of awareness, subject to varying degrees of manipulation.

While the resolution suggested by 'Hitchcock' is that male dominance fosters female knowledge of male fantasies, the film does not explore female fantasies beyond bonding and nesting. Without this initial step of reciprocity in the representation 'Hitchcock' makes of the complexity of the hero's and heroine's desires and strategies, the question of whether either party has the skills for negotiation and compromise is never posed. A feminist consciousness is lacking to conceive terms of empathic pleasure rather than control/dominance. Hitchcock's male protagonist lacks the self-awareness to resist manipulation, offering the female spectator a measure of critical amusement not provided by *noir* films. although in both *film noir* and *Rear Window* women gain power by manipulating the projection fantasies of men.[6] In *film noir*, the power of women's sexuality and the self-awareness that fuels their manipulative leverage is the basis of deep fear and suspicion; the *noir* woman must be destroyed. In *Rear Window* the atmosphere of a comedy of manners permeates much of the film; the patina of wit, however, does not belie the seriousness of psychic needs represented in the melodramatic mode, heightened by violence, suicide and murder.

In heterosexual relationships, the fantasies of both sides address certain needs. But the unacknowledged quality of male needs is the basis of a denial which deforms both men and women – the Big Lie of patriarchy, which enforces on women the constructed necessity of a 'female nature' that will service males' needs without negotiation or reciprocity. The game as the 'Hitchcock' characters play it is zero-sum, however playful in appearance, not a co-operative mutuality. Its competitive individualism is patriarchal.

While narrative structures are determinative in constructing spectator meaning, audiences used to decoding social psychology from character behaviour more readily sense the structural relations of character in a highly illusionistic mode of story-telling. If Thorwald is Jefferies's dark double in fantasy, Lisa's match on the other side of the windows, her feared future self, is Miss Lonelyhearts, who first fantasizes a lover, then pursues one who disappoints her, and finally prepares to commit suicide. In her apartment directly beneath Thorwald's, Miss Lonelyhearts goes to the window at exactly the moment and place that Lisa does in Thorwald's apartment above her. (Earlier Miss Lonelyhearts has served wine to her fantasy lover, just as Lisa presented Jefferies with his glass.) Hitchcock's spatial parallel is an immediately accessible structural relation, one which is heightened by Jefferies's lack of empathy for Miss Lonelyhearts's ghostly ritual. Hitchcock allows us to read character relations in terms of space without dialogue; the latter may dissemble as much as disclose.

If we accept the hypothesis that Miss Lonelyhearts is Lisa's feared double, then Miss Lonelyhearts's approaching suicide, noted by Jefferies's nurse, Stella, but ignored by Jefferies as inconsequential, demonstrates his self-absorbed excitement, watching his moll perform before his eyes, but oblivious of the pain of a character who enacts Lisa's inner fears. A musician's compelling performance distracts her from suicide, but does not alter the fact of Jefferies's obsessive unavailability to concerns other than his own. The other dimension of Lisa, the one Jefferies regards as men's pleasure in women's objectified existence in competitive games of conquest, is externalized by the character of Miss Torso of whom Lisa says, 'She's performing a woman's most difficult task: balancing roles', as Miss Torso hostesses, flirts, pleases, and wards off various suitors.

Besides the structural parallels between Jefferies, Lisa and the neighbours (Wood has noted that all the neighbours represent various kinds and stages of coupling[7]), each character has an ally/friend. Vladimir Propp's study of the Russian folk-tale disclosed the presence of such helpers as a common motif in the formulaic consistency with which basic units of narrative followed each other.[8] Peter Wollen's study of *North by Northwest*[9] indicates some relationships between Proppian and Hitchcockian construction that might prove a valid basis for seeing a Utopian or fairy-tale-like function in the friendly alliances presented in this film.

Lisa's helper is Stella, the no-nonsense visiting nurse who doles out marital advice along with hot meals and massages, while Jefferies's ally is Tom Doyle, a former war buddy turned detective. Buddy friendship is suggested with lines like, 'How did we put up with each other in the same plane for three years?' This 'marriage' of compatible personalities enables the men to accept each other's heckling while perpetuating a dread of women's nagging'. The shift of Jefferies's bond from Doyle to Lisa is made strategically possible by the narration as soon as (a) her nagging about marriage gives way to deductive reasoning about crime, (b) her masculinely reckless pursuit of evidence yields results, and (c) her loyal seconding of Jefferies's judgement out-points Doyle's obtuseness and resistance. In the duel with Jefferies's doppelgänger, Lisa replaces Doyle in the cockpit.

Despite the narrative's resolution in favour of Lisa as the supposed 'winner', we gain little insight from *Rear Window* into Lisa's motivations and desires, other than that they are hopelessly incompatible with Jefferies's, until she subjugates them to gain access to his. She is on the screen only as a performer in his line of sight. The dependency of Lisa's visual presence on Jefferies's attention invites the use of semiotic criticism to explore the construction of connotations in her image. Her first appearance is coded as fantasy. The camera offers her not as a mortal entering the two-room apartment, but suddenly appearing before the sleeping Jefferies – a waking dream. Cutting to their profiles, the stepped camera[10] encases her in slow motion as she rises to press her lips to his, a mermaid phantasm from a sea of sleep. Her murmured questions are all about his bodily needs; she is the ultimate sexual fantasy, maternally devoted to his every physical impulse: 'Are you hungry? Does it hurt anywhere?' Like Marilyn Monroe's entrance in a cloud of face powder a few years later in *The Prince and the Showgirl*, Kelly appears as the ultimate Imaginary, a pre-Oedipal desired object completely merged, the breast of abundance that simultaneously offers enveloping security and anxiety-producing engulfment. Psychoanalytically speaking, this is the point in the film where the simultaneity of lure and trap is most explicit.

Lisa performs as a model, introducing herself as she flashes the apartment lamps on her face (as Carol Burnett said of Elizabeth Taylor, 'She's a professional; she knows her light'). She is continually performing, seducing, charming her way into indispensability, that is interdependency. She competes openly with the show in the other windows until, failing this, she consents to enter it. Jefferies's lack of empathy is evident in his response to Miss Lonelyhearts and Miss Torso. Bonding for him occurs only when Lisa is trapped and endangered, ambiguously also the moment of his greatest narcissistic projection. She is performing at his command, offering her body for his use, allowing him a quasi-sexual control over her.

The narrative is most non-committal about the circumstances under which Lisa is 'rescued' by the police and Jefferies is left to face his doppelgänger, who very nearly destroys him or at least leaves him more maimed physically and psychically, than he has Lisa. The female spectator may read Lisa's escape and Jefferies's subsequent endangerment as his 'punishment', but the ambivalence of whether it is an unintentional act or a constructed strategy by Lisa (who could have accused Thorwald on the spot, rather than letting the police leave without him) is underlined by Thorwald's line: 'What do you want from me? Your girl could have turned me in. Do you want money?' Thorwald *assumes* Jefferies is the director, but this has been Lisa's decision. *What did she want*? To have him take the consequences of his own dark fantasy? To be almost destroyed by his own obsession/creation? The narrative's consistent refusal of Lisa's point of view leaves us to interpret only the consequences, not the motivations, of her behaviour.

Hitchcock's win–lose confrontation as the mode of heterosexual incompatibility and power struggle presents the sudden reversals which are the trademark of the suspense-thriller. The male protagonist seems to be winning until he suddenly finds himself imperilled. Through analogy and metaphor, Hitchcock combines and transforms the threat of physical violence or death at the hands of 'criminals' into the threat of psychic violence – the impending loss of selfhood – in the domestic setting. By doing so he combines four gender-specific genres: the female-oriented comedy of manners and melodrama, and the male-oriented suspense-thriller and crime-detective genres. His combination not only suggests a valuable commercial strategy but a comment on the way that genres associated with gender specificity might be related to each other as points of view on the same problem. The manner of this relation has been suggested by analyses of the horror film and the haunted house genre as similarly revolving around psychoanalytic displacement and condensation: the monster as female sexuality[11], the haunted house as the inescapable site of domestic struggle in the family of origin.[12]

While Jefferies's is the dominant point of view of the film in terms of close following (the narrational camera stays with his character on the screen and in reaction shots), other aspects of narrative construction open a gap between the protagonist and spectator in terms of moral sympathies. 'Hitchcock' frequently gave us the attractiveness of stars enacting somewhat unsavoury characters. Like Cary Grant in *Notorious*, Jefferies is at times ruthless, obtuse and narcissistic. The viewer's distance from him is a result of cues provided by characters: in the film: Stella's 'We should get on the outside of ourselves and take a look inside,' Lisa's 'It's more than a little ghoulish to be disappointed that a man did not kill his wife' and Jefferies's own comment to Lisa, 'How would you start to cut up a human body?' Distance is also formally constructed through point-of-view shots, which take the spectator outside of Jefferies, giving us information he does not have: a) what we see while Jefferies is sleeping, b) Stella's view of Miss Lonelyheart's drawing down the blinds, about to commit suicide, c) Thorwald's view of Jefferies talking to Doyle on the phone, unknown to Jefferies, and d) Lisa's abiding satisfaction, surveying the sleeping Jefferies at the film's close.

The spectator's consciousness of this gap between protagonist and viewer, particularly that of the feminist spectator aware of the critical distance that is opened, may turn us to an awareness of dialogue with a directorial consciousness that assesses and comments. The very subject matter that 'Hitchcock' selects elicits the interest of the feminist spectator as does the wit and skill of his analysis. The capacity 'Hitchcock' has for sudden reversals of point of view in other films, (not the least of which are those in which the bodies of women are the most physically abused, for example in *Psycho* and *Frenzy*), as well as his ability to portray either male or female protagonists whose superficial sophistication or deter-mined naiveté deny opportunities for self-knowledge, approaches an objective critique of gender dynamics. But his assessment of the struc-tured incompatibilities of heterosexual romance – its traps and lures – is not matched by his ability to construct alternative routes out of the maze. The exit or the reconstruction of a route that is not entrapment requires a separation of the partners, their developing self-reliance in order that mutual self-reliance can be attained.

In *Rear Window*, Hitchcock's subject is the struggle between partners for privacy *and* intimacy, one to which female spectators and feminists are particularly sensitive, because the pressures of patriarchy require strategies rather than mere assertion. Voyeurism is an invasion of privacy, an undeserved or unwanted intimacy. Privacy and intimacy require self-knowledge and trust; without each other their meaning is altered. Privacy without intimacy becomes isolation, and intimacy without privacy becomes fusion, the loss of self. The necessary boundary of the self encountering another with understanding is the real mystery at the core of this 'Hitchcock' masterpiece of 'light entertainment' as suspense thriller.

Boundaries between selves are reinforced by Hitchcock by the maintenance of stereotyped sex roles, an opposition which sustains tension and a kind of excitement at the price of a non-negotiated incompatibility, an absence of elasticity. The shifting of gender-marked characteristics in an elastic system of circulation based on the choices of the participants is not conceivable in this construction of ambivalence. Hitchcock's ability to shift the point of view in this structured ambivalence suggests a potentially dialogic or relational capacity of the kind set up by Carol Gilligan's gender-specific 'different voice' in negotiating interpersonal decisions.[13] But Hitchcock's ambivalence betrays a pleasure in the control over a sustained opposition. And finally, the quasi-sexual control of 'Hitchcock', mirroring that of Jefferies's is not compatible with the feminist mode described here. Formalistically pleasurable, often witty in its stylistic aspect, (Hitchcock synchronizes the point-of-view shot from the sole of Jefferies's casted foot as he strains to scratch his toes with the off-screen soprano's aria, her attainment of the top of her octave), this drive to control also underlay the ability that 'Hitchcock' had to survive and prevail in the studio system.

The 'Hitchcock' persona constructed by Hitchcock, David Selznick, the press and television was an image of absolute control of those artistic and industrial commercial processes of which he was a part. Our culture continues to admire the famous 'actors are cattle' persona of 'Hitchcock', and his claims to have made the film in his mind before shooting began may be echoed in the spectator's mental game with a director, to whom she/ he happily and pleasurably surrenders her/his 'as-if-it-were-real' emotions for a time. Do Hitchcock's parallel structures connecting Jefferies with the director lead the feminist spectator to a consideration of the way in which our spectator position submits to his vision, precluding other possibilities? Are we quite happy to act in his programmatic spectator's experience? Indeed, the biographical Hitchcock went on record many times as saying that his films were constructed to elicit certain audience responses. Or can the feminist spectator, like Lisa, learn the scenario and convert it at a crucial moment? Will this conversion transmit certain strategies for countering patriarchal games of control, or will it offer different models for constructing an alternative social reality? Are both skills not elemental for feminist processes? Do they exist in tandem within the same social project of representation?

In teaching feminist film criticism and its method of 'reading against the grain', I ask students to select, from a film they have seen in the class, a scene which they believe offers a crucial moment of conversion. They explain why they believe this and reconceive that scene along different lines, providing a rationale for its alteration. The calculated inadequacy of the 'happy endings' that 'Hitchcock' favours seem to me a call for a frustrated spectator who is not content, but who does what the narative did not: reconceives the struggle along different lines. By beginning the project this way, feminist spectator/critics learn how much the ending plays out the terms which earlier scenes have set, where a conversion must begin and in what ways the terms must change.

François Truffaut said in his interviews with Hitchcock that the latter's sense of terror was primal, a childhood psychic experience intensified by the child's sense of powerlessness and desire for control.[14] That tension becomes the 'Hitchcock' balance between the eruption of chaos and the stylistic mastery of the medium. It is part of spectator pleasure in his films, a pleasure like that of the analyst's client who enters the childhood room of fear, faces a monster and leaves. An encounter with 'Hitchcock' is a disturbing pleasure because one has not defused the monster's power but has simply left the room, saying, 'It's just a movie.'

The refusal of mutual reliance for the manipulative leverage of maintained dependency is enacted by characters and offered to spectators. The latter most emphatically are brought to that point by the film's ending, which presents the male protagonist blissfully crippled and sleeping under the watchful eye of his reclining but alert lover-companion. As Robin Wood points out,[15] the lines of spectator identification and implication in the foibles and weaknesses of the 'Hitchcock' characters (the 'Grendl' mode of narrational point of view) invite us back into the womb that the protagonist has re-entered, however contemptuously we are beckoned by the authorial hand, testing our longing for security at whatever risk. The film's ending returns the 'hero', with near perfect symmetry, to his condition at the film's opening, neither healed nor enlightened about what healing might entail. 'Hitchcock' does not take us across the chasm he has opened – the failure to reconceptualize the social relations of intimacy – but leaves the task to spectatorial imagination. For the feminist spectator the pale pleasure of an inadequate 'happy ending' – as Godard said in *Tout Va Bien* quoting Brecht, an ending for the fool who needs one – may lead to the edge of that abyss and to the strength of our imaginations to do what 'he' could/would not.

'Hitchcock' never found his own best analyst, his critically transforming audience. Recalling André Bazin's remark that Jean Renoir made the same film over and over again, 'Hitchcock', too, made his film several times, repeating the experience, perhaps looking for a way out. Lacking a solution, he delights us with his manner of coping, through wit, intelligence, formal beauty and technical control. But for the feminist spectator, male or female, for whom the film's ending is an inadequate resolution of the terror it has disclosed, there is an invitation to go beyond. Not so much to save 'Hitchcock' or 'to save Hitchcock for feminism' but to stimulate the Utopian moment of feminist imagination, to push film to fulfil its promise of representing viscerally the moment when the capacity for reciprocally voiced needs and desires is attained.

Mark Schorer once wrote that artists construct a world in representation which suits their needs better than reality and which they can manipulate and control.[16] Such creativity may be fuelled by boredom or pain, some discontent that pushes us into the creative act, forces us back upon ourselves, because where we are has grown claustrophobic and uncomfortable and we need to be 'out there' inventing, seeing without the scales of what we already know to blind us. Tillie Olson tells us in *Silences*[17] that women may replace the lone Romantic artist creating out of the pain of isolation with a dream of relational creativity growing together in a healthy place with psychic reserves we did not know we had. It should not surprise anyone who knows the position of women in this culture that black women writers like Alice Walker and Toni Morrison are currently our credible speakers and dreamers. They have the credentials to make hope a possibility.

But this invitation to another vision must confront the contradictions of being 'locked within the fortress'[18] if the mode of film production, the institution of consumption and commodification, the social relations constructed by the apparatus and technology in its broadest sense, are contrary to the social relations which a different vision represents. The pleasure of the feminist spectator is finally a pleasure that not only 'reads against the grain' but constructs the possibility of a meta-communication of shared social responsibility and justice within the 'technology' of socially determined practice. The pleasure of the feminist spectator in *Rear Window* is being brought to the moment of critical necessity, when she is launched into the conversion of dominance/submission structures of interpersonal relationships (in Hitchcock's case, moments of sudden reversal) into reciprocal negotiation and empathic compromise.

Notes

'Hitchcock' appears in quotes throughout this essay as a gesture of distinction between Hitchcock as a person and 'Hitchcock' as a set of textual structures operating under an authorial signature.

1. Richard Dyer, 'Entertainment and Utopia', *Movies and Methods*, Bill Nichols (ed.), Berkeley: University of California Press, 1985, pp. 220–32.

2. Robin Wood, 'Fear of Spying', *American Film*, vol. 9, no. 2 (November 1983), pp. 28–35.

3. Ed Buscombe, 'The Idea of Authorship', *Theories of Authorship*, John Caughie (ed.), London: British Film Institute, 1981, pp. 22–34. Roland Barthes, 'The Death of the Author', *Image/Music/Text*, Stephen Heath (trans.), New York: Hill and Wang, 1977. pp. 142–8. Michel Foucault, 'What Is an author?', *Language, Counter-Memory, Practice*, Donald F. Bouchard (ed.), Ithaca, New York: Cornell University Press, 1977, pp. 113–38.

4. Roland Barthes, *S/Z*, Richard Miller (trans.), New York: Farrar, Straus, Giroux, 1974.

5. Vittorio Giacci, 'Alfred Hitchcock: Allegory of Ambiguous Sexuality', Michele S. de Cruz-Saenz (trans.), *Wide Angle*, vol. 4, no. 1, pp. 4–11.

6. Janey Place, 'Women in Film Noir', *Women in Film Noir*, E. Ann Kaplan (ed.), London: British Film Institute, 1978, pp. 35–67.

7. Robin Wood, 'Rear Window', *Hitchcock's Films*, New York: A.S. Barnes, 1965, pp. 61–70.

8. Vladimir Propp, *A Morphology of the Russian Folktale*, Laurence Scott (trans.), Bloomington: University of Indiana Press, 1958.

9. Peter Wollen, '"North by Northwest": A Morphological Analysis', *Readings and Writings: Semiotic Counter Strategies*, London: Verso 1982, pp. 18–33.

10. Stepped camera is an optical effect produced by photographing individual frames at regularly specified intervals and duplicating those single frames a second time. The result is not the slowed-down but smooth effect of slow motion (frames shot twice as fast or twice as many as the usual twenty-four frames per second) but a more erratic slowed-down effect which nevertheless produces a sense of manipulation other than the convention of realism, thereby implying a subjective or psychological dimension of time and reality.

11. Linda Williams, 'When the Woman Looks', *Re-vision: Essays in Feminist Film Criticism*, Mary Anne Doane, Patricia Mellancamp and Linda Williams (eds.), Frederick, Maryland: University Publications of America, in association with the American Film Institute, 1984, pp. 83–99.

12. Thomas Elsaesser, 'Tales of Sound and Fury: Observations on the Family Melodrama', *Monogram*, no. 4, pp. 2–15.

13. Carol Gilligan, *In a Different Voice: Psychological Theory and Women's Development*, Cambridge, Massachusetts: Harvard University Press, 1982.

14. François Truffaut, *Hitchcock*, Helen G. Scott (collaborator), New York: Simon and Schuster, 1983, p. 25.

15. Robin Wood, 'Psycho', *Hitchcock's Films*, New York: A.S. Barnes, 1965.

16. Mark Schorer, *The World We Imagine*, New York: Farrar, Straus, Giroux, 1968, pp. 385–402.

17. Tillie Olson, *Silences*, New York: Delacorte Press, 1978.

18. Fernando Solanas and Octavior Gettino, 'Towards a Third Cinema', *Movies and Methods*, Bill Nicols (ed.), Berkeley: University of California Press, 1976, pp. 44–64.

3

Women's Film Production: Going Mainstream

Michelle Citron

A recent issue of *Time* magazine contains an article about women directors in Hollywood: Martha Coolidge, Susan Seidelman, Amy Heckerling, Barbra Streisand, Elaine May, Penelope Spheeris, Lee Grant, Donna Deitch, Joyce Chopra, Joan Micklin Silver, and others.[1] The article has a self-congratulatory tone; there are plenty of anecdotes to prove that things are still tough for women directors, yet the conditions are getting measurably better. The women mentioned in the article arrived at their current positions from a variety of places. Some started in the women's political-documentary independent film movement of the 1960s and 1970s (Coolidge, Deitch, Chopra). A few came from within the ranks of Hollywood itself (Grant, Streisand and May are actresses, Silver is married to a producer). The remainder are the first post-feminist generation of women to come out of film schools (Heckerling, Seidelman). The journalistic approach taken by *Time* is entertaining – in our still disenfranchised state there is a certain pleasure derived from a good horror story with a clear villain, in this case the male power structure in Hollywood – but not very insightful. The real question that must be asked is: What does it mean for women to decide to enter into the production of mainstream popular culture?[2]

I want to try and answer this question with the interweaving of two different perspectives. One is the macro-view: to look historically and politically at women in film-making in the United States, particularly as it relates to the broader movements of feminism and feminist film theory. The second is the micro-view: to analyse my own development as an American feminist film-maker and to look at this development both at a personal level and as a member of this larger group. I use myself not to suggest that my development was either particularly

45

unique or common, but rather as an entry into certain ideas about the relationship of the personal and psychological to the social and political.

What Does It Mean?

The question, 'What does it mean for a significant number of women to be making narrative films?', immediately presents a problem. The question is abstract and implies some kind of homogeneity, while the motivations, decisions and experiences of each woman entering into narrative film-making are concrete and diverse. This question implies one thing if asked by an intellectual/theorist and something quite different if asked by a film-maker making a decision about her next project. Even among film-makers the question is slippery. As asked by a woman who has worked her way up through the Hollywood hierarchy it has a different implication than as asked by me, a film-maker who comes out of the political film-making movement of the 1960s and 1970s, has a university teaching job, and is well aware of semiotics, psychoanalysis and feminist aesthetic issues. I am now in the process of making a narrative film more mainstream than my previous work. I have yet to find funding and thus it is not yet produced. My perspective on the issues is obviously influenced by where I am in this process. I find I move easily between cynicism and optimism. And I am aware that if I had already completed and exhibited a mainstream narrative film, my analysis might be quite different.

The first problem is terminology. Director, producer/director, filmmaker ... each word implies not only a particular relationship to the product and defines a different degree of control and power, but an ideology as well. When I made avant-garde films in the early 1970s, I called myself a film-maker, a designation that implied I was the sole controlling force behind the work. When my work evolved into films that were more conventionally (though not entirely) narrative in form, I was still a film-maker, still solely responsible for the work. I conceptualized and wrote the film, raised the money, directed the actors, and shot and edited it. I needed people to assist me, to load the magazines, help hang lights and record sound, but it was truly my film, and I took pride in understanding all aspects of the film-making process. In this sense the term 'film-maker' implies artisan: it is associated with the long history of independent film-making and with a deliberate dissociation from what Hollywood, with its job specification and hierarchy, produced. When I made *Daughter Rite* in 1978 I was a film-maker. When I made *What You Take For Granted* ... in 1983 I went into the project as a filmmaker but came out of it thinking of myself as a producer/director. I conceptualized and wrote it, raised the money and directed the actors. But the film was much larger in scope, too big for me to do everything. I needed others to light it, do the cinematography, record the sound, even assistant-direct. This film, more complex to produce, necessitated job specificity and some structure whereby all the different people could work efficiently with each other. Yet there is another level at work here, because when people now, ten years later, ask me what my role was on *Daughter Rite* I answer, 'producer/director'.

In the United States at least, the term 'film-maker' has lost some of its currency and, with the exception perhaps of small avant-garde films, is now rarely used. Its replacement with 'director' implies a shift towards a desire to associate oneself with Hollywood, or at least with the power that implies. In addition, the term 'director' has gained popular recognition and mythical status in our culture. This has been aided by the prevalence of the *auteur* theory regarding Hollywood directors, as indicated by mass media promotion of directors as superstars: feature articles in *People* magazine, entire television programmes devoted to various directors on *At the Movies* and *Sneak Previews*. My use of the term 'film-maker' as opposed to 'director' in this essay is of necessity inconsistent: but hopefully the context will supply the appropriate meaning and resonance.

Mainstream narrative film is also a slippery term. Should it be defined by the text itself, by its mode of production, or by the nature of its distribution and exhibition? Both Hollywood-produced and independently produced films are theatrically distributed. For example, Donna Deitch's *Desert Hearts* (1985) was produced independently and distributed by Samuel Goldwyn, Jr, mainly to theatrical venues in large cities. Independent films can also be lower budget/alternative works, such as Bette Gordon's *Variety* (1983) or Lizzie Borden's *Born In Flames* (1983). Such films will never be shown in mass-audience theatrical distribution, but will be exhibited internationally on the art house circuit, or on the festival and museum circuit, and on foreign television. What I mean here by a mainstream narrative film is one that is aesthetically accessible to a broad audience and relies to a large extent on classical narrative conventions (whether of plot, of characterization, or of cinematic techniques). I also mean a film which is theatrically distributed: that is, seen in venues other than museums, film festivals and the like. A mainstream narrative is defined by the text itself and by its distribution and exhibition pattern and not necessarily by its production history. The simplest test is to ask, 'Is it likely to be reviewed in the mainstream press and on television?' If the answer is yes, for my purposes it is a mainstream narrative film.

Except for the earliest years of film-making, before film became a large-scale business, there have been only two women 'directors' (and here I mean directors of classic Hollywood mainstream narratives): Dorothy Arzner in the 1930s and 1940s, and Ida Lupino in the 1950s. The remaining smattering of women film-makers worked within the avant-garde (for example, Maya Deren), in documentary (for example, Shirley Clarke), or in small entrepreneurial operations (such as educational films, industrial films and commercials). All of these practices were more marginal and thus, in differing degrees, more accessible to women. There were relatively few women film-makers until the 1960s, when increasing numbers of us stepped behind the camera.

I was one of those women in the early 1970s who could suddenly conceive of herself as a film-maker. This was made possible by the general climate of feminism which was challenging the limited options we had previously seen for ourselves. In the film department at the university I was attending, there was also a shift in attitude in response to demands from women for more access to this traditionally male programme. Even so, in the two production classes I took as a student – both classes of twenty-five students – there was only one other woman besides myself.

I was immediately attracted to the avant-garde. I analysed my attraction with the simplistic phrase: new forms for new feminist contents. I wanted to make films that articulated women's experiences and saw the need for a new film language with which to do so. In retrospect, I realize there was another, deeper reason – my attraction to the avant-garde was one manifestation of an almost relentless intellectual upward mobility.

I was determined to rise above my working-class family by proving I was an intellectual. I would make ART, not movies. Movies I associated with all the other cultural products that abounded in my childhood home – *Reader's Digest Condensed Books, Popular Mechanics, Queen for a Day, The Price is Right* and *Mantovani's 101 Strings*. The making of ART was the clearest way for me to put distance between my parents (who embarrassed me) and myself. It was my tool of self-definition and it allowed me to create a world they could not enter. In a house where too many people lived in too few rooms, where I always shared a bedroom with my sister, where most of the rooms didn't have doors that could be closed, ART was a world that separated me from them. I vividly remember bringing my early films home to show my parents, who were very confused by what they saw. And even after viewing them, they insisted to all their friends that their daughter made educational films. It was the label that in their limited experience was the most accurate; although, with my film experience, I knew it wasn't accurate at all. I was secretly pleased by the misunderstanding. My choice of avant-garde was not psychologically self-indulgent. It was tied to an analysis of the regressive ideology of traditional narrative (that is, Hollywood) forms. But my choice of avant-garde over the more popular choice of documentary was also shaped by my personal history.

I was very much influenced by the 'expanded cinema'[3] movement of the 1960s and tried, in isolation, to synthesize it with feminist politics of the early 1970s and my own notions of a feminist aesthetic. At the time I was unaware of the feminist film conference being held in Edinburgh in 1972 and did not read the articles generated by that meeting until 1974 or 1975. I was working, then, in isolation from the film theorists who were using semiotics and psychoanalysis to develop a feminist film theory and feminist aesthetic. In this I was no different from other women film-makers in the United States. Even my position within a major university did not give me an advantage over my community-based contemporaries in terms of access to theoretical work; an indication, perhaps, of the slow filter-down process that usually occurs with intellectual thought.

I made *Self-Defense* in 1972–3. This is a film that presents, through the metaphor of self-defence, women's anger, their coming to consciousness and their ultimate bonding in sisterhood. These ideas are expressed with images of women that have been manipulated through various techniques of optical printing, layering, filtering, and so on (Fig. 4). The images in the first half of the film consist of shapes or moving colours that slowly transform into a woman practising T'ai Chi. The later images of the film are silhouettes of women, first one then two, then three, performing karate forms. The silhouettes are played against highly saturated images of women's 'finery' – jewellery, make-up, fabric – which at first exist within the figures, then outside of the figures, and ultimately disappear altogether. I was surprised by the audience's re-action to my film. It was not, I discovered, just my parents who were confused. On the one hand, the women for whom the film was intended were befuddled and alienated by *Self-Defense*. They had no experience with avant-garde film language and therefore no entry into the film. On the other hand, my fellow film-makers, all men, had no inkling that there was a deeper metaphorical level at work in the film. All they saw were the optically printed images and the technical expertise they implied.

In reaction to this response I separated out the two audiences by making two distinct films – *Integration* (completed in 1974) for the male film-makers, *Parthenogenesis* (completed in 1975) for the women. *Integration* is a structuralist film, once again using techniques of the optical printer. It is an avant-garde film exploring the manipulation of form, detached from feminist concerns at the levels of both medium and content (it is not an example of an attempt at a political 'alternative film practice').

Parthenogenesis, my only documentary, was a conscious attempt to place myself in the context of the feminist film movement of the early 1970s. In the United States, documentaries were seen by feminists as the politically appropriate film form. There were many reasons for this. Documentary, particularly in the 1950s and 1960s, allowed 'outsiders' some access into the relatively closed world of film production. These two decades saw a broadening of the documentary form (influenced by the Free Cinema movement, *cinéma vérité*, television and new technologies), in terms of production techniques, subjects and aesthetics. This atmosphere of experimentation and openness permitted the entry of some women, particularly at the lower levels of the hierarchy, as editors and associate producers. Ironically, the editor turned out to have a position of creative control, and thus of power, since many of these films were, in effect, shaped in a fundamental way during the editing process. By the time the feminist movement of the 1960s emerged with its changing notions of what women could achieve, a group of trained and experienced women documentary film-makers already existed.[4] In addition, documentary's changing and broadening of aesthetic standards and production values had very practical implications. Provided the topic was of compelling interest, a film could be made for less money than, and could look different from, a mainstream narrative yet still be accessible to audiences and critics. This made the documentary form seem even more desirable to film-makers, especially to women with no previous film-making experience.

But there were also clear political reasons why women chose to make documentary films. Documentary, with its long political history and didactic potential, was – given the political situation that motivated most women film-makers at the time – an appropriate form. Documentary film was also seen, particularly in the United States, as a healthy and necessary reaction to the 'unreality' of mainstream narrative film. Women, finally becoming politically aware and self-aware, desired to present 'real' women on the screen, something that Hollywood not only failed to do, but actively worked against. Film theory of the 1970s, with its analysis of realism and ideology, put to rest the naive notion that film is a transparent reflection of reality. And yet documentary film seemed able to be a viable, accessible and powerful means of capturing, or representing, a certain 'lived experience'.

In making *Parthenogenesis*, I saw myself as part of the feminist film movement in the United States. The film follows a week of daily violin lessons between a female teacher and her young female student as they learn the Bach Double Violin Concerto in D minor. It explores the teacher/student interaction, the importance of women as artistic role models, and seeks to demystify the 'creative' process. This last was represented by the one avant-garde technique of the film. The film starts with an abstract image that recurs at various points during the learning of the piece. With each of its appearances, this image becomes more concrete so that by the end of the film it is clearly identifiable as the student and teacher performing the piece they have been practising. This final image of the film represents, simultaneously, the demystified abstracted image and the end result of the learning process documented in the film. With this final image, documentary and avant-garde become one. Although flawed as a film, *Parthenogenesis* was very satisfying in terms of audience response. Not only was it highly accessible, but the device and meaning of the abstracted image were always a focus of viewer response so that awareness of form, as well as of content, was an important aspect of audience discussion.

The political climate of the 1970s also created an environment that encouraged the production of avant-garde films. The use of semiotics and psychoanalysis in analysing classical Hollywood film led to a desire to develop a film practice – defined as avant-garde – that transcended the traditional regressive nature of the medium. I found this investigation of form inspired by feminist film theory very exciting. Examples include the films of Laura Mulvey and Peter Wollen – *Penthesilia* (1974) and *Riddles of the Sphinx* (1976), although many other films and film-makers could be cited as well. Their theoretical investigation offered a more thorough analysis and understanding of the importance of avant-garde film than did the 'expanded cinema' context in which I had been working; and, in making theory concrete, they were very important for what they taught about that theory. I found these films intellectually stimulating and visually beautiful. And yet I also found them lacking; they suppressed the affective, that is the emotional, sphere. But this is precisely the point of these films – which were, as a result, theoretically interesting and politically sound, but flat. They offer intellectual pleasure but rarely emotional pleasure, the consequences of which are both theoretical and practical.

I hadn't always wanted to be a film-maker. In 1970, after completing an undergraduate degree in psychology, I had started graduate work in cognitive psychology at the University of Wisconsin in Madison. Academic psychology was in the grip of behaviourism and I was directed to design empirical experiments – the only methodology recognized by the institution – to research the subtle phenomenon of cognition. My master's thesis was intended to investigate the way in which we synthesize complex concepts from multiple channels of information. I created a multi-media presentation about water that included the simultaneous projection of five slides and three channels of sound. Experimental method required that I project the stimuli in different arrangements (for instance, simultaneous versus linear) to unsuspecting eight-year-olds. I then performed sophisticated multi-variance statistical analysis on the data. I received my degree for the work, but the numbers that emerged from the computer told me nothing about how we make sense out of our experiences: the behaviourist approach, in other words, seemed futile and wrong to me. I concluded that empiricism might be helpful in understanding the brain, but was useless for understanding the mind. My discontent inspired many confrontations with the faculty in my department. Finally, I turned in frustration to a study of the underlying assumptions of empiricism – a study of the history and philosophy of science. In 1974, I was awarded my PhD and immediately became a film-maker, leaving behind for ever the intellectual mire created by committing onself to an empirical methodology – or so I thought.

Years later, while watching feminist avant-garde films grounded in contemporary film theory, I was struck by their similarity to empiricism. Positivism – as manifested in empiricism, which had had its genesis in philosophy and the hard sciences and had subsequently moved into the social sciences in the late 1940s and early 1950s – had finally, so it seemed to me, reached the humanities. These avant-garde films perpetuated one of the dichotomies that underlies positivism: the higher world of the mind (the intellect) over the baser world of the body (the emotions). They represented a kind of artistic empiricism.[5] Useful and intellectually pleasurable as these films and the theory informing them are, both are limited because their underlying meaning is one of separation, not integration. This separation of the intellectual from the emotional and the implied subordination of the latter to the former in some ways paralleled my own attraction, as a beginning film-maker, to ART and not to movies.

Daughter Rite (1978) should be seen in this context. The film is the story of two pairs of sisters and their relationship to their respective mothers. The themes of betrayal, anger, love and manipulation between mothers and daughters and between sisters are presented through an interweaving of cinematic techniques: scripted and acted scenes shot in the visual language of *cinéma vérité* and optically printed home movie images accompanied as voice-over by a narrator reading entries from her journal.

My experiences with audience reactions to my earlier work, as well as my intellectual development in graduate school, led me to want to make accessible avant-garde films. For *Daughter Rite* I tried to solve the problem of accessibility through the device of mixing modes (documentary, narrative and avant-garde) and genres (*cinéma vérité* and melodrama), in order both to critique film language itself and also to open it up to non-avant-garde audiences (Fig. 5). A play on genres, with its mass culture familiarity and appeal, seemed to offer a way of entry into what would otherwise be an avant-garde film. It would allow me to use conventions (of visual style, acting technique, narrative scene pacing and development, characterization) familiar enough to audiences to provide a 'hook'. And by juxtaposing different generic conventions, I hoped to critique and illuminate, as well as to entertain (or perhaps give pleasure). My understanding of accessibility involved embryonic ideas about the validity of the emotional sphere and its importance in film. When I chose to use melodramatic conventions, my choice was dictated by the fact that melodrama is a genre historically associated with women, and was among the earliest issues addressed by feminist film theory and criticism. It is also a genre infused with a highly charged emotional layer. My use of it reflected my desire to integrate the intel-lectual and affective realms.

Many feminist avant-garde films are inaccessible in that they strain the tenuous relationship of communication which binds the film-maker, through the film, to the audience. Through its use of popular genres, this relationship is stronger in narrative film than in other forms. Feminist avant-garde films reject generic convention, relying on the subject-matter of the film to provide entry into an otherwise inaccessible work. But the language and style of the avant-garde, being unfamiliar, create a gap that many viewers cannot bridge. *Daughter Rite* is usually programmed with a second more purely avant-garde feminist film, often Sally Potter's *Thriller* (1979) or Su Fredrich's *The Ties That Bind* (1985), two very important works. Though both are avant-garde, these two films come from different traditions. *Thriller*, a feminist reworking of the story of Puccini's opera *La Bohème*, makes its consciousness of contemporary feminist film theory evident in both sound and image, and uses an avant-garde film language to suppress a potential emotional response from the viewer despite its wonderful use of humour. *The Ties That Bind* is more in keeping with the American avant-garde tradition; it is consciously aware of its use of an unconscious or intuitive language as opposed to a theoretical langue in expressing and encouraging an emotional response from the viewer. Both these avant-garde approaches – whether the separation of the emotional from the intellectual or the use of a personal language to explore the emotional – create a distance from the film for the viewer. If the audience is an art museum or cinema audience having previous experience with avant-garde film language, there is usually little problem with either film. But if the viewers are a general non-film gathering (for instance a women's centre), or a community based group), I often find myself having to explain and defend these films to a confused and sometimes hostile group, angry at being shut out. There is no question that these audiences learn a lot from the experience of viewing and then discussing these avant-garde films. But the experience is dependent upon teaching; the film cannot stand alone. This in itself is not bad, and does in fact expand the audience for future films. I in no way think that all films should reach all audiences and I love and staunchly defend avant-garde work; but from my own political perspective, this kind of avant-garde film practice, although important and necessary, is inevitably circumscribed.

I don't mean to imply that *Daughter Rite* never suffers misunderstanding on the part of 'general' audiences. This is not in fact true, although misunderstanding seems to happen in a somewhat limited way. Of particular difficulty are the home movies/narration sequences in the film. Individual viewers seem to attend *either* to the visual channel *or* to the auditory channel. This does not seem to close the viewer off entirely from the film's meaning and experience, rather it creates a 'hole' for them in an otherwise accessible film.

The film *What You Take for Granted* ... (1983) was my attempt to resolve further this issue of accessibility. It concerns the contradictions of women working in non-traditional blue-collar and professional jobs. Structurally, the film consists of the interweaving of three cinematic components: first, six women who talk directly to camera about their lives and jobs; secondly, two of the six women – a truck-driver and a doctor – engaged in a narrative; and thirdly, documentary footage of women doing various types of work. Thus, cinematic tension is set up which parallels the tension between the public and private spheres of the characters' lives. But while *What You Take For Granted* ... merges cinematic styles, it is nevertheless the most conventionally narrative of my work.

Women's independent/political films in the 1970s, whether documentary or avant-garde, existed in a larger social/political context. This broad context included such varied elements as grassroots political movements (civil rights, anti-war, feminist, gay rights, labour, and so on) with their numerous centres and identifiable members; a more liberal and responsive government agenda than at present regarding social and art programmes; and a lively intellectual environment fuelled by a new political awareness. This made possible independent/political film funding (from government as well as from alternative sources, such as progressive private foundations like the Film Fund), distribution and exhibition.

The context has changed since the 1970s, so those of us working within it must also change. On the simplest level, we have lost our audiences as previously defined (for example, the large network of broad-based women's centres has greatly diminished). Serious Business Company and Iris Films, two important distributors of women's films throughout the 1970s, have ceased to exist (Serious Business ceased trading in 1983, Iris in 1985).[6] Only two distributors of women's films remain in the United States: New Day Films (which has expanded to include labour movement and health films) and Women Make Movies. Other films are occasionally picked up by broader-based independent distributors; this in itself is a kind of mainstreaming. In such a context, films are seen not as women's films but as independent films. In some cases, this can have the advantage of broadening a film's audience; in others, it can bury them out of sight.

But no matter who distributes 'alternative' films, there are fewer companies handling fewer films and exhibiting to smaller audiences. This is in response to a changing market. Women Make Movies can serve as an example. Although their revenues have increased, it is due to an expanded list (they took over a number of Serious Business and Iris films) and a few films that subsidize the rest of the collection by frequent university film department rentals. Demand by women's groups, centres, and so on, has declined as these groups have decreased in number in the United States. Those audiences we reached in the 1970s are no longer out there in the same simply defined way. In this changed context, one could say that women entering into the production of mainstream narrative films are film-makers following their audience. This may be questionable as a political strategy – certanly as judged by the criteria of the 1970s – but it is at least pragmatic. If a film-maker wants her films to be seen by women, she must reach out to them in a different way in the 1980s. She can do this by exploring different distribution strategies – exploiting the half-inch home video market for instance – or more easily by making films that fit into current distribution and exhibition markets, usually meaning mainstream narrative.

For fifteen years feminists have made films which allowed for a privileged communication between film-maker and audience. The film-maker might have travelled with the film and engaged with the audience, answering questions after the screening. Sometimes such a dialogue took place in the classroom between teacher (the film-maker's surrogate) and students. This kind of film-maker/film/audience relationship is difficult to maintain with changing distribution patterns and the decrease in exhibition venues. There are now fewer women's or feminist exhibition situations and less money at universities for film rental or women's studies programmes. My own experience is that over the past ten years or so invitations to screen my films have clearly shifted from women's organizations and women's studies departments to university film and English departments.

Mainstream narrative film, a popular form relying on accepted conventions, has always allowed for an immediate relationship between audience and film. Traditionally, the only mediating devices have been those of the popular film critic and audience word of mouth, which are useful but not necessary for an individual viewer's understanding of a particular film. Given the decrease in political and educational outlets in the United States, narrative film's traditionally unmediated relationship to an audience is increasingly appealing.

One further point may be made about the changed context: the political atmosphere of the 1970s and early 1980s fostered dialogue between film-makers and film-makers, film-makers and audiences, film-makers and film theorists. This dialogue took place at film festivals (Edinburgh Festival in 1972 and 1979), at conferences (the Alternative Cinema Conference at Bard in 1979, the Milwaukee conferences in the late 1970s and early 1980s, the International Conference of Feminist Film and Video Makers in Amsterdam in 1981, to name just a few), in university classes and grassroots community meetings everywhere. This activity was linked to a focused and broad-based feminist political movement. What I see as the mainstreaming of film, whether in terms of film theory or in terms of production, is part of a larger mainstreaming of feminism.

Mainstreaming

Independent production can mean many things, but particularly important is independence of the need for large sums of money. I think the magic number is probably around $200,000 for production costs alone. Less than that a film-maker can probably raise and thus maintain personal control of a project and remain a 'film-maker', in the sense discussed above. More than that necessitates different sources of, and strategies for, obtaining money and consequently a loss of total control over the production. The exception to this would be the director who has a lot of power in the industry, which few women in Hollywood have.[7] In the past I did not need to be concerned with my films selling advertising on television or returning an investment. At my level of financing the profit margin was quickly reached and, once there, I defined the meaning of profit. This gave me the freedom to make what I wanted when I wanted. I still needed resources, but these were attainable. I could get a grant for $6,000 or $20,000. I could use the equipment at the institution where I taught, or borrow a camera for a week from a friend who was not working. Of course this was not easy. A film took four years to make instead of one. I paid heavily with free labour, my own and that of my friends. I was marginal (which had its own special status) but I also took full responsibility for what I produced.

I was a 'film-maker', not a 'director'. I controlled the entire process of making a product that was small enough for control to be maintained. Every film I started I knew I would finish, and I did finish because completion depended solely on my own tenacity. For a director, the situation is different. Within the institution of mainstream theatrical narrative production (whether one works under a studio or independently, in Hollywood, New York or elsewhere) the script can be great, but still unmarketable. A script can be sold, but not produced. A film can be shot but not finished. And a film can be completed yet not distributed or adequately marketed. These become financial, not aesthetic decisions, decisions made by people who probably do not share my priorities regarding film.

The shift from film-maker to director can be seen as trading control for power. The director has the power fed by large sums of money, experienced crew and actors, good equipment, and so on. The director works in a form and with production values that can reach large audiences because the product is familiar to audiences and thus is what theatrical distributors want. In this context, power means a number of things: the opportunity to reach a larger audience, the potential of using mainstream culture to critique or subvert it, the freedom to define and test one's own personal boundaries as film-maker. This is all very seductive. But in the hierarchy of mainstream narrative film the director, in gaining this power, relinquishes control to the producer, to the distributor. Will the film get made and distributed? Who will make the really pivotal decisions? What kinds of compromises to the market-place will have to be made?

A lot of women now desire the kind of power available through mainstream narrative film-making. This change of priorities is one manifestation of our changing social/political context. If women are no longer a clearly definable political movement, then the focus shifts from the group to the individual. This is one understanding of the phenomenon of mainstreaming. When a defined political group is dispersed and submerged within a dominant culture, it can then only be defined by its individual members; power can be exercised only in an individualistic manner. Ironically such personal power is now possible because women collectively have obtained film-making experience and a new level of self-confidence: this is one consequence of the women's movement. It is easier to contemplate making a mainstream narrative film when you've shot a $250,000 documentary or have been to film school and learned to direct a large crew.

But power is double-edged. A desire to make mainstream narrative films can also indicate an acceptance of our culture's definition of progress and success. The myth is that bigger is better: more money for production, higher production values, stars, wider distribution and larger audiences means a BIGGER film which means progress and thus a better product.

The politics of the 1970s provided us with alternative myths to those of the dominant culture: politically correct is better; the artisan grounded in the community, however small, is better. Feminist film-makers had little desire to enter into the mainstream film world; our goal was to make films in direct opposition to that world. We wanted to make films that challenged the status quo. Whether documentary or avant-garde, these were films for a purpose, for political organizing and consciousness-raising in the broadest sense. This film practice challenged ideas about film language, the relationship between viewer and film, and the function of cinema in our society. But in a changing political context, the dominant film world has become more enticing. This is not to argue that the desire to make mainstream narrative features has no legitimacy. But it does reflect part of the paradox and contradiction of wanting to do so.

One interpretation of women's move into the production of narrative film is that women now feel a willingness to take different kinds of risks: to perhaps be the woman who, while accepting the parameters of main-stream narrative film as dictated by both the market-place and the strong psychological pull of narrative, can subvert it. In one way, this acceptance of power can be seen as a desire, reinforced by self-confi-dence, to 'win on our own terms'. This might be easier for younger women who are entering into narrative production today, the field changed by the women who came before them; they enter film-making with a kind of self-confidence bred of their age and environment. These women can build on a now visible history of women film-makers and directors, including directors of feature films, both narrative and documentary. In entering film-making through mainstream narrative production, they do not have to first reassess, and in a sense reject, their own prior non-narrative work. These women can define compromise differently because, both personally and culturally, they have come out of a different historical moment.

The situation is different for women who have already worked in film and are moving into narrative production from other forms. Any kind of film production is a compromise forged on a constantly shifting matrix of content, aesthetics, accessibility, access to financial and production resources, distribution and exhibition potential, and so on. As political film-makers of independent avant-garde and documentary films, our choices were based on our priorities at the time. What we sacrificed in a particular compromise was not in that context as important as what we gained. A film-maker might make a seventeen-minute film that would be seen by no more than 10,000 women. But the film had a clarity of political and aesthetic vision completely in the film-maker's control. Audience size was augmented if the film could be used as an educational or organizing tool. But the shifting historical moment creates both a willingness and a need to make different compromises. Today, a woman director can make a low-budget feature which gets theatrically distributed and seen by hundreds of thousands of women. But in this case, the demands of the market as 'safeguarded' by the producer circumscribe risks at the level of either form or content. The contradictions here are unlimited. Martha Coolidge tells of a conversation she had with the producer of *City Girl*, a film she directed in 1981 but which has never been completed. 'The first thing the producer said to me was, "Are you a feminist?" Well, of course I'm a feminist. But I knew that if I said yes, I'd lose the job. So I said no.'[8]

How do the compromises made by women working within Hollywood with limitations imposed from above differ from those faced by women working independently? At what point does a practical compromise become a betrayal of past goals, experience and work? When is a compromise valuable? The answers to these questions are difficult, as they are shaped by continually shifting cultural contexts and the changing experiences of women film-makers. Nevertheless, it is important that women are entering into narrative film production; though I make this statement with full awareness of its contradictions and ambiguities.

What Is the Meaning of Narrative?

Narrative film's enduring quality as popular art implies some deep psychological attraction which the form holds for us: attempts to understand this phenomenon have provided a central focus for contemporary film theory. This has often meant a study of genre. With women's entry into the production of mainstream narrative films, understanding genre becomes doubly important, since to make a mainstream narrative film today is to work within a genre. The questions raised by women's move into mainstream narrative film production are therefore not only about accepting power and losing or relinquishing control, but about the power of genre itself. What is our attraction to genre? Can women create new genres? Can we work within the context of old genres, while creating a different point of view or subverting it in some other way? I would like to look at Martha Coolidge's film *Valley Girl* (1983) as an example.

Valley Girl is a romantic comedy about Los Angeles Valley high schooler Julie, who is bored with her Valley steady Tommy, a conservative egocentric stud. Julie becomes attracted to Randy, a working-class punk from the inner city (Hollywood). Her romance with Randy is played out in the context of the values of her own upper-middle-class culture, as represented by her friends who greatly discourage her new romance because Randy comes from the 'wrong side' of the Hollywood Hills.

Early in the film there is a party scene. Tommy, recently rejected by Julie, responds by cornering Loryn, one of Julie's close friends. He coaxes her away from the party into an upstairs bedroom where he comes on to her sexually. At first Loryn resists, insisting it would be wrong for them to make out because of her loyalty to Julie. Tommy tells her he is emotionally devastated, that it is Julie's fault, and that he needs the solace that only Loryn, with her sexual favours, can provide. His flattery gradually breaks down Loryn's initial protests, and he succeeds in getting her to undress. At the point when Loryn is most vulnerable, lying on the bed with her breasts exposed, she asks, 'Tommy, does this mean we're going together?' Tommy, who by now has got what he wants from Loryn replies, 'No. I think it means you're a pretty lousy friend ... messing around with your girlfriend's boyfriend while he's in a bad way. But I'll tell you what. I won't tell anybody if you won't. 'Loryn is stunned by the betrayal but before she can respond, Tommy bolts, leaving her alone on the bed crying.

This bedroom scene, composed of only one shot – camera angled slightly above Loryn and Tommy as they lie on the bed – is presented exclusively from the emotional point of view of Loryn. The characters are positioned in the frame with Loryn beneath Tommy so that we clearly see Loryn's full face and body. Tommy, looming over her, is little more than a barely identified male back. This shot set-up privileges Loryn's emotional point of view by enabling us to see her changing body language and facial expressions as the scene unfolds. We see her vulnerability, humiliation and doubt of her own perception as she trusts Tommy, yielding to his need to be nurtured and succumbing to his flattery, only to be used by him. In this context, Loryn's nudity becomes an indictment of Tommy's sexist manipulations, and not the presentation of a women's body for male visual pleasure. The female nudity in this film was a demand made by the producer, a demand to which Coolidge knew she would have to acquiesce. In this particular instance Coolidge's only choice was how to film the nudity. Coolidge took the producer's demand for female nudity and used it towards her own feminist ends.

This scene, moreover, is intercut with the party going on downstairs and the first verbal interaction between Julie and Randy, her new romantic interest. This meeting is initiated by Julie's aggressive gaze at Randy across the crowded room. The scene between Loryn and Tommy in the bedroom makes public a common exchange experienced privately by women in the male/female sexual game. The scene between Julie and Randy at the party presents an alternative scenario for female/male interaction. The intercutting of the meeting downstairs with the scene of sexual humiliation upstairs presents a sequence in which a young woman's relationship to sex and power is explored in a strong and unusual manner.

However, this scene occurs in a film which is, for the most part, fairly conventional. *Valley Girl* falls into the genre of romantic comedy in its presentation of a female protagonist who must make a decision about her life, a decision defined by conventionality versus individuality. But the choice is only between two boys: should she date the young, upper-class stud Tommy, who comes from and represents the conservative values of her own class, or should she date the young, working-class punk Randy and so choose the 'other'? Despite peer group pressure she chooses the punk, thus affirming her strength of character and imagination. Yet ultimately, the choice can be framed only in the context of a conventional male/female relationship. The film is not particularly progressive on a narrative level, but rather is similar to others in the romantic comedy genre, from *The Philadelphia Story* (1940) to *Kiss Me Goodbye* (1982) to *Desperately Seeking Susan* (1985).

The nudity in *Valley Girl*, as well as the genre itself, were demands made by the producer, not choices made by the director. But Coolidge is able to work within the constraints of a popular genre and subvert it in small but significant ways by offering a point of view informed by a feminist awareness. She is able to work within an established genre and deliberately play on audience expectations. I am not suggesting that all women directors wish, or have the ability, insight or position, to twist formulas, just as subversion cannot be assured simply because a woman director works independently. But the potential for subversion in a mainstream context nevertheless does exist.

Most women directors working in Hollywood have been confined to traditional women's genres such as melodrama – Lee Grant's *Tell Me a Riddle* (1980), Amy Jones's *Love Letters* (1983); or comedy – Amy Heckerling's *National Lampoon's European Vacation* (1983), Lisa Gottlieb's *One of the Boys* (1985), Susan Seidelman's *Desperately Seeking Susan* (1985). Few have been allowed to direct detective films, thrillers, or science fiction, genres which are 'male' as well as more expensive to produce. The exceptions have been light comic science fiction such as Seidelman's *Making Mr Right* (1987) and Coolidge's *Real Genius* (1985), and Penelope Spheeris's two low-budget exploitation films *Hollywood Vice Squad* (1985) and *The Boys Next Door* (1984). But even women working independently outside Hollywood have chosen for the most part to work within traditional women's genres. For example, both Donna Deitch's *Desert Hearts* and Joyce Chopra's *Smooth Talk* (1985) are melodramas.

What does this mean? Is it some recognition of the psychological validity of these genres that have historically been regarded as women's domain? Or is it a result of what will 'sell' and therefore be safe? What is the relationship between the psychological, the social, the political and the historical? What is so compelling about specific genres? What is so compelling about narratives? Can stories and myths be created that are different from the ones currently popular? What is the relationship between the meaning of the form and the meaning of the myth? How can point of view function? Contemporary film theory has attempted to answer some of these questions. But we need to broaden our theoretical approach to include along with work on film texts, analyses of their social, economic, political and historical dimensions. The consequences of this broadening will become clear only when we are in a position to examine a large body of narrative films directed by women. Only then can we ask different questions, or ask the same questions in a different way.

The social and political thought and activity of the 1960s and 1970s provided a focus for what we, as film-makers, wanted to say. Documentary, the form of the didactic, flourished. The theoretical analysis of film in the 1970s provided a focus for the experimentation of the avant-garde. These two approaches and the resultant film practices had an underlying assumption of 'political correctness'. Narrative film, however, is more ambiguous. It allows for contradictions, paradoxes, uncertainties. My own desire to explore narrative is an acknowledgement and acceptance that all is not clearly understood. It is an attempt consciously to explore the meaning of myth and ambiguity, and it is only at the present historical and personal moment that I can do so. This is not to imply that all women going 'Hollywood' share my motives, nor that all women film-makers should be making narrative films. Women should not focus exclusively on narrative films: documentary and avant-garde films still need to be made. I only suggest that the entry of women into mainstream narrative film-making will broaden the work we do and expand our understanding of visual culture and of ourselves. Ultimately, my argument is for heterogeneity; to add to the production of documentary and avant-garde, not to replace it.

To make narrative films is to take risks. However, these are risks we need now to take. We will lose a certain amount of control of our films, despite our best intentions and preparedness. We will make bad judgements. We will even make bad films. But we need new 'data' in order to refine our understanding of film and our relationship to it. By making narrative films, we can accumulate such material. What we need now are narrative films made by as many women as possible in as many ways as possible about as many things as possible.

Notes

I would like to thank Fina Bathrick and Chuck Kleinhans for their valuable feedback on earlier drafts of this essay.

1. *Time*, 24 March 1986, pp. 82–3.

2. For two other approaches, written by film-makers concerned with experimental narrative, see Jill Godmillow, 'A Little Something on Narrativity', the *Independent*, vol. 9, no. 3 (April 1986). And Yvonne Rainer, 'Some Ruminations around Cinematic Antidotes to the Oedipal Net(tles) while Playing with De Lauraedipus Mulvey, or, He May Be Off Screen, But ...', the *Independent*, vol. 9, no. 3 (April 1986).

3. 'Expanded Cinema' was a label coined by Gene Youngblood in the early 1970s to describe a varied body of avant-garde film work being produced in the United States. The work, which included the films of Stan Brakhage, Scot Bartlett, Bruce Baillie, and Will Hindle, among others, was noted for its use of varied formal experimentation which reflected the 'expanded consciousness' of the film-maker in the 1960s.

4. It is not surprising that New Day Films, the first feminist film distributor in the United States, had its inception at a Flaherty Seminar; its creation was motivated by the sense of disenfranchisement felt by a number of women documentary film-makers at the time.

5. Terry Lovell has a much more refined discussion of the similarities between empiricism and contemporary film theory in her book *Pictures of Reality: Aesthetics, Politics and Pleasure*, London: British Film Institute, 1980. What I call empiricism, Lovell more accurately defines as three different intellectual approaches (empiricism, conventionalism and realism). In addition, my analysis comes from a viewing of contemporary avant-garde feminist films, products of the theory, while Lovell's analysis is based on an analysis of the theory itself. Empiricism is even more transparent in mainstream communication studies as practised by the majority of radio–television–film departments in universities in the United States. This is analogous to my experiences of psychology in the late 1960s and early 1970s; the embracing of a methodology that represents a simplistic understanding of the powers of empiricism and a misplaced attempt to make the intellectual work of cultural studies 'scientific'.

6. Two good articles on the reality of independent film funding, production, distribution and exhibition are Freude Bartlett's, 'Distributing Independent Films', *Jump Cut*, no. 31, and 'Freude Bartlett Interviewed: Doing Serious Business', *Jump Cut*, no. 31 (1986).

7. The May 1986 issue of *Life* magazine is devoted entirely to Hollywood. The cover shows a group photo captioned 'Hollywood's most powerful women'. Pictured are five actresses: Sally Field, Jane Fonda, Goldie Hawn, Jessica Lange and Barbra Streisand.

8. *Time*, p. 83.

4

Pleasurable Negotiations

Christine Gledhill

This essay takes as its starting-point the recent renewal of feminist interest in mainstream popular culture. Whereas the ideological analysis of
the late 1970s and early 1980s, influenced by post-structuralism and
cine-psychoanalysis, had rejected mainstream cinema for its production
of patriarchal/bourgeois spectatorship and simultaneous repression of
femininity, other approaches, developing in parallel, and sometimes in
opposition to, psychoanalytic theories argued for socio-culturally differentiated modes of meaning production and reading.[1] Feminist analysis
has focused in particular on forms directed at women. While feminist
literary criticism recovers women's fiction – both Victorian and contemporary, written by women and/or for women, feminist work on film and
television has particularly explored the woman's film, melodrama and
soap opera.[2] A frequent aim of this enterprise, which relates commonly
derided popular forms to the conditions of their consumption in the lives
of socio-historically constituted audiences, is to elucidate women's
cultural forms, and thereby to challenge the male canon of cultural
worth. In this respect, feminist analysis of the woman's film and soap
opera is beginning to counter more negative cine-psychoanalytic views
of female spectatorship.

Cine-psychoanalysis and Feminism

The theoretical convergence of psychoanalysis and cinema has been
problematic for feminism in that it has been theorised largely from the
perspective of masculinity and its constructions. Notions of cinematic
voyeurism and fetishism serve as norms for the analysis of classic

64

narrative cinema, and early cine-psychoanalysis found it difficult to theorize the feminine as anything other than 'lack', 'absence', 'otherness'. Underpinning these concepts lay the homology uncovered between certain features of cinematic spectatorship and textual organization, and the Oedipal psycho-linguistic scenario theorized by Jacques Lacan in which the child simultaneously acquires identity, language and the Unconscious.[3] In this structure, the child's perception of sexual difference as the maternal figure's castration and the consequent repression of this perception are linked to the similarly hidden role of phonological and linguistic difference in the operation of language and production of meaning (it is the difference between 't' and 'd' that enables the formation of different words, and the difference between 'sheep' and 'mutton' that enables meaning to arise from such linguistic forms). This homology between the psychic and the linguistic, it is argued, enables the (male) child both to enter the symbolic order and to master language. It also, however, results in the repression of femininity. Thus the patriarchal subject is constructed as a unified, consistent, but illusory identity – a 'self' whose words appear to give it control of a world to which it is central. (In this respect, the identity of the patriarchal subject coalesces with the centrality of the 'individual' in bourgeois ideology.) Underlying these constructs there exists another reality – language and subjectivity as processes that produce each other, ever in flux, and based in linguistic and psychic 'difference'. Self, speech and meaning can never coincide with each other and fail to provide more than the illusion of mastery. For both bourgeois and patriarchal subjects, 'difference' – gender, sex, class, race, age, and so on – is alienated as 'otherness' and repressed. The repressed threatens to return, however, through the processes of the 'Unconscious'.

According to cine-psychoanalysis, classic narrative cinema reproduces such psycho-linguistic and ideological structures, offering the surface illusion of unity, plenitude and identity as compensation for the underlying realities of separation and difference.[4] The subject of mainstream narrative is the patriarchal, bourgeois individual: that unified, centred point from which the world is organized and given meaning. Narrative organization hierarchizes the different aesthetic and ideological discourses which intersect in the processes of the text, to produce a unifying, authoritative voice or viewpoint. This is the position – constructed outside the processes of contradiction, difference and meaning production – which the spectator must occupy in order to participate in the pleasures and meaning of the text.

Since in this argument narrative organization is patriarchal, the spectator constructed by the text is masculine. Pleasure is largely organized to flatter or console the patriarchal ego and its Unconscious.

Simultaneous sublimation and repression of femininity is literally re-enacted in the way plot and camera place the female figure in situations of fetishistic idealization or voyeuristic punishment. This has led to the argument that female representations do not represent women at all, but are figures cut to the measure of the patriarchal Unconscious. In particular the 'look' of the camera – mediated through the 'gaze' of a generally male hero – has been identified as male.[5] While these arguments have attracted feminists for their power to explain the alternate misogyny and idealization of cinema's female representations, they offer largely negative accounts of female spectatorship, suggesting colonized, alienated or masochistic positions of identification. Moreover, given the absorption of class struggle within patriarchal narrative structures – the textual spectator is a trans-class construct – this perspective has difficulty in dealing with the female image or spectator in terms of class difference.

While the theoretical gap between textual and social subject may seem unproblematic when considering male spectatorship – perhaps because the account of the male spectator fits our experience of the social subject – this distinction is crucial for feminist criticism, with its investment in cultural and political change for women in society. The psycho-linguistic location of the feminine in the repressed semiotic processes of signification leads to the advocacy of the 'feminine' avant-garde or the 'deconstructive' text as a means of countering the patriarchal mainstream. Such works, it is argued, counteract the power of the classic narrative text to reduce the play of semiotic and sexual difference to the 'fixed position' and 'identity' of the patriarchal subject. The avant-garde or deconstructive text foregrounds the means of its construction, refuses stable points of identification, puts 'the subject into process' and invites the spectator into a play with language, form and identity. The more politically tendentious work literally 'deconstructs' the text, taking it apart to expose the mechanisms of mainstream narrative.[6] However, such procedures do not, in my view, avoid the problems of positioning. While the political avant-garde audience deconstructs the pleasures and identities offered by the mainstream text, it participates in the comforting identity of critic or *cognoscente*, positioned in the sphere of 'the ideologically correct', and the 'radical' – a position which is defined by its difference from the ideological mystification attributed to the audiences of the mass media. This suggests that the political problem is not positioning as such, but which positions are put on offer, or audiences enter into.

Recent initiatives in feminist film theory – drawing on the work of feminist psychoanalysts and social psychologists such as Luce Irigary, Julia Kristeva, Nancy Chodorow and Dorothy Dinnerstein – have made possible considerable revisions to the cine-psychoanalytic construction of the classic narrative text, facilitating attempts to take account of the 'female spectator'.[7] However, as Annette Kuhn points out, this work draws on theoretically divergent analytical approaches. 'Female spect-atorship' elides conceptually distinct notions: the 'feminine spectator', constructed by the text, and the female audience, constructed by the socio-historical categories of gender, class, race, and so on.[8] The ques-tion now confronting feminist theory is how to conceive their relationship.

One approach to the problem of their elision is to question the ident-ification of mainstream narrative structures with patriarchal/bourgeois ideology on which it is based. For while avant-garde practices may produce a spectator 'fixed' in the avant-garde, recent work suggests that the textual possibilities of resistant or deconstructive reading exist in the processes of the mainstream text. To pursue this avenue, however, we require a theory of texts which can also accommodate the historical existence of social audiences. For 'femininity' is not simply an abstract textual position; and what women's history tells us about femininity lived as a socio-culturally, as well as a psychically differentiated category, must have consequences for our understanding of the form-ation of feminine subjectivity, of the feminine textual spectator and the viewing/reading of female audiences. Work on women's cultural forms, female audiences and female spectatorship poses this problem in acute form.

Culture as Negotiation

Arguments which support the notion of a specific, socio-historically constructed female cultural space come from diverse intellectual contexts and traditions and do not yet form a coherent theory. A range of concepts have been drawn on, including sub-cultural reading, cultural competence, decoding position and so on. A notion frequently deployed in various contexts is that of 'negotiation'.[9] It is the purpose of this piece to suggest that this concept might take a central place in rethinking the relations between media products, ideologies and audiences – perhaps bridging the gap between textual and social subject. The value of this notion lies in its avoidance of an overly deterministic view of cultural production, whether economistic (the media product reflects dominant economic interests outside the text), or cine-psychoanalytic (the text constructs spectators through the psycho-linguistic mechanisms of the patriarchal Unconscious). For the term 'negotiation' implies the holding together of opposite sides in an ongoing process of give-and-take. As a model of meaning production, negotiation conceives cultural exchange as the intersection of processes of production and reception, in which overlapping but non-matching determinations operate. Meaning is neither imposed, nor passively imbibed, but arises out of a struggle or negotiation between competing frames of reference, motivation and experience. This can be analysed at three different levels: institutions, texts and audiences – although distinctions between levels are ones of emphasis, rather than of rigid separation.

A theory of 'negotiation' as a tool for analysing meaning production would draw on a number of tenets of neo-Marxism, semiotics and psychoanalysis, while at the same time challenging the textual determinism and formalism of these approaches in the ideological analyses of the 1970s. In place of 'dominant ideology' – with its suggestion either of conspiratorial imposition or of unconscious interpellation – the concept of 'hegemony', as developed by Antonio Gramsci, underpins the model of negotiation.[10] According to Gramsci, since ideological power in bourgeois society is as much a matter of persuasion as of force, it is never secured once and for all, but has continually to be re-established in a constant to and fro between contesting groups. 'Hegemony' describes the ever shifting, ever negotiating play of ideological, social and political forces through which power is maintained and contested. The culture industries of bourgeois democracy can be conceptualized in a similar way: ideologies are not simply imposed – although this possibility always remains an institutional option through mechanisms such as censorship – but are subject to continuous (re-)negotiation.

Institutional Negotiations

The economics and ideologies of the 'free market' produce a contradictory situation which lays capitalist production open to the necessity of negotiation. Terry Lovell argues that the search for new markets requires new products, exchanged for a range of ever extending use-values.[11] But these values vary according to particular groups of users and contexts of use. Even consumer products such as cars or washing-machines, which might seem predictable and amenable to ideological control (through advertising, for instance), may have unforeseen social and cultural uses for specific social groups.[12] If this is true of consumer products, then the use values of media texts (which lie in a complex of pleasures and meanings operating at different levels – aesthetic, emotional, ideological, intellectual) are far less easily predicted and controlled. Thus the use-value to a particular group of a profitable (in the short-term) media product may be in contradiction with the ideologies which in the long term maintain capitalism. An obvious example of this is the publishing industry, for certain branches of which Marxist and feminist books make profitable commodities.

Negotiation at the point of production is not, however, simply a matter of potential contradiction between the needs of the media industries and user groups. Within media institutions, the professional and aesthetic practices of 'creative' personnel operate within different frameworks from, and often in conflict with, the economic or ideological purposes of companies and shareholders. Such conflict is, indeed, part of the ideology of creativity itself. Aesthetic practice includes, as well as formal and generic traditions, codes of professional and technical performance, of cultural value and, moreover, must satisfy the pressure towards contemporary renewal and innovation. These traditions, codes and pressures produce their own conflicts which media professionals must attempt to solve.

An example of the kind of negotiation provoked by the inherent contradictoriness of the media industries is offered in Julie D'Acci's chronicle of struggles over the American television series, *Cagney and Lacey*, between CBS network executives and their advertisers, its independent writing/producing team (two women friends, plus a husband) and sections of the American women's movement.[13] According to D'Acci, the series would not have originated without the public spread of ideas circulated by the women's movement – with which the producing trio identified and which could be called on in times of trouble to support the programme. What made the series saleable was not its incipient 'feminism', but the innovation of a female buddy pairing in the cop show – an idea inspired by Molly Haskell's critique of the 1960s–1970s male buddy movie for its displacement of good female roles.[14] The series, however, despite successful ratings and an Emmy award, had been under frequent threat of cancellation from CBS, in large part, D'Acci argues, because of the problematic definitions of 'woman' and female sexuality that it invokes, particularly in relation to the unmarried Christine Cagney, whose fierce independence and intense relation to another woman has led to three changes of actress in an effort to bring the series under control and reduce the charge of lesbianism – something such strategies have singularly failed to do.

Textual Negotiations

The example of *Cagney and Lacey* suggests how the product itself becomes a site of textual negotiation. Contradictory pressures towards programming that is both recognizably familiar (that conforms to tradition, to formal or generic convention) and also innovative and realistic (offering a twist on, or modernizing, traditional genres) leads to complex technical, formal and ideological negotiations in mainstream media texts. For example, the decision by the makers of *Cagney and Lacey* to put a female buddy pair inside a cop series, as well as using gender reversal to breathe new life into an established genre, immediately raises aesthetic and ideological problems. Conflicting codes of recognition are demanded by the different generic motifs and stereotypes drawn into the series: the cop show, the buddy relationship, the woman's film, the independent heroine. Moreover, the female 'buddy' relationship can be 'realistically' constructed only by drawing on the sub-cultural codes of women's social intercourse and culture. Inside a soap opera, such codes are taken for granted. Inside a police series, however, they have a range of consequences for both genre and ideology. When female protagonists have to operate in a fictional world organized by male authority and criminality, gender conflict is inevitable. But the series could not evoke such gender conflict with any credibility if it did not acknowledge discourses about sexism already made public by the women's movement in America. Such discourses in their turn become an inevitable source of drama and ideological explanation. The plotting of *Cagney and Lacey* is itself made out of a negotiation, or series of negotiations, around definitions of gender roles and sexuality, definitions of heterosexual relations and female friendships, as well as around the nature of the law and policing.

Crucial to such a conception of the text are the semiotic notions of textual production, work and process. According to this perspective, meanings are not fixed entities to be deployed at the will of a communicator, but products of textual interactions shaped by a range of economic, aesthetic and ideological factors that often operate unconsciously, are unpredictable and difficult to control.

Reception as Negotiation

To the institutional and aesthetic vagaries of production is added the frequent diminution of textual control at the third level of media analysis – reception. The viewing or reading situation affects the meanings and pleasures of a work by introducing into the cultural exchange a range of determinations, potentially resistant or contradictory, arising from the differential social and cultural constitution of readers or viewers – by class, gender, race, age, personal history, and so on. This is potentially the most radical moment of negotiation, because the most variable and unpredictable. Moreover we are not dealing with solitary viewers or readers. Ien Ang and Janice Radway, writing respectively on soap opera viewing and romance reading, discuss viewing and reading as a social practice, which differs between groups and historical periods and shapes the meanings which audiences derive from cultural products. This line of argument points beyond textual analysis, to the field of anthropological and ethnographic work with 'real' audiences.[15]

A frequent aim of this research is to rescue the female sub-cultural activity, resistance and pleasure that may be embedded in popular, mainstream culture. However, to start from the perspective of audiences and their putative pleasures is not without problems of its own. Such an approach is open to charges of relativism – in other words, there is no point to ideological analysis because meaning is so dependent on variable contexts. Or it may be accused of populism – a media product cannot be critiqued if audiences demonstrably enjoy it.[16] Counter-readings of popular texts often get caught up in arguments about whether particular films or television programmes are 'progressive' or 'subversive'. And concern with the pleasures or identifications of actual audiences seems to ignore the long-term task of overthrowing dominant structures, within which resistant or emergent voices struggle on unequal terms. In any case, it is often argued, capitalism cannot ignore the potential market represented by groups emerging into new public self-identity and its processes invariably turn alternative life-styles and identities into commodities, through which they are subtly modified and thereby recuperated for the status quo. Thus the media appropriate images and ideas circulating within the women's movement to supply a necessary aura of novelty and contemporaneity. In this process, bourgeois society adapts to new pressures, while at the same time bringing them under control.[17] To such criticisms, cine-psychoanalysis adds the argument that approaches from the perspective of the audience ignore the role of language and the Unconscious in the construction of subjectivity, assuming that external socio-economic or cultural determinations provide material for the class or gender consciousness of otherwise free-thinking subjects.

To characterize cultural exchange between text and reader as one of negotiation, however, does not necessitate a return to an economistic view of language and cultural form as transparent instruments of subjective expression. The concept of negotiation allows space to the play of unconscious processes in cultural forms, but refuses them an undue determination. For if ideologies operate on an unconscious level through the forms of language, the role of the 'other' in these processes is not passively suffered. The everyday working of argument and misunderstanding – in which contesting parties are positioned by, and struggle to resist, the unarticulated, 'unconscious' meanings running through their opponents' words, tones and gestures – demonstrates the extent to which 'otherness' may be negotiated. In this process, such constraints may become available to conscious understanding. A similar struggle can be posited of cultural exchange. Language and cultural forms are sites in which different subjectivities struggle to impose or challenge, to confirm, negotiate or displace, definitions and identities. In this respect, the figure of woman, the look of the camera, the gestures and signs of human interaction, are not given over once and for all to a particular ideology – unconscious or otherwise. They are cultural signs and therefore sites of struggle; struggle between male and female voices, between class voices, ethnic voices, and so on.

Negotiation and Cultural Analysis

The value of 'negotiation', then, as an analytical concept is that it allows space to the subjectivities, identities and pleasures of audiences. While acknowledging the cine-psychoanalytic critique of the notion 'selfhood' – of 'fixed' and centred identity – the concept of negotiation stops short at the dissolution of identity suggested by avant-garde aesthetics. For if arguments about the non-identity of self and language, words and meaning, desire and its objects challenge bourgeois notions of the centrality and stability of the ego and the transparency of language, the political consequence is not to abandon the search for identity. As has been frequently noted, social out-groups seeking to identify themselves against dominant representations – the working class, women, blacks, gays – need clearly articulated, recognizable and self-respecting self-images. To adopt a political position is of necessity to assume for the moment a consistent and answerable identity. The object of attack should not be identity as such but its dominant construction as total, non-contradictory and unchanging. We need representations that take account of identities – representations that work with a degree of fluidity and contradiction – and we need to forge different identities – ones that help us to make productive use of the contradictions of our lives. This means entering socio-economic, cultural and linguistic struggle to define and establish them in the media, which function as centres for the production and circulation of identity.

However, knowledge of the instability of identity, its continual process of construction and reconstruction, warns the cultural critic not to look for final and achieved models of representation. Paradoxically, cine-psychoanalytic arguments about ideological effects, in their dependence on the centrality of language acquisition to the formation of subjectivity, make the text a moment of 'fixation' in the process of cultural exchange. Too frequently, cine-psychoanalytic analyses suggest that to read a mainstream text, to 'submit' to its pleasures, is to take a single position from which it can be read or enjoyed – that of the textual (patriarchal) subject, bound into ideological submission. However such analysis relies on a complete reading, on tracing the play of narrative processes through to narrative closure, which it is assumed conclusively ties up any ambiguity or enigmatic 'false' trails generated by the processes of the text. Such textual analysis depends on total consumption of the cultural product and merges with the economistic critique of the spectator as passive consumer. Janice Radway, in her work on romance reading, has pointed to the 'culinary fallacy' in the notion of viewer as consumer – one who, meeting with the media product as a discrete object, swallows it whole, an already textually processed package of the same order as a television dinner. It seems highly improbable that cultural experiences are 'consumed' in quite this totalistic way. The notion of 'process' suggests flux, discontinuities, digressions, rather than fixed positions. It suggests that a range of positions of identification may exist within any text; and that, within the social situation of their viewing, audiences may shift subject positions as they interact with the text. Such processes – far from being confined to the 'high art' or political avant-garde work – are also a crucial source of cultural and formal regeneration, without which the culture industries would dry up.

The complete reading – from narrative disruption, to enigma development, to resolution – that arises from repeated viewings and close analysis is the product of the critical profession and does not replicate the 'raw' reading/viewing of audiences. The notion that the last word of the text is also the final memory of the audience – a notion frequently critiqued from Molly Haskell's account of classic romantic comedy, onwards – derives more from the exigencies of the critical essay than from the *experience* of films, which has no such neat boundaries. It is this haphazard, unsystematic viewing experience, and its aftermath that the cultural analyst must investigate if she/he wants to determine the political *effects* of textual ideologies. The text alone does not provide sufficient evidence for conclusions on such questions, but requires the researches of the anthropologist or ethnographer.

Negotiation and Textual Criticism

This returns me to a final question concerning the role of textual criticism in cultural analysis – a particularly pressing question in that I want to go on to consider the film *Coma* as an example of textual negotiation and do not have ethnographic skills. To limit the textual critic's authority in the analysis of *ideological effects* need not, however, lead to critical relativism, passivity, nor even unemployment – even if it does mean that textual analysis cannot alone determine the progressiveness or otherwise of a particular work. Semioticians argue that while the majority of cultural products are polysemic, they are not open to any and every interpretation. Aesthetic constraints intersect with the institutional in conscious or unconscious effort to contain or to open out the possibilities of negotiation. By studying the history and forms of aesthetic practices, codes and traditions as they operate within institutions, by studying narrative forms and genres, or the interpretative frameworks and viewing habits suggested by ethnographic research, the textual critic analyses the *conditions and possibilities of reading.*

Approached from this perspective, the cultural 'work' of the text concerns the generation of different readings; readings which challenge each other, provoke social negotiation of meanings, definitions and identities. Cultural history demonstrates that changes in context can render previous 'dominant' readings outmoded, enabling texts to be restructured in preference for alternative readings. For example, film criticism in the 1960s struggled to win 'commercial' Hollywood cinema for 'art', a project rejected by the ideological concerns of the 1970s as 'bourgeois humanism'. While some films disappeared from view (for instance, Fred Zinneman's social problem western, *High Noon*) others were saved by a re-evaluation and re-reading of their textual operations (John Ford's *Young Mr Lincoln*), and yet others were 'discovered' for the critical canon (for instance, Douglas Sirk's family melodrama, *Written on the Wind*).[18] In this respect criticism represents the professionalization of meaning production. The critic, attuned by training to the semiotic and social possibilities of texts, produces sophisticated, specialist readings. To the critical enterprise, ethnographic work contributes knowledge of the network of cultural relations and interactions in which texts are caught and which help shape their possibilities, suggesting what they are capable of generating for different social audiences. But the critical act is not finished with the 'reading' or 'evaluation' of a text. It generates new cycles of meaning production and negotiation – journalistic features, 'letters to the editor', classroom lectures, critical responses, changes in distribution or publication policy, more critical activity, and so on. In this way traditions are broken and remade. Thus critical activity itself participates in social negotiation of meaning, definition, identity. The circulation of the mainstream Hollywood film *Coma* into the orbit of feminist debates about cinema offers a good example of this interchange between general and specialized critical discourses.[19]

Feminist Film Analysis

A problem for feminist analysis is that it enters critical negotiation from a specific political position, often beginning with the aim of distinguishing 'progressive' from 'reactionary' texts. Yet, as we have seen, any attempt to fix meaning is illusory. Moreover, the feminist project seeks to open up definitions and identities, not to diminish them. While the attempt to define the ideological status of texts may stimulate debate, such judgements also threaten to foreclose prematurely on critical and textual negotiation. It is necessary, then, for feminist criticism to perform a dual operation. In the first instance, the critic uses textual and contextual analysis to determine the conditions and possibilities of gendered readings. The critic opens up the negotiations of the text in order to animate the contradictions in play. But the feminist critic is also interested in some readings more than others. She enters into the polemics of negotiation, exploiting textual contradiction to put into circulation readings that draw the text into a female and/or feminist orbit. For example, *Coma* (Michael Crichton, 1977) was conceived, publicized and discussed critically as a futuristic thriller exploiting public concern about organ transplants. But the film also makes the central investigative protagonist a woman doctor. This produces a series of textual negotiations which are both ideologically interesting to feminists and a considerable source of the film's generic pleasure. My analysis of the film is partisan to the extent that it focuses on these considerations at the expense of the issues of medical science.

Conditions and Possibilities of Textual Negotiation

A major issue for the analysis of textual negotiations is how 'textual' and 'social' subjects intersect in a cultural product; how the aesthetic and fictional practices engaged by a particular text meet and negotiate with extra-textual social practices; and, more specifically, how we can distinguish the patriarchal *symbol* of 'woman' from those discourses which speak from and to the historical socio-cultural experience of 'women'.

It is my argument that a considerable source of textual negotiation lies in the use by many mainstream film and television genres of both melodramatic and realist modes.[20] This dual constitution enables a text to work both on a symbolic, 'imaginary' level, internal to fictional production and on a 'realist' level, referring to the socio-historical world outside the text. Thus two aesthetic projects may co-exist in the same work. Popular culture draws on a melodramatic framework to provide archetypal and atavistic symbolic enactments; for the focus of melodrama is a moral order constructed out of the conflict of Manichaean, polar opposites – a struggle between good and evil, personified in the conflicts of villain, heroine and hero. At the same time such conflicts have power only on the premiss of a recognizable, socially constructed world; the pressure towards realism and contemporaneity means that a popular text must also conform to ever shifting criteria of relevance and credibility.

If, however, melodramatic conflicts still have imaginative resonance in twentieth-century culture, melodrama as a category is rejected for its association with a discarded Victorianism – for its simplistically polarized personifications of good and evil and 'feminized' sentimentalism. In order, therefore, to find credible articulations of such conflict, which will re-solicit the recognition of continually shifting audiences, current melo-dramatic forms draw on those contemporary discourses which apportion responsibility, guilt and innocence in 'modern' terms – psychoanalysis, for example, marriage guidance, medical ethics, politics, even feminism. The modern popular drama, then, exists as a negotiation between the terms of melodrama's Manichaean moral frameworks and conflicts and those contemporary discourses which will ground the drama in a recognizable verisimilitude. These conditions of aesthetic existence ensure the continuing renewal of popular forms, the generation of renewed use values that will bring audiences back to the screen.

Gender representation is at the heart of such cultural negotiation. For during a period of active feminism, of social legislation for greater sexual equality and corresponding shifts in gender roles, gender and sexual definitions themselves become the focus of intense cultural negotiation. Central to such negotiation is the figure of woman, which has long served as a powerful and ambivalent patriarchal symbol, heavily over-determined as expression of the male psyche. But while film theory suggests how narrative, visual and melodramatic pleasures are organized round this symbol, feminist cultural history also shows that the figure of woman cannot be fixed in her function as patriarchal value. The 'image of woman' has also been a site of gendered discourse, drawn from the specific socio-cultural experiences of women and shared by women, which negotiates a space within, and sometimes resists, patriarchal domination. At the same time new definitions of gender and sexuality circulated by the women's movement contest the value and meaning of the female image, struggling for different, female recognitions and ident-ifications. When popular cultural forms, operating within a melo-dramatic framework, attempt to engage contemporary discourses about women or draw on women's cultural forms in order to renew their gender verisimilitude and solicit the recognition of a female audience, the negotiation between 'woman' as patriarchal symbol and woman as generator of women's discourse is intensified. While melodrama orches-trates gender conflicts on a highly symbolic level to produce the clash of identities that will adumbrate its moral universe, the codes of women's discourse work in a more direct and articulate register to produce realist and gendered recognitions. Arguably this is the terrain on which *Coma* is grounded.

Coma: **Woman-as-Victim versus Independent Heroine**

The generic base of *Coma* is the suspense thriller, a melodramatic sub-genre which involves a race against time between 'villain' and 'hero' – the one to conceal and get away with, the other to solve and expose, a criminal plot. In this case, a hospital provides the context for a futuristic crime in which selected patients are deliberately put into and maintained in coma, so that their organs can be auctioned to the highest bidder. The villain, George Harrison, Chief of Surgery (Richard Widmark), has so far got away with turning a public good into something sinister and evil – not simply because of his power and cunning, but because the medical world is shot through with ambition, careerism, politics and cynicism. Read as melodrama, such a world requires a heroic protagonist who can embody medical innocence and thereby confront and unseat the villain through the force of natural ethical conviction. Given the function of 'woman' as symbol of moral value in melodrama, the film supports a female rather than male doctor for this central role. For Dr Susan Wheeler (Genevieve Bujold), helping people and the pursuit of medical truth comes before any careerist or political consideration. In this respect she occupies the typical role of the melodramatic heroine/victim – whose perseverance to the end, against danger and public opinion, leads to public recognition of the truth.[21] Correspondingly, in order to create narrative space for the heroine's activity, the 'good' male doctor, Mark Bellows (Michael Douglas), is cast in a role typical of the Vic-torian melodramatic hero: supportive but impercipient and therefore a hindrance rather than a help – until everything is explained and he leaps in for the last-minute rescue.

In terms of textual negotiation, the issue is how this atavistic melo-dramatic framework will renew itself as the basis of recognizable contemporary conflict. In the first instance, *Coma* successfully regener-ates and disguises this format in contemporary and controversial terms by recourse to public debate about the ethics of organ transplants. It is this drama which was the source of the director's interest in the film and which has largely concerned mainstream critics.[22] However, the deploy-ment of a central female protagonist as upholder of 'truth', while conforming to the demands of melodrama, produces problems on the level of 'authentication'. In generic terms, the film must draw on the 'independent heroine' stereotype, established in screwball and romantic comedies of the 1930s. However, 'independence' is not just a formal attribute, but must be established in relation to current social definitions. For an American movie, made in the late 1970s, and seeking to address a white middle-class professional audience, contemporary reference is inevitably supplied by the discourses on sexism and medical practice, made publicly visible by the activity of the American women's movement. At the same time, however, such reference, while giving the film a 'controversial' dimension, makes it also the subject of feminist debate – giving rise to claims and counter-claims as to the film's progressiveness or sexism. I want to explore the textual conditions which make both sets of claims possible as part of a wider and continuing process of cultural negotiation.

Medical Practice and Sexism

This process is entered at the film's opening which sets the terms of narrative credibility, while at the same time preparing the audience for the ensuing melodrama. In the first instance this means negotiating the melodramatic 'woman-as-victim' with a modern 'independent heroine' stereotype. Contemporary discourses around sexism and medicine contribute to the solution of this aesthetic problem. The film opens in a teasingly ambiguous fashion. The establishment of Dr Susan Wheeler/ Genevieve Bujold attempts to suggest a female protagonist who combines aspects of the typically 'feminine' with an equally recognizable 'new' independence. Bujold's physique and performance style is crucial here: petite features and soft voice, combined with an obstinate lower jaw and fractious manner. The characterization she offers is of a woman both vulnerable and tough.

Our first encounter with Dr Wheeler is constructed to disturb expectation both of the conventional and the feminist image of woman. She offers an impersonal and mechanistically efficient run-down on the condition of a middle-aged, visibly bewildered and abashed female patient to a group of male students and their tutor. Susan's professional competence is established in relation to the impersonal, male authority of medical discourse, and the value of both thereby accrues a degree of ambiguity. Our next encounter with Susan introduces her private life: here the film must engineer a second ambivalence around Susan's heterosexuality, in order to confirm Susan's 'femininity' and at the same time motivate the marginalized role of the hero in the coming drama. For this, the film draws on the estrangement produced by Susan's struggle against sexism, both in her personal and institutional relationships. In the scene which introduces Mark Bellows/Michael Douglas, convention is once more disturbed, as Susan ungraciously resists – in phrases of women's movement discourse – her lover's claim that the burdens of his day entitle him to first call on her attention and the shower. The situation has a touch of the screwball exchange, except that her serious-ness and ill-humour allow little space in which to preserve the hero's self-esteem.

This context of struggle, defined by sexism, is continued the following day when, after her previous evening's departure (provoked by Mark's unwillingness to start dinner), Susan insists that her aerobics class take precedence over his hopes for a conciliatory lunch. A further element in the struggle is introduced here, in that she attends an all-woman class with her closest friend, Nancy, with whom she shares a brief exchange about the difficulties of relating to Mark. This sketch of an alternative female world, to which Susan gives considerable priority – activity with women, insistence on a space for personal relaxation, female friendship, as against the rigours and problems of the workplace with which the heterosexual relationship is aligned – draws on the oppositional stance of the women's movement in a way that both gives the film contempor-aneity *and* contributes motivation to the melodramatic heroine's pursuit of the truth underlying the plot that is about to unfold.

The needs of contemporaneity and melodrama are drawn together in the following parallel sequences, during which Nancy undergoes the abortion that will put her into a fatal coma, while Susan reassures a child about his imminent kidney transplant. Any ambiguity about the align-ment of medical and gender values will be clarified by the end of this episode. For the hospital plot, the choice of abortion as the exemplary coma-inducing operation introduces an ethical and futuristic dimension – medicine's power over life and death – which will found the coming melodrama. However, for feminism abortion is a highly resonant, politi-cized choice. Given the plot's later exposure of medical perversion at the Jefferson Institute, where coma cases are stored and life is preserved in death for huge profit – an institution, moreover, superintended by an archetypal 'bad mother' – it is perhaps surprising that the negotiational processes of the film do little to pull the abortion into a patriarchal equation with its images of death. If, however, this ideological linkage is not foregrounded, but lies inert, it is not because the film is taking a 'progressive' stance as such. On the one hand, the film gains credibility for its modern 'independent heroine' by touching on controversial issues raised by the women's movement. The conversation between medical personnel during the operation suggests, for those in the audience who can hear, the patient's need for concealment from both the medical authorities and from her husband (the official reason for a D & C is 'menstrual irregularity'). The jocular patronage of the male doctors, instructing a group of male students – 'I'm going to get her out of a helluva mess'; 'Let's get this mother off the table' – and Nancy's humiliating posture, on her back, her legs up in stirrups, demonstrate in a way open to a range of responses – anger, amused cynicism, fear, and so on – the place of 'woman as victim' within a patriarchally controlled medical practice.[23] At the same time, the film's melodramatic premisses require of the hospital a credibly villainous ambiance and a female sacrificial victim. In this respect, Nancy's abortion and medical chauvinism serve melodramatic plotting as well as the need for contemporary reference, diverting ultimate sacrifice from the 'independent heroine', while motivating Susan's pursuit of the truth against the advice of her male colleagues and lover. Ideologically, because Susan is melodrama's innocent heroine, the abortion that motivates her heroic action must also be perceived as innocent for the melodrama to work.

The Melodramatic Scenario: Misrecognition and Sexism

Nancy's unexplained coma and subsequent death open out on to a melodramatic scenario, which starts with a simple desire on Susan's part to understand what has caused her friend's death. She finds her quest blocked in a way that quickly suggests something sinister afoot. Susan's position within the unfolding mystery is characteristic of the melodramatic heroine. She stands by the principle that no unexplained medical event can be ignored and that 'truth' overrides bureaucratic procedures, hospital politics and personal feelings. The clash of her values with those of the medical hierarchy leads her to suspect malpractice. At the same time, she is opposed by the Chief of Surgery, a seductively paternalistic villain as yet unrecognized by heroine and audience, who deliberately engineers public misrecognition of her motives and actions. Susan's function as a melodramatic heroine is to hang on to, and keep asserting, her demand for truth and its public recognition, despite unknown and intensifying dangers, both physical and moral, which she must undergo alone. These dangers are appreciated only by the film's audience to whom sufficient privileged knowledge is given to invoke melodrama's structures of suspense and pathos.

Susan's role as independent heroine, however, complicates her melodramatic construction as victim. She is both insightful in her unravelling of the medical mystery and resourceful in dealing with physical danger. Why then does no one believe her? In its search for answers which will be consonant with 'the changing position of women', the film draws women's movement discourses into its plotting. For the Chief of Surgery engineers misrecognition of Susan's questions, insights and intentions by recourse to sexism. Susan is a victim not only because there is a hired assassin roaming the hospital seeking to eliminate her, but because of the hold that gendered (mis)definitions have over what counts as knowledge, reason and emotion, over who has which and in what circumstances. Thus the success of the villain's designs is not simply a matter of personal evil, but is due to the range of male misconceptions, ambitions, desires and fears he can rely on or motivate in his colleagues, including the hero.

The start of this process is heavily marked in a male colleague's comment to Mark on Susan's 'surprising' response to Nancy's coma; 'if it had been a friend I don't know I'd have been that cool'. The exchange between Mark and Susan that follows lays out the stakes that are being played. Mark assumes that Susan, as a woman, will be emotionally overwhelmed by her friend's death, and hopes to renew their intimacy by offering his comforting support. Susan's reply frustrates him: 'I'm not upset. You think because I am a woman I'm going to be upset. I just want to understand the variables as they apply to this patient.' Refusing his definition of what constitutes an appropriate response to the occasion, Susan, instead of going to supper with Mark, proceeds to contravene regulations concerning access to computer statistics and so to discover a string of unexplained coma cases. This in turn brings her up against her boss, the silver-haired Chief of Surgery, George Harrison. Paternal concern and patriarchal power meet in his representation of her 'reason' as the mark of personal stress (Fig. 6). If she is to continue at the hospital, he threatens, she must see the hospital psychiatrist. The (Black) psychiatrist deflects her concern to understand the comas by questioning her about how she feels.[24] To Harrison he explains her behaviour as the result of a 'crisis in her personal life'; her conflicts with Mark and her refusal to face her 'grief' over Nancy have led her into 'paranoia'. Here Susan's situation is 'read' within the film through conventional, repressive, culture-bound gender definitions, which the plot will have to negotiate if it is to continue.

The head anaesthetist, Dr. George, to whom Susan next goes for information, confronts her questions in a sinister, defensive (not to say paranoid) manner, protecting his professional, and male, preserve from her desire to know what he has not yet been able to find out. Mark, as her lover, is called on to bring her into line. He attempts to persuade Susan to drop her investigations in terms of the *realpolitik* of the hospital as it affects their careers – particularly his prospects of becoming Chief Resident. Her second disciplinary interview with the Chief of

Surgery, in which he again insistently and overbearingly probes her feelings, finally reduces her to womanly tears, undermining, for the moment, her solitary resistance. Once she has broken down, he sends her off for a 'recuperative' weekend with Mark: 'I'll take care of the politics; you take care of yourself ... our emotions make us human.' In these different encounters, which are about Susan demanding she be listened to and the different ways in which that demand is blocked, the drama is enacted as one of misunderstanding – of translation from one discourse or identity into another – a process dominated by gender definitions and politics. Thus the nature of knowledge – its relations with feeling, reason and power – becomes itself an object of gendered conflict.

Pathos, Suspense and the Independent Heroine

Blockage and misrecognition are the source of two melodramatic narrative strategies – *suspense* and *pathos* – through which the symbolic and referential roles played by Susan are further negotiated. As *Coma* is a suspense thriller, *suspense* is the stronger of the two and has been critiqued for undermining Susan's command of the narrative, in that it depends on the audience having privileged knowledge of the dangers that encompass her.[25] However, the giving and withholding of audience knowledge is carefully controlled in an attempt to maintain the independent heroine within the suspense structure. And the credibility required for this negotiation to work depends on the operation of the film's pathos. Both suspense and pathos rely on our sympathy for the potentially victimized protagonist. Susan wins our sympathy because she represents good medical practice and takes a moral stand. Like suspense, *pathos* also depends on privileged audience knowledge. Pathos is not merely a matter of identification with, nor of pity for, another; it is a formal construct in which a protagonist is held at a distance which allows the audience to experience and understand, on her or his behalf, oppressive or threatening forces of which the protagonist is not fully aware.[26] In order to believe that Susan is right – and thereby to participate in the suspense – the audience must participate in the pathos of her misrecognition, acknowledging dangers that threaten her not only physically, but also intellectually and emotionally. The question is posed: do we think she is stupid, or can we understand her dilemma? If the audience concedes that she is right about the conspiracy, it is then in a position to see the danger that comes from patriarchal/sexist forces – from the power of male definition, which leads Susan to doubt what we know she knows.

In this respect suspense is created out of the conditions of subjectivity. Susan's identity and what she thinks she knows shifts from encounter to encounter. She is, by turns and according to whose perception is operative, female hysteric, cool professional, needy lover and a woman struggling with patriarchy. In a privileged moment, the audience is allowed a glimpse of George Harrison's villainy when, after sending Susan off for the weekend with Mark, he explodes, 'Women! Christ!' Misogyny becomes an indicator of evil and, following this outburst, the weekend itself becomes ambiguous, its 'idyllic' advertising images and soupy music tinged with a mixture of nostalgia, irony and threat. Its escapism is confirmed as the couple's reconciliation is broken abruptly on their homeward journey, when the chance appearance of a signpost to the Jefferson Institute pulls Susan out of 'romance' and back into the investigation.

If the viewer does not engage in the negotiations around sexism to which the 'pathos' of Susan's situation invites us, the structures of suspense open up another route into this territory. Because the suspense thriller depends on a play with the giving and withholding of knowledge, potential guilt is distributed between nearly all the film's male protagonists, and the misrecognition to which Susan is subjected and which founds the pathos is shared or perpetrated – we are not sure which till the film's end – by her superiors, colleagues and lover. In the world constructed by *Coma*, men are dangerous; even Mark may be part of the plot against the heroine. We see Susan in battle with a 'male' other who appears in many guises; lover, boss, father, assassin. The shifts are often highly overdetermined. After her nightmarish entrapment in a deserted lecture theatre, where her suspected attacker switches on one light after another till he forces her into the open, Susan escapes into fully lit corridors and the apparent safety of a male colleague, to find only a familiar, fatherly security guard following her. But almost immediately she is subjected to a second pursuit, from which she escapes by burying her would-be assassin under a pile of cadavers, to fall – in a shock cut that links her pursuer's yells with Mark's towering figure – into her lover's arms, as he opens his apartment door. In the swings between normality, security and comfort on the one hand, and futuristic medical crime, nightmare and danger on the other, the melodrama throws up images from the underside of conventional wisdoms about the 'caring professions' and protective paternalism. The lover becomes an assassin, doctors become murderers, the preservation of life a financial racket, and – given the rows of male cadavers in the dissection room, or stored in the deep-freeze – the male body itself an image of death.

Susan's persistent pursuit of knowledge, despite dangers within and without, uncovers what the crime is, and how and why it is being committed. But she makes a near-fatal mistake about the *who*, taking her newly found solution of the plot to the principal villain himself. For the melodrama this is less a mistake than a rendering of her innocence – it is her trust that is abused by a corrupt paternalism. But her mistake also brings about melodrama's culminating confrontation between villain and heroine, in which evil is recognized and the true identities of the protagonists made visible. Leaning back with her (drugged) whisky, Susan listens to the telephone call that interrupts her third and final interview with the Chief Surgeon and idly scans his certificates framed on the wall. As her eyes rest on his full name, *George* Harrison, she also recognizes the emphatic use of his colleague's Christian name over the phone as the mode of interchange between senior colleagues. By the time the call is ended, she knows, and he knows she knows, that her identification of *Dr George*, the anaesthetist, as villain – derived from overhearing another conversation – was a mistake in social coding. As she succumbs to the drug, and sees a 'true' perception of the surgeon, distorted by a fish-eye lens, the irony of the conflict over knowledge and identity strikes her; reversing his earlier recommendation for her, she laughs, '*you* need to see someone.' She then announces the truth: 'You are killing people!', a truth which he has tried to render as the paranoid fantasy of an upset woman.

Negotiational Pleasures

Negotiation between symbolic and referential roles in *Coma* is not only a critical means of generic renewal; it is also a source of aesthetic pleasure. Some of the film's pleasures have been identified as patriarchal constructions, thereby denying the space of negotiation. Most readily critiqued are early moments in the construction of Bujold as heroine – the shower and aerobics episodes – which focus on her body as an object of desire. However, these moments are potentially under negotiation as the film struggles to align woman as melodramatic symbol with the independent heroine's reference to women's struggles in the real world. Moreover, to deny the spectacle of the body is to deny not only male desire for the female body but women's too. In these particular instances this critique also ignores their narrative placement at moments of female resistance. Susan both grabs the shower first and offers us the pleasure of the female body. If the look of the camera at Susan's blurred outline through the shower screen is already and only male, negotiation ends here. However, the camera remains with the disconsolate hero, left outside, on the losing end of this particular argument. To identify with the male look here opens up a position of desire, rejection, frustration and annoyance with the woman. For a woman, however, following the line of the hero's gaze may offer an identification with Susan's resistance, ungraciously claiming rights to the shower and the body's comfort (much as the left-wing viewer of television news, watching picket-line 'violence' through a camera positioned behind police lines, may reinterpret 'violence' as 'resistance' to state power). To identify with Susan offers a stake in a female claim to the body and its image, of resistance to male demand or amusement in his frustration. In other words, to take up a gendered position of identification here is to enter – humorously or resistingly, pleasurably or unpleasurably – into a struggle for the meaning and possession of the female image.

The aerobics class – another instance of Susan's resistance to Mark's demands – similarly puts at issue the gendering and possession of the 'look'. As well as pleasure in looking at women's bodies, the session also suggests a different order of being from heterosexual strife: women together, pleasure in physical being, intimate friendship. These are 'moments' from the subculture of women in the social spaces where they meet and talk, made publicly recognizable through the cultural forms of the women's movement which are increasingly, as here, brought into wider circulation in the mainstream media. The Bujold character is offered as a woman caught in the contradictory demands of independence, of professional practice, of female community, of heterosexual intimacy and, later, dependence. In Susan's continuing arguments with Mark, male and female perspectives and priorities conflict as they each struggle to define the other. It is, however, impossible to say that the image is claimed either for patriarchy or for feminism. The struggle continues because each character continues to desire the other, while not giving up their positions – until perhaps at the film's end. What I am suggesting for the moment is that the intermeshing of symbolizing and referential modes constructs the female image as an object of contest, of negotiation, for the characters and for the audience.

A second pleasure is offered by the suspense structure's negotiations between the melodramatic need for woman as victim and *Coma*'s deployment of the 'independent heroine'. Indeed the film cannot work for audiences not prepared to enter into the world of the suspense thriller. It assumes we take pleasure in certain kinds of dramatic enactments, emotional situations, aesthetic frissons – the chase, off-screen threats, suspense, shock cuts. Deploying a woman doctor protagonist regenerates these enactments, by bringing pressure to bear on and renegotiating many of the assumptions involved in them. For instance, the intersection of suspense with the independent heroine raises the question, how will a woman deal with the tough action and physical violence which are the hallmark of the thriller? In the pursuit sequences, the camera positions the audience with Susan at the onset of imminent danger, but then cuts to her pursuer. Suspense is generated from the audience's ignorance of her whereabouts and consequent expectation of seeing her succumb to the victim's role. But suspense must also negotiate a heroine who is 'independent' and consequently teases expectation by playing the victim motif off against Susan's ingenious methods of defence and escape.

The Last-Minute Rescue

Such negotiational play is taken to extremes at the end of the film, when identification of the villain leads into the suspenseful coda of the last-minute rescue. For some, this ending represents the putting into patriarchal place of the would-be independent heroine: Susan becomes the ultimate victim, drugged and supine on the operating table, while Mark tracks down the carbon monoxide inlet and calls the police. Analysed in terms of negotiation, however, the attempt to bring to conclusion such a strongly generic film, that also engages discourses running counter to the ideological balance of gender roles in our society, leads to an almost frantic intensification of its textual processes. Susan, drugged, knows that she is herself, under guise of an appendectomy, being taken to the operating theatre where comas are induced, while Mark continues blandly reassuring her. By the time he understands what Susan is telling him, he is trapped into assisting at the operation. It is the female victim who, by pressing his beeper, provides him with the excuse to leave the operating theatre. And it is Susan's earlier investigation which guides him in voice-over to the lethal gas input. Susan may be supine, while Mark breathlessly charges about the hospital engineering plant, but without her earlier calm, logical tracing of pipelines, she could not be saved now. Mark finds nothing for himself, but depends on memories of her recounting her discoveries and a clue which that investigation left behind – her tights abandoned during her climb of the hospital works. All is safe at the end, when Mark, holding Susan's hand, quiets her attempts to continue her self-justification with an acknowledgement of the truth she has discovered: 'I know, baby' – hardly the feminist last word. She is not given the recognition the melodrama owes her, perhaps because it cannot – given its embrace of women's movement discourse – find the terms to produce the image of a loving heterosexual couple and an accepting, united community such as closes traditional melodrama, though it attempts to do so with a close-up of a 'clenched' hand-clasp. Instead, the film closes on the recognition by a public apparatus, the law, of the villain who earlier has been explicitly identified with paternalism and misogyny, and who now puts out the lights of the operating theatre and the film. This ending is perhaps symptomatic of the state of gender conflict in our culture. The culture can acknowledge what we don't want; rejection and contestation produces drama. Imagining the new future in popular images is more difficult.

Clearly the ambivalence of textual negotiation produces a wider address – more servicable to a capitalist industry – than a more purely feminist text, or counter-text, could. If for many – not necessarily feminist – women, Susan's struggles with sexism at home and at work, and the formal negotiations of the woman-as-victim role, produce echoes of recognition and pleasure, viewers who support sexist attitudes have a route through the film in the humorous exasperation of Mark – 'what you want is a wife, not a lover!' – and can take comfort in the fact that identification of the culprit expels both male and medical villainy: Mark is exonerated. On the other hand, if we accept the role of the mass media in making cultural definitions – and also post-structural theory's exposure of the ideologically 'pure' and full representation, whether feminist or dominant, as an illusory goal – perhaps we may take a more positive stance towards the spaces of negotiation in mainstream production. For into dominant typifications and aesthetic structures are locked both atavistic and Utopian desires; archetypal and futuristic motifs; sensibility and reason; melodrama and realism. The productivity of popular culture lies in its capacity to bring these different dimensions into contact and contest; their negotiations contribute to its pleasures. We need to attend to such pleasures if we are to appreciate what holds us back as well as what impels us forward, and if cultural struggle is to take place at the centre of cultural production as well as on the margins. Thus critical readings made under the rubric of negotiation offer not so much resistant readings, made against the grain, as animations of possibilities arising from the negotiations into which the text enters. Such readings work with the pleasures of the text, rather than suppressing or deconstructing them. The pleasures *Coma* offers feminism are in many ways gruesome; its atavistic desires for protective paternalism, enacted in Susan's moments of exhaustion from the loneliness of her struggle, are rendered in the context of the thriller as sources of nightmare, producing a kind of feminine horror film. There are of course other pleasures of various ideological complexions in play in the film: of gender role reversal, of the victimization of women, and so on. No doubt these pleasures, too, can be read in their double-sidedness; but the point of a feminist reading is to pull the symbolic enactments of popular fictions into frameworks which interpret the psychic, emotional and social forces at work in women's lives.

Notes

1. For example, cultural studies in England, and reader-response theory in the United States have explored the cultural processes and textural procedures that make differential readings possible.

2. For examples of feminist analysis of women's fiction, see: Nina Baym, *Woman's Fiction: A Guide to Novels by and About Women in America, 1920–1970*, Ithaca: Cornell University Press, 1978; Janice A. Radway, *Reading the Romance: Women, Patriarchy, and Popular Literature*, London: Verso, 1987; Jane Tompkins, *Sensational Designs: The Cultural Work of American Fiction, 1790–1860s*, Oxford: Oxford University Press, 1985. For feminist work on the woman's film, melodrama and soap opera, see: Tania Modleski, *Loving with a Vengeance*, Hamden, Connecticut: The Shoe String Press, 1982; Charlotte Brunsdon, 'Crossroads: Notes on Soap Opera', in E. Ann Kaplan (ed.), *Regarding Television: Critical Approaches – An Anthology*, Los Angeles: American Film Institute, 1983; Dorothy Hobson, *Crossroads: The Drama of a Soap Opera*, London: Methuen, 1982; Ien Ang, *Watching Dallas*, London: Methuen, 1985; Maria LaPlace, 'Producing and Consuming the Woman's Film: Discursive Struggle in *Now, Voyager*', and Linda Williams, '"Something Else Besides a Mother": *Stella Dallas* and the Maternal Melodrama', both in Christine Gledhill (ed.), *Home Is Where the Heart Is*, London: British Film Institute, 1987.

3. For an account of Lacanian psychoanalysis, see Steve Burniston, Frank Mort and Christine Weedon, 'Psychoanalysis and the Cultural Acquisition of Sexuality and Subjectivity', in Women's Studies Group, Centre for Contemporary Cultural Studies, University of Birmingham (ed.), *Women Take Issue*, London: Hutchinson, 1978.

4. The psychoanalytic underpinnings of classic narrative cinema were first signalled in a special issue of *Screen*, vol. 14 no. 1/2 (Spring/Summer 1973), dealing with semiotics and cinema, and were developed by Colin MacCabe in 'The Politics of Separation', and by Stephen Heath in 'Lessons from Brecht', both in *Screen*, vol. 15, no. 2 (Summer 1974). *Screen*, vol. 16, no. 2, translated Christian Metz's 'The Imaginary Signifier' in a special issue on psychoanalysis and the cinema.

5. Claire Johnston's 'Women's Cinema as Counter-Cinema', *Screen* Pamphlet, no. 2, September 1972, is an early and influential exposition of this view. Laura Mulvey's 'Visual Pleasure and Narrative Cinema' in *Screen*, vol. 16, no. 3 (Autumn 1975), provided an influential development of feminist cine-psychoanalysis. Annette Kuhn's book *Women's Pictures: Feminism and Cinema*, London: Routledge and Kegan Paul, 1982 offers succinct and critical introduction to this work, and Ann Kaplan's *Women and Film: Both Sides of the Camera*, New York: Methuen, 1983, a distinctive development of it, dealing in particular with the notion of the 'male gaze' in classic narrative cinema. See also my 'Recent Developments in Feminist Film Criticism' in Mary Ann Doane, Patricia Mellencamp and Linda Williams (eds), *Re-Vision: Essays in Feminist Film Criticism*, Frederick, Maryland: University Publications of America, in association with the American Film Institute, 1984, for an account of feminist engagement with psychoanalysis.

6. See Annette Kuhn, *Women's Pictures*.

7. For example, Tania Modleski, 'Never To Be Thirty-Six Years Old: *Rebecca* as Female Oedipal Drama', *Wide Angle*, vol. 5, no. 1 (1982), and Linda Williams, '"Something Else Besides a Mother": *Stella Dallas* and the Maternal Melodrama', and Tania Modleski, 'Time and Desire in the Woman's Film', in Gledhill.

8. Annette Kuhn, 'Women's Genres: Melodrama, Soap Opera and Theory', *Screen*, vol. 25, no. 1 (1984), reprinted in Gledhill.

9. For example, Stuart Hall, 'Encoding/Decoding', in Hall *et al.* (eds.), *Culture, Media, Language*, London: Hutchinson, 1980, David Morley, *The Nationwide Audience*, London: British Film Institute Television Monograph II, 1980, Richard Dyer, *Stars*, London: British Film Institute, 1980.

10. See Antonio Gramsci, *Selections from the Prison Notebooks*, Quintin Hoare and Geoffrey Nowell-Smith (ed. and trans.), London: Lawrence and Wishart, 1971. For discussion and application of the notion of hegemony to cultural products, see Terry Lovell, 'Ideology and Coronation Street', in Richard Dyer *et al.*, *Coronation Street*,

London: British Film Institute Television Monograph 13, 1981, and Geoff Hurd, 'Notes on Hegemony, the War and Cinema', in *National Fictions: World War Two in British Films and Television*, London: British Film Institute, 1985.

11. See Terry Lovell, *Pictures of Reality: Aesthetics, Politics and Pleasure*, London: British Film Institute, 1980, pp. 56–63. She defines the 'use-value' of a commodity as 'the ability of the commodity to satisfy some human want', which, according to Marx, 'may spring from the stomach or from the fancy'. 'The use-value of a commodity is realised only when it is consumed, or used' (p. 57).

12. See Maria LaPlace, 'Producing and Consuming the Woman's Film: Discursive Struggle in *Now, Voyager*', in Gledhill, for a discussion of the contradictions of consumerism for women.

13. Julie D'Acci, 'The Case of *Cagney and Lacey*', in Helen Baehr and Gillian Dyer (eds), *Boxed In: Women and Television*, London: Pandora, 1987.

14. Molly Haskell, *From Reverence to Rape: The Treatment of Women in the Movies*, Harmondsworth: Penguin, 1979.

15. Ien Ang, *Watching Dallas*, London: Methuen, 1985, and Janice Radway, *Reading the Romance: Women, Patriarchy and Popular Literature*, London: Verso, 1987.

16. See, for example, Judith Williamson, 'The Problems of Being Popular', *New Socialist*, September 1986.

17. For examples of fully developed textual analysis of the 'recuperative' strategies of mainstream cinema, see Peter Steven (ed.), *Jump Cut: Hollywood, Politics and Counter-Cinema*, New York, Praeger, 1985.

18. For a translation of the seminal analysis of *Young Mr. Lincoln* by the editors of *Cahiers du Cinéma*, see *Screen*, vol. 13, no. 3 (Autumn 1972), reprinted in Bill Nichols (ed.) *Movies and Methods*, Berkeley: University of California Press, 1976. For work on Douglas Sirk, see Jon Halliday (ed.), *Sirk on Sirk*, London: Secker and Warburg/British Film Institute, 1971, a special issue of *Screen*, vol. 12, no. 2 (Summer 1971), and Laura Mulvey and Jon Halliday (eds), *Douglas Sirk*, Edinburgh: Edinburgh Film Festival, 1972.

19. See, for example, Elizabeth Cowie's account of press coverage of *Coma* in 'The Popular Film as a Progressive Text – a discussion of *Coma* Part 1', *m/f*, no. 3, 1979. Part 2 of this article appeared in *m/f*, no. 4, 1980. *Coma* was discussed by Christine Geraghty under the heading, 'Three Women's Films', in *Movie*, nos. 27/28, Winter/Spring 1980–81, an article which is reprinted in Charlotte Brunsdon (ed.), *Films for Women*, London: British Film Institute, 1986, as is also an extract from Part 1 of Elizabeth Cowie's piece. The film frequently appears in film study courses dealing with feminism and cinema.

20. See 'The Melodramatic Field: An Investigation', in Gledhill.

21. This account of melodramatic narrative structure is drawn from Peter Brooks, *The Melodramatic Imagination: Balzac, Henry James, Melodrama and the Mode of Excess*, New Haven: Yale University Press, 1976, and Thomas Elsaesser, 'Tales of Sound and Fury: Observations on the Family Melodrama', *Monogram*, no. 4, 1972, reprinted in Gledhill.

22. See the interview with Michael Crichton by Ralph Appelbaum, 'Genetic Genocide', in *Films and Filming*, vol. 24, no. 4 (1978).

23. I am indebted to Christine Panks for discussion of this episode.

24. In so far as the psychiatrist is the only Black character in the film, the coupling of ethnicity with this particular role is marked. How precisely this strategy is to be read, however, is unclear and must depend on which negotiational routes the viewer is taking through the film.

25. See Cowie.

26. This discussion of pathos is drawn from Elsaesser, 'Tales of Sound and Fury' in Gledhill.

5

The Color Purple: Black Women as Cultural Readers

Jacqueline Bobo

Tony Brown, a syndicated columnist and the host of the television programme *Tony Brown's Journal* has called the film *The Color Purple* 'the most racist depiction of Black men since *The Birth of a Nation* and the most anti-Black family film of the modern film era'. Ishmael Reed, a Black novelist, has labelled the film and the book 'a Nazi conspiracy'.[1] Since its première in December 1985, *The Color Purple* has provoked constant controversy, debate and appraisals of its effects on the image of Black people in the US.

The film also has incited a face-off between Black feminist critics and Black male reviewers. The women defend the work, or more precisely, defend Alice Walker's book and the right of the film to exist. Black males vehemently denounce both works and cite the film's stereotypical representations. In the main, adverse criticisms have revolved around three issues: a) that the film does not examine class, b) that Black men are portrayed unnecessarily as harsh and brutal, the consequence of which is to further the split between the Black female and the Black male; and c) that Black people as a whole are depicted as perverse, sexually wanton, and irresponsible. In these days of massive cutbacks in federal support to social agencies, according to some rebukes, the film's representation of the Black family was especially harmful.

Most left-wing publications in the United States, the *Guardian*, *Frontline* and *In These Times*, denounced the film, but mildly. *The Nation*, in fact, commended the film and its director for fitting the work's threatening content into a safe and familiar form.[2] Articles in the other publications praised particular scenes but on the whole disparaged the film for its lack of class authenticity. Black people of that era were poor, the left-wing critics stated, and Steven Spielberg failed to portray that fact. (Uh-uh, says Walker. She said she wrote here about people who owned land, property and dealt in commerce.)

Jill Nelson, a Black journalist who reviewed the film for the *Guardian*, felt that the film's Black protestors were naïve to think that 'at this late date in our history ... Hollywood would ever consciously offer Black Americans literal tools for our emancipation.[3] Furthermore, Nelson refuted the charge that the film would for ever set the race back in white viewers' minds by observing that most viewers would only leave the theatre commenting on whether or not they liked the film. Articles counter to Nelson's were published in a following issue of the *Guardian* and they emphasized the film's distorted perspective on class and the ideological use to which the film would be put to show the Black family's instability.

The December première of *The Color Purple* was picketed in Los Angeles by an activist group named the Coalition Against Black Exploitation. The group protested against the savage and brutal depiction of Black men in the film.[4] That complaint was carried further by a Black columnist in the *Washington Post*, Courtland Milloy, who wrote that some Black women would enjoy seeing Black men shown as 'brutal bastards', and that furthermore, the book was demeaning. Milloy stated: 'I got tired, a long time ago, of white men publishing books by Black women about how screwed up Black men are.'[5] Other hostile views about the film were expressed by representatives of the NAACP, Black male columnists, and a law professor, Leroy Clark of Catholic University, who called it dangerous. (When Ntozake Shange's choreopoem *For Colored Girls Who Have Considered Suicide/When the Rainbow Is Enuf* opened on Broadway in autumn 1976, the response from Black male critics was similar.)

Black female reviewers were not as critical of the film in its treatment of gender issues. Although Barbara Smith attacked the film for its class distortions, she felt that 'sexual politics and sexual violence' in the Black community were matters that needed to be confronted and changed.[6] Jill Nelson, emphasizing that those who did not like what the messenger (the film) said about Black men should look at the facts, provided statistics on female-headed Black households, lack of child support, and so on.[7]

Michele Wallace, a professor of Afro-American literature and creative writing at the University of Oklahoma and author of *Black Macho: The Myth of the Superwoman*, stated that the film had some 'positive feminist influences and some positive import for Black audiences in this country'.[8]

However, in an earlier article in the *Village Voice*, 18 March 1986, Michele Wallace was less charitable to the film. Although she gives a very lucid explication of Walker's novel, citing its attempt to 'reconstruct Black female experience as positive ground', Wallace wrote of the film, 'Spielberg juggles film clichés and racial stereotypes fast and loose, until all signs of a Black feminist agenda are banished, or ridiculed beyond repair.' Wallace also noted that the film used mostly cinematic types reminiscent of earlier films. She writes: 'Instead of serious men and women encountering consequential dilemmas, we're almost always minstrels, more than a little ridiculous; we dance and sing without continuity, as if on the end of a string. It seems white people are never going to forget Stepin Fetchit, no matter how many times he dies.'[9]

Wallace both sees something positive in the film and points to its flaws. I agree with her in both instances, especially in her analysis of how it is predictable that the film 'has given rise to controversy and debate within the Black community, ostensibly focused on the eminently printable issue of the film's image of Black men.'

In an attempt to explain why people liked *The Color Purple* in spite of its sometimes clichéd characters, Donald Bogle, on the Phil Donahue show, put it down to the novelty of seeing Black actors in roles not previously available to them:

> for Black viewers there is a schizophrenic reaction. You're torn in two. On the one hand you see the character of Mister and you're disturbed by the stereotype. Yet, on the other hand, and this is the basis of the appeal of that film for so many people, is that the women you see in the movie, you have never seen Black women like this put on the screen before. I'm not talking about what happens to them in the film, I'm talking about the visual statement itself. When you see Whoopi Goldberg in close-up, a loving close-up, you look at this woman, you know that in American films in the past, in the 1930s, 1940s, she would have played a maid. She would have been a comic maid. Suddenly, the camera is focusing on her and we say, 'I've seen this woman some place, I know her.'[10]

It appears to me that one of the problems most of the film's reviewers have in trying to analyse the film, with all of its faults, is to make sense of the overwhelming positive response from Black female viewers.

The Color Purple was a small quiet book when it emerged on the literary scene in 1982. The subject of the book is a young, abused, uneducated Black girl who evolves into womanhood and a sense of her own worth gained by bonding with the women around her. When Alice Walker won the American Book Award and the Pulitzer Prize for Fiction in 1983, the sales of the novel increased to over two million copies, placing the book on the *New York Times* best-seller lists for a number of weeks.[11] Still the book did not have as wide an audience or the impact the film would have. In December 1985 Steven Spielberg's *The Color Purple* exploded with the force of a land-mine on the landscape of cultural production. Many commentators on the film have pointed out that the film created discussion and controversy about the image of Black people in media, the likes of which had not been seen since the films *The Birth of a Nation* (1915) and *Gone With the Wind* (1939).

One of the reasons Alice Walker sold the screen rights was that she understood that people who would not read the book would go to see the film. Walker and her advisers thought that the book's critical message needed to be exposed to a wider audience. The readership for the novel was a very specific one and drastically different from the mass audience toward which the film is directed. However, the film is a commercial venture produced in Hollywood by a white male according to all of the tenets and conventions of commercial cultural production in the United States. The manner in which an audience responds to such a film is varied, diverse and complex. I am especially concerned with analysing how Black women have responded.

My aim is to examine the way in which a specific audience creates meaning from a mainstream text and uses the reconstructed meaning to empower themselves and their social group. This analysis will show how Black women as audience members and cultural consumers have connected up with what has been characterized as the 'renaissance of Black women writers'.[12] The predominant element of this movement is the creation and maintenance of images of Black women that are based upon Black women's constructions, history and real-life experiences.

As part of a larger study I am doing on *The Color Purple* I conducted a group interview with selected Black women viewers of the film.[13] Statements from members of the group focused on how moved they were by the fact that Celie eventually triumphs in the film. One woman talked about the variety of emotions she experienced: 'I had different feelings all the way through the film, because first I was very angry, and then I started to feel so sad I wanted to cry because of the way Celie was being treated. It just upset me the way she was being treated and the way she was so totally dominated. But gradually, as time went on, she began to realize that she could do something for herself, that she could start moving and progressing, that she could start reasoning and thinking things out for herself.' Another woman stated that she was proud of Celie for her growth: 'The lady was a strong lady, like I am. And she hung in there and she overcame.'

One of the women in the group talked about the scene where Shug tells Celie that she has a beautiful smile and that she should stop covering up her face. This woman said that she could relate to that part because it made Celie's transformation in the film so much more powerful. At first, she said, everybody who loved Celie [Shug and Nettie], and everyone that Celie loved, kept telling her to put her hand down. The woman then pointed out 'that last time that Celie put her hand down nobody told her to put her hand down. She had started coming into her own. So when she grabbed that knife she was ready to use it.' This comment refers to the scene in the film at the dinner table, when Celie and Shug are about to leave for Memphis. Mister begins to chastise Celie telling her that she will be back. He says, 'You ugly, you skinny, you shaped funny and you scared to open your mouth to people.' Celie sits there quietly and takes Mister's verbal abuse. Then she asks him, 'Any more letters come?' She is talking about Nettie's letters from Africa that Mister has been hiding from Celie and that Celie and Shug had recently found. Mister replies, 'Could be, could be not.' Celie jumps up at that point, grabs the knife, and sticks it to Mister's throat.

The woman who found this scene significant continued: 'But had she not got to that point, built up to that point [of feeling herself worthwhile], she could have grabbed the knife and turned it the other way for all that it mattered to her. She wouldn't have been any worse off. But she saw herself getting better. So when she grabbed that knife she was getting ready to use it and it wasn't on herself.'

Other comments from the women were expressions of outrage at criticisms made against the film. The women were especially disturbed by vicious attacks against Alice Walker and against Black women critics and scholars who were publicly defending the film. One of the women in the interview session commented that she was surprised that there was such controversy over the film: 'I had such a positive feeling about it, I couldn't imagine someone saying that they didn't like it.' Another said that she was shocked at the outcry from some Black men: 'I didn't look at it as being stereotypically Black or all Black men are this way' (referring to the portrayal of the character Mister).

Another related a story that shows how two people can watch the same film and have opposite reactions: 'I was thinking about how men felt about it [*The Color Purple*] and I was surprised. But I related it to something that happened to me sometime ago when I was married. I went to see a movie called *Three in the Attic.* I don't know if any of you ever saw it. But I remember that on the way home – I thought it was funny – but my husband was so angry he wouldn't even talk to me on the way home. He said, "You thought that was funny." I said that I sure did. He felt it was really hostile because these ladies had taken this man up in the attic and made him go to bed with all of them until he was ... blue. Because he had been running around with all of these ladies. But he [her husband] was livid because I thought it was funny. And I think now, some men I talked to had a similar reaction to *The Color Purple.*

That it was ... all the men in there were dummies or horrible. And none of the men, they felt, were portrayed in a positive light. And then I started thinking about it and I said, "well ... I felt that somebody had to be the hero or the heroine, and in this case it just happened to be the woman."'

I have found that on the whole Black women have discovered something progressive and useful in the film. It is crucial to understand how this is possible when viewing a work made according to the encoding of dominant ideology. Black women's responses to *The Color Purple* loom as an extreme contrast to those of many other viewers. Not only is the difference in reception noteworthy but Black women's responses confront and challenge a prevalent method of media audience analysis which insists that viewers of mainstream works have no control or influence over a cultural product. Recent developments in media audience analysis demonstrate that there is a complex process of negotiation whereby specific members of a culture construct meaning from a mainstream text that is different from the meanings others would produce. These different readings are based, in part, on viewers' various histories and experiences.

Oppositional Readings

The encoding/decoding model is useful for understanding how a cultural product can evoke such different viewer reactions. The model was developed by the University of Birmingham Centre for Contemporary Cultural Studies, under the direction of Stuart Hall, in an attempt to synthesize various perspectives on media audience analysis and to incorporate theory from sociology and cultural studies. This model is concerned with an understanding of the communication process as it operates in a specific cultural context. It analyses ideological and cultural power and the way in which meaning is produced in that context. The researchers at the Centre felt that media analysts should not look simply at the meaning of a text but should also investigate the social and cultural framework in which communication takes place.[14]

From political sociology, the encoding/decoding model was drawn from the work of Frank Parkin, who developed a theory of meaning systems.[15] This theory delineates three potential responses to a media message: dominant, negotiated or oppositional. A dominant (or preferred) reading of a text accepts the content of the cultural product without question. A negotiated reading questions parts of the content of the text but does not question the dominant ideology which underlies the production of the text. An oppositional response to a cultural

96

product is one in which the recipient of the text understands that the system that produced the text is one with which she/he is fundamentally at odds.[16]

A viewer of a film (reader of a text) comes to the moment of engagement with the work with a knowledge of the world and a knowledge of other texts, or media products. What this means is that when a person comes to view a film, she/he does not leave her/his histories, whether social, cultural, economic, racial, or sexual at the door. An audience member from a marginalized group (people of colour, women, the poor, and so on) has an oppositional stance as they participate in mainstream media. The motivation for this counter-reception is that we understand that mainstream media has never rendered our segment of the population faithfully. We have as evidence our years of watching films and television programmes and reading plays and books. Out of habit, as readers of mainstream texts, we have learned to ferret out the beneficial and put up blinders against the rest.

From this wary viewing standpoint, a subversive reading of a text can occur. This alternative reading comes from something in the work that strikes the viewer as amiss, that appears 'strange'. Behind the idea of subversion lies a reader-oriented notion of 'making strange'.[17] When things appear strange to the viewer, she/he may then bring other viewpoints to bear on the watching of the film and may see things other than what the film-makers intended. The viewer, that is, will read 'against the grain' of the film.

Producers of mainstream media products are not aligned in a conspiracy against an audience. When they construct a work they draw on their own background, experience and social and cultural milieu. They are therefore under 'ideological pressure' to reproduce the familiar.[18] When Steven Spielberg made *The Color Purple* he did not intend to make a film that would be in the mould of previous films that were directed by a successful white director and had an all-Black or mostly Black cast.

Spielberg states that he deliberately cast the characters in *The Color Purple* in a way that they would not carry the taint of negative stereotypes:

I didn't want to cast traditional Black movie stars, which I thought would create their own stereotypes. I won't mention any names because it wouldn't be kind, but there were people who wanted to play these parts very much. It would have made it seem as if these were the only Black people accepted in white world's mainstream. I didn't want to do that. That's why I cast so many unknowns like Whoopi Goldberg, Oprah Winfrey, Margaret Avery.[19]

But it is interesting that while the director of the film made a conscious decision to cast against type, he could not break away from his culturally acquired conceptions of how Black people are and how they should act. Barbara Christian, Professor of Afro-American Studies at University of California, Berkeley, contends that the most maligned figure in the film is the character Harpo. She points out that in the book he cannot become the patriarch that society demands he be.[20] Apparently Spielberg could not conceive of a man uncomfortable with the requirements of patriarchy, and consequently depicts Harpo as a buffoon. Christian comments that 'the movie makes a negative statement about men who show some measure of sensitivity to women'. The film uses the husband and wife characters, Harpo and Sofia, as comic relief. Some of the criticisms against the film from Black viewers concerned Harpo's ineptness in repairing a roof. If the film-makers have Harpo fall once, it seems they decided that it was even funnier if he fell three times.

In her *Village Voice* review, Michele Wallace attributed motives other than comic relief to the film's representations of the couple. Wallace considered their appearances to be the result of 'white patriarchal interventions'. She wrote:

> In the book Sofia is the epitome of a woman with masculine powers, the martyr to sexual injustice who eventually triumphs through the realignment of the community. In the movie she is an occasion for humor. She and Harpo are the reincarnations of Amos and Sapphire; they alternately fight and fuck their way to a house full of pickaninnies. Harpo is always falling through a roof he's chronically unable to repair. Sofia is always shoving a baby into his arms, swinging her large hips, and talking a mile a minute. Harpo, who is dying to marry Sofia in the book, seems bamboozled into marriage in the film. Sofia's only masculine power is her contentiousness. Encircled by the mayor, his wife and an angry mob, she is knocked down and her dress flies up providing us with a timely reminder that she is just a woman.[21]

The depiction of Sofia lying in the street with her dress up is almost an exact replica of a picture published in a national mass-circulation magazine of a large Black woman lying dead in her home after she had been killed by her husband in a domestic argument. Coincidence or not, this image among others in the film makes one wonder about Spielberg's unconscious store of associations.

Black People's Representation in Film

While a film-maker draws on her/his background and experience, she/he also draws on a history of other films. *The Color Purple* follows in the footsteps of earlier films with a Black storyline and/or an all Black cast which were directed by a white male for mass consumption by a white American audience. The criticisms against the film repeatedly invoked the names of such racist films as *The Birth of a Nation* (1915), *Hallelujah* (1929) and *Cabin in the Sky* (1943). One reviewer in the *Village Voice* wrote that *The Color Purple* was 'a revisionist *Cabin in the Sky*, with the God-fearing, long-suffering Ethel Waters (read Celie) and the delectable temptress Lena Horne (known as Shug Avery) falling for each other rather than wrestling over the soul of feckless (here sadistic) Eddie Anderson'.[22]

According to Donald Bogle in *Toms, Coons, Mulattoes, Mammies and Bucks*, Nina Mae McKinney's character in *Hallelujah* executing 'gyrations and groans' and sensuous 'bumps and grinds' became a standard for almost every Black 'leading lady' in motion pictures, from Lena Horne in *Cabin in the Sky* to Lola Falana in *The Liberation of L.B. Jones*.[23] The corollary of this stereotype can be seen acted out by Margaret Avery as Shug in the juke-joint scenes in *The Color Purple*. Here we see Shug singing in the juke-joint and later leading the 'jointers' singing and prancing down the road to her father's church. One viewer of The Color Purple wondered, in reference to this scene, if it were obligatory in every film that contained Black actors and actresses that they sing and dance.[24]

As Spielberg called on his store of media memories in making *The Color Purple*, he used a cinematic technique that made D.W. Griffith famous, cross-cutting, toward the same end as Griffith – that of portraying the 'savage' nature of Black people. At the beginning of *The Color Purple* the young Celie gives birth to a child fathered by the man she thinks is her father. The viewer can recall the beads of sweat on Celie's face and the blood in the pan of water as Nettie wrings out the cloth she is using to wash Celie. The next shot of blood is on the rock that one of Mister's bad kids throws and hits the young Celie with. We look at Celie and then there is a close-up of the blood on the rock. Later in the film, there is a scene of the grown Celie taking up a knife that she will use to shave Mister. It should be noted that this scene was not in the book and was entirely the film's invention. As Celie brings the knife closer to Mister's neck there is continual cross-cutting with scenes of the initiation rites of Adam (Celie's son) and Pasha in Africa. This cross-cutting is interspersed with shots of Shug dressed in a red dress running across a field to stop Celie from cutting Mister's throat. As the back and forth action of the three scenes progresses, the kids' cheeks are cut and we see a trickle of blood running down one of their faces.

In fictional film-making, scripts utilize what is known as the rule of threes: first there is the introduction to a concept that is significant, then the set-up, then the pay-off. Without reaching too hard for significance, we can see in the meaning of the shots of blood with the blood-red of Shug's dress as she runs to rescue Celie, and then the bloodletting of the African initiation rite, that these shots and their use of red culminate in the pay-off: these are 'savage' people. This connects up later in the film with the overall red tone to the juke-joint sequences and the red dress that Shug wears while she is performing there. As Barbara Christian put it, the gross inaccuracy of the African initiation ceremony coupled with the shots of Celie going after Mister with the sharpened knife seemed intended to depict a 'primordial blood urge shared by dark peoples in Africa and Afro-Americans'.

Other films that have formed the foundation of Black people's demeaning cinematic heritage are *Hearts of Dixie* (1929), *The Green Pastures* (1936), *Carmen Jones* (1954) and *Porgy and Bess* (1959). *Porgy and Bess* is especially interesting because of the similarity of its reception to that of *The Color Purple*. The playwright Lorraine Hansberry figures prominently in Black people's negative reaction to *Porgy and Bess*. Hansberry was the only Black person who confronted the director, Otto Preminger, in a public debate about the film. At the time of the debate, Hansberry was well known because of the success of her play, *A Raisin in the Sun* (1959). Hansberry's condemnation of the film and its director was the catalyst for a scathing article in *Ebony* magazine, criticizing not only the makers of the film, but also the Black stars who had defended the film as a commendable work of art.[25]

There is a sense of *déja vu* in considering the success of Lorraine Hansberry, her view of Black people's representation in commercial films, and her deliberations about having her work turned into a Hollywood property. Hansberry's concern almost twenty-five years before the release of *The Color Purple* reads as if it could have been written about the contemporary film. Both Hansberry and Alice Walker were hesitant about turning their works, which were successful in another medium, over to a white director in Hollywood. Hansberry wrote about this in 1961:

> My twenty years of memory of Hollywood treatment of 'Negro material' plus the more commonly decried aspects of Hollywood tradition, led me to visualize slit skirts and rolling eyeballs, with the latest night club singer playing the family's college daughter. I did not feel it was my right or duty to help present the American public with yet another latter-day minstrel show.[26]

The negative assumptions that Hansberry was confronting and that she countered in her works is the myth of the exotic primitive.[27] I label it a myth not because of the concept's falseness but because of its wide acceptance, and because of the manner in which it functions as a cultural belief system.

In contemporary terms, a myth is a narrative that accompanies an historical sequence of events or actions. A body of political writings and literature develops around this narrative. This becomes the formulated myth. The myth is constructed of images and symbols which have the force to activate a cultural belief system. This means that if a culture believes a myth to be true or operable in their society, a body of tradition, folk-lore, laws and social rules is developed around this mythology. In this way myths serve to organize, unify and clarify a culture's history in a manner that is satisfactory to a culture.

Mark Schorer, in *Myth and Mythmaking*, states that all convictions (belief systems), whether personal or societal, involve mythology. The mythology, although historically grounded, does not have to be historically accurate. The truth or falsity of the myth is not important when considering the function of the myth (that of validating history), as the cultural system of beliefs is not rational but based on the assumptions in the myth-making process. As Schorer indicates: 'Belief organizes experience not because it is rational but because all belief depends on a controlling imagery and rational belief is the intellectual formalization of that imagery.'[28] In other words, we believe first, and then we create a rationale for our beliefs and subsequent actions. The formal expression of our beliefs can be seen in the imagery used by a culture.

The characteristics of the myth of the exotic primitive are these: a) Black people are naturally childlike. Thus they adjust easily to the most unsatisfactory social conditions, which they accept readily and even happily; b) Black people are oversexed, carnal sensualists dominated by violent passions; c) Black people are savages taken from a culture relatively low on the scale of human civilization.[29]

As a panellist on *The Negro in American Culture*, a radio programme aired on WABI-F, in New York in January 1961, Lorraine Hansberry spoke eloquently about mainstream artists' need to portray Black people in a negative light:

> And it seems to me that one of the things that has been done in the American mentality is to create this escape valve of the exotic Negro, wherein it is possible to exalt abandon on all levels, and to imagine that while I am dealing with the perplexities of the universe, look over there, coming down from the trees is a Negro who knows none of this, and wouldn't it be marvelous if I could be my naked, brutal, savage self again?[30]

Knowing that this concept of exoticism underlies the products of mainstream cultural production, I think this is one of the reasons that many viewers of a film such as *The Color Purple* have what Bogle described earlier as a schizophrenic reaction. The film did have something progressive and useful for a Black audience but at the same time some of the caricatures and representations cause the viewer to wince. It is my contention that a Black audience through a history of theatre-going and film-watching knows that at some point an expression of the exotic primitive is going to be presented to us. Since this is the case, we have one of two options available to us. One is to never indulge in media products, an impossibility in an age of media blitz. Another option, and I think this is more an unconscious reaction to and defense against racist depictions of Black people, is to filter out that which is negative and select from the work elements we can relate to.

Black Women's Response

Given the similarities of *The Color Purple* to past films that have portrayed Black people negatively, Black women's positive reaction to the film seems inconceivable. However, their stated comments and published reports prove that Black women not only like the film but have formed a strong attachment to it. The film is significant in their lives.

John Fiske provides a useful explanation of what is meant by the term 'the subject' in cultural analysis. 'The subject' is different from the individual. The individual is the biological being produced by nature; the 'subject' is a social and theoretical construction that is used to designate individuals as they become significant in a political or theoretical sense. When considering a text – a cultural product – the subject is defined as the political being who is affected by the ideological construction of the text.[31]

Black women, as subjects for the text, *The Color Purple*, have a different history and consequently a different perspective from other viewers of the film. This became evident in the controversy surrounding the film, and in the critical comments from some Black males about what they perceived as the detrimental depiction of Black men. In contrast to this view, Black women have demonstrated that they found something useful and positive in the film. Barbara Christian relates that the most frequent statement from Black women has been: 'Finally, somebody says something about us.'[32] This sense of identification with what was in the film would provide an impetus for Black women to form an engagement with the film. This engagement could have been either positive or negative. That it was favourable indicates something about the way in which Black women have constructed meaning from this text.

It would be too easy, I think, to categorize Black women's reaction to the film as an example of 'false consciousness'; to consider Black women as cultural dupes in the path of a media barrage who cannot figure out when a media product portrays them and their race in a negative manner. Black women are aware, along with others, of the oppression and harm that comes from a negative media history. But Black women are also aware that their specific experience, as Black people, as women, in a rigid class/caste state, has never been adequately dealt with in mainstream media.

One of the Black women that I interviewed talked about this cultural past and how it affected her reaction to the *The Color Purple*: 'When I went to the movie, I thought, here I am. I grew up looking at Elvis Presley kissing on all these white girls. I grew up listening to "Tammy, Tammy, Tammy". [She sings the song that Debbie Reynolds sang in the movie of the same name.] And it wasn't that I had anything projected before me on the screen to really give me something that I could grow up to be like. Or even wanted to be. Because I knew I wasn't Goldilocks, you know, and I had heard those stories all my life. So when I got to the movie, the first thing I said was "God, this is good acting." And I liked that. I felt a lot of pride in my Black brothers and sisters.... By the end of the movie I was totally emotionally drained.... The emotional things were all in the book, but the movie just took every one of my emotions.... Towards the end, when she looks up and sees her sister Nettie ... I had gotten so emotionally high at that point ... when she saw her sister, when she started to call her name and to recognize who she was, the hairs on my neck started to stick up. I had never had a movie do that to me before.'

The concept 'interpellation' sheds light on the process by which Black women were able to form a positive engagement with *The Color Purple*. Interpellation is the way in which the subject is hailed by the text; it is the method by which ideological discourses constitute subjects and draw them into the text/subject relationship. John Fiske describes 'hailing' as similar to hailing a cab. The viewer is hailed by a particular work; if she/he gives a co-operative response to the beckoning, then not only are they constructed as a subject, but the text then becomes a text, in the sense that the subject begins to construct meaning from the work and is constructed by the work.[33]

The moment of the encounter of the text and the subject is known as the 'interdiscourse'. David Morley explains this concept, developed by Michel Pêcheux, as the space, the specific moment when subjects bring their histories to bear on meaning production in a text.[34] Within this interdiscursive space, cultural competencies come into play. A cultural competency is the repertoire of discursive strategies, the range of knowledge, that a viewer brings to the act of watching a film and creating meaning from a work. As has been stated before, the meanings of a text will be constructed differently depending on the various backgrounds of the viewers. The viewers' position in the social structure determines, in part, what sets of discourses or interpretive strategies they will bring to their encounter with the text. A specific cultural competency will set some of the boundaries to meaning construction.

The cultural competency perspective has allowed media researchers to understand how elements in a viewer's background play a determining role in the way in which she/he interprets a text. Stuart Hall, David Morley and others utilize the theories of Dell Hymes, Basil Bernstein and Pierre Bourdieu for an understanding of the ways in which a social structure distributes different forms of cultural decoding strategies throughout the different sections of the media audience. These understandings are not the same for everyone in the audience because they are shaped by the individual's history, both media and cultural, and by the individual's social affiliations such as race, class, gender, and so on.[35]

As I see it, there can be two aspects to a cultural competency, or the store of understandings that a marginalized viewer brings to interpreting a cultural product. One is a positive response where the viewer constructs something useful from the work by negotiating her/his response, and/or gives a subversive reading to the work. The other is a negative response in which the viewer rejects the work. Both types of oppositional readings are prompted by the store of negative images that have come from prior mainstream media experience; in the case of *The Color Purple*, from Black people's negative history in Hollywood films.

A positive engagement with a work could come from an intertextual cultural experience. This is true, I think, with the way in which Black women constructed meaning from *The Color Purple*. Creative works by Black women are proliferating now. This intense level of productivity is not accidental nor coincidental. It stems from a desire on the part of Black women to construct works more in keeping with their experiences, their history, and with the daily lives of other Black women. And Black women, as cultural consumers, are receptive to these works. This intertextual cultural knowledge is forming Black women's store of decoding strategies for films that are about them. This is the cultural competency that Black women brought to their favourable readings of *The Color Purple*.

Black Women's Writing Tradition: Community and Articulation

The historical moment in which the film *The Color Purple* was produced and received is what one Black feminist scholar has categorized the 'renaissance of Black women writers' of the 1970s and 1980s. Within this renaissance the central concern of the writers has been the personal lives and collective histories of Black women. The writers are reconstructing a heritage that has either been distorted or ignored. In this reconstruction, Black women are both audience and subject.[36]

A major difference in the current period of writing from that of the well known Harlem Renaissance of the 1920s, the protest literature of the 1940s and the Black activist literature of the 1960s, is that Black women writers are getting more exposure and recognition today, and the target of their works is different. In the earlier periods of Black writing, male writers were given dominant exposure and the audience to whom they addressed their works was white. The writers believed that because Black people's oppression was the direct result of white racism, exposing this fact to white people would result in change. By contrast, for Black women writers within the last forty years, the Black community has been the major focus of their work.

Hortense J. Spillers writes that the community of Black women writing is a vivid new fact of national life. Spillers includes in this community not only the writers but Black women critics, scholars, and audience members. This community, which Spillers labels a community of 'cultural workers' is fashioning its own tradition. Its writers and its readers are, she writes, creating their works against the established canons and are excavating a legacy that is more appropriate to their lives. Spillers argues compellingly that traditions are made, not born. Traditions do not arise spontaneously out of nature, but are created social events. She insists that traditions exist not only because there are writers there to make them, but also because there is a 'strategic audience of heightened consciousness prepared to read and interpret the works as such'.[37]

Spillers adds that traditions need to be maintained by an audience if they are to survive, and she argues that this is currently happening. She writes that 'we are called upon to witness' the formation of a new social order of Black women as a community conscious of itself. This is not a random association of writers creating in isolation or readers consuming the works in a vacuum. According to Spillers, the group views itself as a community and is aware that it is creating new symbolic values and a new sense of empowerment for itself and the members of the group.

Stuart Hall has defined the principle of 'articulation', developed by Ernesto Laclau, to explain how individuals within a particular society at a specific historical moment wrest control away from the dominant forces in a culture and attain authority over their lives for themselves and for others within their social group. The way in which an articulation is accomplished, and its significance, has bearing on this examination of the film *The Color Purple*. An articulation is defined as the form of a connection, a linkage, that can establish a unity among different elements within a culture, under certain conditions.[38] In the case of a cultural product such as the film *The Color Purple*, the unity that is formed links a discourse (the film) and a specific social group (Black women or, more precisely, what Spillers has defined as the Black women's writing community). Such unity is flexible, but not for all time. It must constantly be strengthened. The strength of the unity formed between a discourse and a social alliance comes from the use to which the group puts the discourse, or the cultural product. In the case of *The Color Purple*, the film has been used to give new meaning to the lives of Black women.

Articulation, as it is normally defined, can have two meanings: 'joining up' in the sense of the limbs of a body or an anatomical structure, or 'giving expression to'.[39] Hall disagrees with the use of articulation to mean 'giving expression to' because it implies that a social group shares an expressive unity which Hall believes it does not. An articulation results from a coming together of separate discourses under certain specific conditions and at specific times. The use of articulation to mean 'giving expression to' implies that the two elements that are linked are the same, but for Hall they are not. The unity formed 'is not that of an identity where one structure perfectly reproduces or recapitulates' the other. The social group and the signifying text are not the same. An articulation occurs because a social alliance forms it, in a political act which makes the group a cohesive one for a time, as long as it goes on acting for a political purpose.

When an articulation arises, old ideologies are disrupted and a cultural transformation is accomplished. The cultural transformation is not something totally new, nor does it have an unbroken line of continuity with the past. It is always in a process of becoming. But at a particular moment the reality of the cultural transformation becomes apparent. The group that is the catalyst for it recognizes that a change is occurring and that they are in the midst of a cultural transition. The formal elements of the transformation are then recognized and consolidated.

The Black women's writing tradition laid a foundation for the way in which Black women formed an articulation through which they interpreted the film *The Color Purple*. The boundaries of the tradition are set from 1850 onward. Although Black women were socially and politically active from the beginning of their enforced presence in the 'new world', their writings, speeches, and lectures, their 'public voice', as Hazel Carby describes it, was not being recorded and preserved. Carby makes the critical point, however, that Black women's voices were being heard.[40] The public voice of nineteenth-century Black women activists resounds now in the creative works of Black women in the 1970s and the 1980s, thus giving contemporary texts all the elements of a tradition.

Barbara Christian's *Black Women Novelists* (1980) was instrumental in identifying the presence of the tradition. In her book Christian not only demonstrated that there was indeed a Black women's writing tradition, but she also proved convincingly, I think, that the reasons that these Black women were little known was that the two established critical institutions, African-American literature and mainstream white literature, had placed Black women in the shadows of literary scholarship. She proved, as Spillers indicated, that tradition is a man-made product and that Black women had been left out.

Christian also looks at the elements of Black women's writing that foreshadowed and formed a foundation for the contemporary writers that she finds most influential: Paule Marshall, Toni Morrison and Alice Walker. The elements of Black life that they portray seem to strike a resonance in the audience for whom the works are written, Black women. Christian argues that Black women's literature is not just a matter of discourse, but is a way of acknowledging one's existence: 'it has to do with giving consolation to oneself that one does exist. It is an attempt to make meaning out of that existence.' And further, 'The way in which I have often described this for myself, as a Black woman, is that this literature helps me to know that I am not hallucinating. Because much of one's life from the point of view of a Black woman could be seen as an hallucination from what society tells you.' She said the way in which the literature connects up with the experiences of other Black women is that, in giving Black women a place as subject, it 'therefore gives them a sense that their lives are in fact *real*'.[41]

Toni Morrison writes of one of her characters: 'She had nothing to fall back on; not maleness, not whiteness, not ladyhood, not anything. And out of the profound desolation of her reality she may well have invented herself.'[42] Out of the profound desolation of Black women's reality, to paraphrase Toni Morrison, Black women cultural producers are beginning to create works more appropriate to their lives and to the daily reality of other Black women. In Ntozake Shange's choreopoem *For Colored Girls Who Have Considered Suicide/When the Rainbow Is Enuf* (1976), one of the characters, the lady in orange, tells her former boyfriend:

> ever since i realized there waz someone callt
> a colored girl an evil woman a bitch or a nag
> i been trying not to be that & leave bitterness
> in somebody else's cup/ come to somebody to love me
> without deep & nasty smellin scald from lye or bein
> left screamin in a street fulla lunatics/whisperin slut bitch bitch niggah/ get outta here wit alla
> that/ ...

Later in the passage the lady in orange delivers what I think is a sign for Black women that the status quo is not for them and that something different is required:

... /but a real dead
lovin is here for you now/ cuz i don't know anymore/how to avoid my own face
wet wit my tears/ cuz i had convinced
myself colored girls had no right to sorrow/ & i lived
& loved that way & kept sorrow on the curb/ allegedly
for you/ but i know i did it for myself/
i cdnt stand it
i cdnt stand bein sorry & colored at the same time it's so redundant in the modern
world.[43]

'I couldn't stand it', the lady in orange says, and she issues an ultimatum that the Black woman was evolving from one place in society's conception of her to another of her own choosing. The Black woman was changing from victim to victor, was placing herself outside of the cocoon for others' constructions of her and, as Alice Walker's character Celie says in *The Color Purple*, entering into 'the Creation'.

Celie's declaration contains the essence of Black women's response to the film *The Color Purple*. There has been a long march from early images of the Black woman in creative works to the reconstruction of the character Celie in Alice Walker's novel. Celie tells Mister, at a turning-point in the novel, that she is leaving the prison that he has created for her and entering into a freer place where she has more control over her own destiny. Black women responded to Celie's statement in their overwhelming positive reaction to both the novel and the film.

Black women's positive response to the film *The Color Purple* is not coincidental, nor is it insignificant. It is in keeping with the recent emergence of a body of critical works about the heritage of Black women writers, the recent appearance of other novels by Black women written in the same vein as *The Color Purple* and, very importantly, the fact that there is a knowledgeable core of Black women readers of both literary and filmic texts. This community of heightened consciousness is in the process of creating new self-images and forming a force for change.

Notes

1. Phil Donahue read a quote by Tony Brown with this statement on his show, *The Phil Donahue Show*, 25 April 1986. Brown was part of a panel along with Donald Bogle, Michele Wallace and Willis Edwards, debating the film. Ishmael Reed's statement was

quoted by Tony Brown on his show *Tony Brown's Journal*, when Reed was a guest there. Reed was debating Barbara Smith on the topic of the show: 'Do Black Feminist Writers Victimize Black Men?' (repeat programme), 2 November 1986.

2. Andrew Kopkind, 'The Color Purple', *The Nation*, 1 February 1986, p. 124. The *Guardian* is a radical journal in the United States.

3. Jill Nelson, 'Spielberg's "Purple" is Still Black', *Guardian*, 29 January 1986, p. 1.

4. E.R. Shipp, 'Blacks in Heated Debate over *The Color Purple*', *New York Times*, 27 January 1986, p. A13.

5. Courtland Milloy, 'A "Purple" Rage Over a Rip-Off', *Washington Post*, 24 December 1985, p. B3.

6. Barbara Smith, '*Color Purple* Distorts Class, Lesbian Issues', *Guardian*, 19 February 1986, p. 19.

7. Jill Nelson, *Guardian*, p. 17.

8. Michele Wallace, *The Phil Donahue Show*, 25 April, 1986.

9. Michele Wallace, 'Blues for Mr Spielberg', *Village Voice*, 18 March 1986, p. 27.

10. Donald Bogle, *The Phil Donahue Show*, 25 April 1986.

11. William Goldstein, 'Alice Walker on the set of *The Color Purple*', *Publisher's Weekly*, 6 September, 1985, p. 48.

12. Mary Helen Washington, 'Book Review of Barbara Christian's *Black Women Novelists*', *Signs: Journal of Women in Culture and Society*, Vol. 8 no. 1 (August 1982), p. 182.

13. I am at present writing a dissertation on Black women's response to the film *The Color Purple*. As part of the study I conducted what will be an ethnography of reading with selected Black women viewers of the film in December 1987 in California. All references to women interviewed come from this study. For a discussion of the issues of readers' response to texts in media audience analysis see Ellen Seiter *et al.* 'Don't Treat Us Like We're So Stupid and Naive: Towards an Ethnograhy of Soap Opera Viewers', in *Rethinking Television Audiences*, Ellen Seiter, (ed.) Chapel Hill: University of North Carolina Press, forthcoming. See also Seiter's use of Umberto Eco's open/closed text distinction to examine the role of the woman reader. Seiter uses Eco's narrative theory to argue for the possibility of 'alternative' readings unintended by their producers in 'Eco's TV Guide: The Soaps', *Tabloid*, no. 6 (1981) pp. 36–43.

14. David Morley, 'Changing Paradigms in Audience Studies', in *Rethinking Television Audiences*, Ellen Seiter (ed.), Chapel Hill: University of North Carolina Press, forthcoming.

15. David Morley, 'Changing Paradigms', p. 4.

16. Lawrence Grossberg, 'Strategies of Marxist Cultural Interpretation', *Critical Studies in Mass Communication*, no. 1 (1984), p. 403.

17. Christine Gledhill explains the idea of 'making strange' in two articles: 'Developments in Feminist Film Criticism', *Re-Vision: Essays in Feminist Film Criticism*, Mary Ann Doane, Patricia Mellencamp and Linda Williams (eds), Frederick, Maryland: University Publications of America, in association with the American Film Institute, 1984; and 'Klute 1: A Contemporary Film Noir and Feminist Criticism', *Women in Film Noir*, E. Ann Kaplan (ed), London: British Film Institute, 1984.

18. Lawrence Grossberg, p. 403.

19. Steven Spielberg, BBC documentary, *Alice Walker and The Color Purple*, 1986.

20. Barbara Christian, 'De-Visioning Spielberg and Walker: *The Color Purple* – The Novel and the Film', Center for the Study of Women in Society, University of Oregon, 20 May 1986.

21. Michele Wallace, 'Blues for Mr Spielberg', p. 25.

22. J. Hoberman, 'Color Me Purple', *Village Voice*, 24 December 1985, p. 76.

23. Donald Bogle, *Toms, Coons, Mulattoes, Mammies and Bucks: An Interpretive History of Blacks in American Films*, New York: Viking Press, 1973, p. 31.

24. Julie Salamon, '... As Spielberg's Film Version Is Released', *Wall Street Journal*, 19 December 1985, p. 20.

25. Era Bell Thompson, 'Why Negroes Don't Like "Porgy and Bess"', *Ebony*, October 1959, p. 51. A rundown of Lorraine Hansberry's debate with Otto Preminger is

also given by Jack Pitman, 'Lorraine Hansberry Deplores "Porgy"', *Variety*, 27 May 1959.

26. Lorraine Hansberry, 'What Could Happen Didn't', *New York Herald-Tribune*, 26 March 1961, p. 8. In this article Lorraine Hansberry writes about the experience of turning her play *A Raisin in the Sun* into a Hollywood movie. Hansberry wrote the screenplay herself and, as far as I know, was the first Black woman to have a Hollywood film based on her work. For a further examination of the political and historical significance of Hansberry, see Jacqueline Bobo, 'Debunking the Myth of the Exotic Primitive: Three Plays by Lorraine Hansberry', unpublished MA thesis, San Francisco State University, 1980.

27. Anthropologist Melville Herskovits gives broader scope to the myth, designating it as the myth of the Negro past. The trait of exotic primitivism can be extrapolated from Herskovits's definition and considered a myth itself in that both concepts are of sufficient potency that the effect in a culture is the same: validating the social processes whereby Black people are considered inferior. Melville Herskovits, *The Myth of the Negro Past*, Boston: Beacon Press, 1958, p. 1.

28. Mark Schorer, 'The Necessity of Myth', *Myth and Mythmaking*, Henry A. Murray (ed.), New York: George Braziller, 1960, p. 356.

29. Herskovits, p. 1.

30. Lorraine Hansberry, 'The Negro in American Culture', reprinted in *The Black American Writer*, C.W.E. Bigsby (ed.), Florida: Everett/Edward, 1969, p. 93.

31. John Fiske, 'British Cultural Studies and Television', *Channels of Discourse: Television and Contemporary Criticism*, Robert C. Allen (ed.), Chapel Hill: University of North Carolina Press, 1987, p. 258.

32. Barbara Christian, University of Oregon, 20 May 1986.

33. John Fiske, 'British Cultural Studies and Television', p. 258.

34. David Morley, 'Texts, Readers, Subjects', *Culture, Media, Language*, Stuart Hall, Dorothy Hobson, Andrew Lowe and Paul Willis (eds), London: Hutchinson, 1980, p. 164.

35. David Morley, 'Changing Paradigms in Audience Studies', p. 4.

36. Barbara Christian, Seminar: 'Black Women's Literature and the Canon', University of Oregon, 7 December 1987.

37. Hortense J. Spillers, 'Cross-Currents, Discontinuities: Black Women's Fiction', *Conjuring: Black Women, Fiction, and Literary Tradition*, Marjorie Pryse and Hortense J. Spillers (eds), Bloomington: Indiana University Press, 1985, p. 250.

38. Stuart Hall discusses the principle of 'articulation' in two articles: 'Race, Articulation and Societies Structured in Dominance', in *Sociological Theories: Race and Colonialism*, UNESCO, 1980, pp. 305–45. Also, Lawrence Grossberg (ed.) 'On Postmodernism and Articulation: An Interview with Stuart Hall', *Journal of Communication Inquiry*, Summer 1986, vol. 10, no. 2, pp. 45–60.

I explore the principle of 'articulation' further in the larger study that I am doing on Black women's response to *The Color Purple*. I see the articulation between Black women as audience, the Black women's writing community and Black women's collective response to the film as constituting a social force that will effect other areas in Black people's lives: politically, economically and socially.

39. Hall, 'Race, Articulation and Societies Structured in Dominance', p. 28.

40. Hazel V. Carby, *Reconstructing Womanhood: The Emergence of the Afro-American Woman Novelist*, New York: Oxford University Press, 1987. Other critical works that examine the Black women's writing tradition are: *The Black Woman* (1970), by Toni Cade; *Black-Eyed Susans* (1975) and *Midnight Birds* (1980), by Mary Helen Washington, *Black Women Writers at Work* (1983), Claudia Tate (ed.); *Black Women Writers* (1984), by Mari Evans; *Invented Lives* (1987), by Mary Helen Washington; and *Specifying* (1987), by Susan Willis.

41. Barbara Christian, Seminar, University of Oregon, 7 December 1987.

42. Toni Morrison, cited in Mary Helen Washington, *Black-Eyed Susans: Classic Stories by and about Black Women*, New York: Anchor Press/Doubleday, 1975, p. vii.

43. Ntozake Shange, *For Colored Girls Who Have Considered Suicide/When the Rainbow Is Enuf*, New York: Macmillan Publishing Co., 1976, p. 43.

6

Gazes/Voices/Power: Expanding Psychoanalysis for Feminist Film and Television Theory

Jackie Byars

In the first words of her book, *In a Different Voice*, on the differences between female and male discourse, Carol Gilligan recounts this experience:

> Over the past ten years, I have been listening to people talking about morality and about themselves. Halfway through that time, I began to hear a distinction in these voices, two ways of speaking about moral problems, two modes of describing the relationship between other and self.... Against the background of the psychological descriptions of identity and moral development which I had read and taught for a number of years, the women's voices sounded distinct. It was then that I began to notice the recurrent problems in interpreting women's development and to connect these problems to the repeated exclusion of women from the critical theory-building studies of psychological research.[1]

Researchers in interpersonal communication have also met with this sort of problem. For instance, Deanna Hall and Kristin Langellier note that research on story-telling has focused on stories gathered primarily from male subjects, and this research has analysed stories from a 'male as norm' perspective. They argue that:

> Women's communication experience has not been considered worthy of study by past researchers; or it has been described as deviant or deficient by comparison to male models. Such research implies that women cannot tell stories 'right' and that what women tell are not 'real' stories.... Data has repeatedly been collected on men's storytelling, usually in public places, and generalized to the entire speech community.[2]

As a result, the structures, purposes, styles, strategies, and functions of women's story-telling have – until recently – been inadequately understood.

A similar problem exists in film theory and, since many film theorists are now turning their attention to television, in television theory. In the 1970s, feminist film theorists and analysts, like their counterparts in history and literary studies, exposed the cinema – especially Hollywood films (indeed, all of 'classic realist cinema') – as oppressive, and women as its victims. But by the mid-1970s, feminist historians and literary analysts had turned away from a preoccupation with explaining women's victimization and towards a 'recuperative' project which soon found evidence of significant female power evident in records of daily life and in literary texts by both male and female writers. But feminist media analysts focused this 'recuperative' project on political and avant-garde film texts; very few looked for evidence of female power in mainstream Hollywood film or in network television programming, dismissing these texts as inherently patriarchal. My work has included analyses of representations of gender in mainstream narratives: financially successful Hollywood family melodramas distributed in the 1950s and contemporary American network television programmes.[3] Over a number of years, it has become increasingly clear that a significant minority of film and television narratives contain elements of resistance which emerge through 'recuperative' reading. My aim here is to explain the ways in which feminist film and television theory may be expanded to account for the presence of different 'voices' in the struggles over gender definition waged in and with these texts.

Laura Mulvey has attempted to explain how the female viewer derives pleasure from a Hollywood genre film which is 'structured around masculine pleasure, offering an identification with the *active* point of view'. She has argued that this allows a woman spectator 'to rediscover that lost [masculine] aspect of her sexual identity', the never fully repressed bedrock of feminine repression. Mulvey insists that such an accomplishment is derived through a 'trans-sex identification' in which the female spectator temporarily remembers her masculine, active stage. Within a theory based on Freudian psychoanalysis, as Mulvey's is, the male/masculine is active and normative, and there is no way to explain the female/feminine except through this 'norm'.[4] Within this realm of film theory, then, there is no way to explain the resisting, different 'voice' that functions at both the narrative and the enunciative levels, and there is no way to explain the pleasure of the female spectator without reference to a masculine 'norm'.

A primary difficulty is the dominance in feminist film theory of Freudian and Lacanian theories of psychoanalysis, which describe personality development from a position which favours the masculine, and as such, operate conservatively to extend and naturalize the repression of women, defining 'woman' in terms of aberrance and deviance and effectively obscuring any variant 'voice'. According to Lacanian psychoanalysis, in fact, sexuality is produced in and through language, and language constructs woman as *not* man. The male – or masculine – voice that dominates our society and structures sexuality and gender also structures the very theories we use to explain them. Not surprisingly, these theories lack an explanation of change and so consign women to an inevitable secondary status.

Mainstream entertainment texts cannot be divorced from the material conditions in which they are produced and consumed nor separated from the ideological struggles of which they are a part. They are not simple texts; they are not ideologically coherent, nor are they monolithically repressive. They are participants in an ongoing ideological process; real ideological struggle goes on in and with mainstream entertainment texts, and ideological struggle goes on in theory as well. In order to understand and explain this struggle and the existence and role of a 'different voice' in Hollywood's family melodramas and in network television programming, it is necessary to read Freudian and Lacanian theories of psychoanalysis through the eyes of contemporary feminism.

In her pioneering book, *The Reproduction of Mothering*, Nancy Chodorow draws on clinical evidence, and a consideration of the context in which it was obtained, to reassess psychoanalytic descriptions of female personality development.[5] She rereads Freudian theory, basing her work in the object relations school of psychoanalysis. Object relations theory, like Lacanian theory, posits that the human subject is a social construction. But unlike Lacanian theory, which minimizes the importance of extralinguistic determinants in the formation of subjectivity, object relations theory assumes that it is the child's social relations that primarily determine psychological growth and personality formation. Chodorow rejects the Freudian emphasis on the child's discovery of anatomical difference between the sexes, focusing more extensively on the pre-Oedipal phase. She argues, for example, that the first identification for both male and female infants is with the primary parent, who in our society is usually the mother. Assuming this, Chodorow reinterprets Freud's Oedipal 'family romance'.

Freud claimed that the male child's relationship with his mother leads him to see his father as a rival: and so fearing paternal retaliation, he denies his love for his mother and identifies with his father, assuming a sense of superiority to all that is feminine. In this process, his identification with his father leads him into a 'normal' and ethically 'superior' object-love, first for his mother and later for other women. However,

Freud saw the female child in a very different light. The female child, he contended, recognizes herself as anatomically 'inferior' and comes to despise herself and all those like her (penisless), most especially her mother, who now becomes identified as a rival for her father's affection. According to Freud, the female may regain self-esteem only through a form of narcissistic vanity. She can never develop 'normal' object-love but may 'artificially' displace her narcissism on to her relations with her children.

Chodorow directly contradicts Freud's analysis of the Oedipal 'family romance' by asserting that the male's development involves a negation of the primary identity, while the female's does not. She insists that the female child does not give up her attachment to her mother during the Oedipal stage, as Freud argues, but develops instead a different model, a triadic model, for relationships. On the other hand, in order to develop 'normally', the male must repress his identification with the mother and develop a sense of himself as different and separate. Because girls are parented by a person of the same sex, Chodorow argues, they experience themselves as more continuous with the external world than do boys. Chodorow finds that female ego boundaries are more flexible than those of males and that their sense of identity is more fluid; females define themselves in terms of relationships rather than in terms of separateness and individuality. In addition, because women do not develop a masculine sense of justice and morality, based in a denial of relationship and connection and dependent on an uncompromising superego, they are more empathetic than males.

Analysing interviews with people on the topic of morality, Carol Gilligan found distinct differences between the way males and females talk, differences strikingly similar to those found by Chodorow. She describes two distinct perspectives, two modes of thinking, two different experiences of self. One, the male, is rooted in objectivity and impartiality, premissed 'on a fundamental separation between other and self', and is characterized by reciprocity, the need to receive in response to one's giving. The other, the female perspective, is based in a blurring of boundaries between self and other, allows feelings to influence thought, and is characterized by response and connectedness. She argues that Freud's desire to eliminate contradictions within his theory 'blinded him to the reality of women's experience' and to the asymmetrical personality development of males and females.[6] He lived in a society 'where women's lives were not considered to inform human possibility', and he worked with a notion of theory construction limited by a 'conception of objectivity in science that led to a series of enforced separations' (the analytic situation) characteristic of the masculine perspective. Chodorow recognizes that even the language of object-relations psychoanalysis is 'grounded in separation' and carries with it a 'vocabulary of borders and boundaries, splitting and fusion' that 'creates an image of love that is indistinguishable from the imagery of war'.[7]

While neither Chodorow nor Gilligan argue that such differences are inherent or essential, they do argue that they are very real in our society. Gilligan, for instance, reports that males and females describe themselves differently – females in terms of relationships, males in terms of separation – but she does not argue that these distinctions are absolute. Rather, she contends that once we see them, we may begin to see the existence of feminine traits in men and vice versa. Chodorow points to the recognition of the social causes of differences between men and women – mothering by women – as the starting-point for social change. She speculates that

> equal parenting [by males and females] would leave people of both genders with the positive capacities each has, but without the destructive extremes these currently tend toward.... Men would be able to retain the autonomy which comes from differentiation without that differentiation being rigid and reactive, and women would have more opportunity to gain it. People's sexual choices might become more flexible, less desperate.[8]

Still, the notion of equal parenting – as Chodorow notes – constitutes a basic challenge to our social, economic and ideological organization, and this 'more positive' development of gender depends on significant social change. An expanded theory of psychoanalysis – one that takes into account the gender differences described by Chodorow and Gilligan – allows for a theorizing of gender construction *and* its representation in terms of hierarchies of power. However, conceptualizing power in object-relations terms challenges Freudian and Lacanian theories of psychoanalysis, and also the film theory based in them.

The earliest strain of psychoanalytically based film theory focused on narrative patterns and produced a method of analysis which traces Freud's Oedipal 'family romance' as it generates and drives the narratives of Hollywood films, especially family melodramas. Since the masculine perspective is dominant in our culture, it is not surprising that the Freudian scenario effectively describes the characters and plots of a good many films.[9] Take, for instance, *Not as a Stranger* (1955).[10] The male protagonist, the bright but self-righteous medical student Luke Marsh (Robert Mitchum), marries the unsophisticated but sincere nurse Kristina Hendrickson (Olivia de Havilland). She has a substantial savings account, while he – because his drunken father has squandered the money saved by his mother for Luke's education – is on the verge of being expelled from medical school for non-payment of tuition fees.

Luke eventually graduates from medical school and, with Kristina, moves to a small town where, unlike his more materialistic classmates, he plans to be a heroic and altruistic doctor. Another woman, Harriet Lang (Gloria Grahame: who else?), enters the scene, and Luke is immediately attracted to the sultry, wealthy widow in a way he's never been to Kristina.[11]

Kristina desperately wants a child, while Luke does not. She finally becomes pregnant but learns of her pregnancy only after they have separated because of his relationship with Harriet. Kristina is willing (though unhappy) to mother alone if necessary. The voice of Luke's superego finally appears in the person of former classmate Alfred (Frank Sinatra), who informs Luke that Kristina is pregnant but unable to tell him herself. Luke tries, without significant sincerity, to reconcile with Kristina, who rejects him. At this point, the story is ruptured by the death of Luke's partner and role-model, Dr Dave Runkleman (Charles Bickford), and by Luke's realization that even *he* could not have saved him. Luke wanders the streets, finally coming to their home. He begs her for help, and Kristina acquiesces; they embrace. A Freudian explanation of this narrative might focus on Luke's replacing the mother – his provider and nurturer – with Kristina. The film's ending might be read as Luke's acknowledgement of Kristina's mothering role. Kristina, herself, might be understood in terms of her 'narcissistic' desire for a child. Certainly, for Freud, women exist only in relationship to men; to each other, they are – as Kristina and Harriet – rivals, enemies.

In the mid to late 1970s, film theory suffered from the sort of faddishness that often resulted in the wholesale rejection of one approach and its replacement with another. Rather than retaining and refining the useful aspects of a theory or analytic methodology, film theorists tended to make entire substitutions.[12] As film theorists turned towards an emphasis on form in this period, the focus on content began to lose favour. Lacanian psychoanalysis, with its linguistic emphasis on signifying processes, became attractive, and indeed Lacanian theory has enriched film analysis. For instance, thinking in terms of Lacan's rereading of Freud, with its focus on symbolic activity, expands the analysis of *Not as a Stranger*. The struggles that result in the playing out of the Freudian 'family romance' may also be read in Lacanian terms. The final scene can be read as Luke's move into adulthood. When his symbolic father, Runkleman, dies despite Luke's efforts to save him, Luke realizes that he is vulnerable, imperfect, alone in the world: fatherless. He must now take responsibility for himself and for the family he has (inadvertently) begun. He finally enters the Symbolic, after an extremely extended adolescence. Both interpretations are convincing. They each have a legitimate base in the text and seem credible; the focus of this film is masculine, as are the theories on which these readings are based, and they reinforce each other. But they do not account for all possible credible readings. While Freud's and Lacan's descriptions of personality formation within the 'family romance' lead to convincing readings of many narratives, the tendency to universalize these theories – to consider the descriptions transhistorically and transculturally applicable – limits their usefulness and obscures the diversity present even within Western European and American cultures. What is needed here is recognition of a minority voice.

A quite different, but still credible, reading can be posited: a feminine voice can be heard even in the male Oedipal drama, *Not as a Stranger*, and this can lead toward a different reading of the film. While Kristina's desire to mother would be interpreted by a Freudian as simply narcissistic, a Chodorowian would interpret it as her inclination toward a triadic relationship. Her pregnancy and her reconciliation with Luke, at the end, cements the triad. But Kristina is not the film's centre; Luke is, and the story – his story – is told from a masculine perspective, one that represents Kristina only in relation to him. The ability to block out certain major aspects of a narrative is not at all unusual. Chodorow's description of male and female relational models is useful in accounting for such readings, both through audience analysis and through textual analysis. It posits not only basically incompatible people but, consequently, basically incompatible sorts of readers, males and females. It can also help to account for the presence in the text of a weak but perceptible 'feminine voice', as well as to account for readings that reject the 'masculine' readings. Her explanation of asymmetrical personality development also accounts for a significant minority of female-oriented family melodramas from the 1950s that tell distinctly different kinds of stories than do male-oriented films.[13]

Female-oriented family melodramas centre on communities of women and children. Chodorowian theory explains such a community, while Freudian and Lacanian theories do not. Chodorow argues that one way women fulfil the needs not met by a dyadic relationship is 'through the creation and maintenance of important personal relations with other women', relationships generally ignored in male-oriented narratives and, indeed, in male-oriented theories:

> Women tend to have closer personal ties with each other than men have, and to spend more time in the company of women than they do with men.... These relationships are one way of resolving and recreating the mother–daughter bond and are an expression of women's general relational capacities and definition of self in relationship.[14]

Typically, female-oriented family melodramas are motivated by a gap in the triad, usually the absence of a patriarchal figure; the 'lack' here is male (indeed, Steven Neale calls attention to the fact that the male is central to this sub-genre[15]). A community of women and children is invaded by a young and virile male 'intruder-redeemer' who identifies the 'problem' (the heroine's single state) and enables its 'solution' (their coupling and the integration of their family unit into the larger community). This narrative feature lends credence to the readings that argue family melodramas operate simply and straightforwardly to reinforce a repressive patriarchy. A reading that focuses on the needs of the female protagonist – needs which, Chodorow argues, include the completion of a triadic relational model – requires an expansion of theory. Completion of a triadic model does participate in the reproduction of a patriarchal sex-gender system. Indeed, contemporary American patriarchy is precisely the status quo Chodorow describes. But unlike Freud and Lacan, she does not describe it as inherent, inevitable or unchangeable. Neither does she describe the masculine (or the feminine) as normative. She sees an asymmetrically organized sex-gender system that privileges the male and the masculine but that also includes rewards for females that encourage, even necessitate, their participation in a system that represses them.

Chodorow's description offers an explanation of the features of mothering usurped by patriarchy for its own ends and speculation concerning how mothering – and patriarchy – can change. Previous theories of psychoanalysis fail to account for the significant changes that have occurred in the past hundred years or so within Western European and American patriarchy.[16] Nor do they account for the continued presence and popularity of narratives oriented toward the concerns and told through the perspectives of strong female protagonists.

Think, for example, of *All That Heaven Allows* (1955) and *Picnic* (1956).[17] *All That Heaven Allows* begins in the feminine sphere, with an interchange between 'best friends' – suburban matrons Cary (Jane Wyman) and Sarah (Agnes Moorehead). Cary, the heroine, is an upper-middle-class widow whose world is largely composed of her two children and her best friend. Her 'solution', Ron Kirby (Rock Hudson) proceeds – through a series of adventures and misadventures brought about because of the differences in Cary's and Ron's ages and social positions – to win her heart and the promise of her hand. In the female-oriented family melodrama, only a certain sort of male character can accomplish this: like the 'intruder-redeemer' common to 'male genres' such as the western, he comes from outside the community and corrects a major structural problem within the community. In westerns this often means righting an imbalance of political power; in the family melodrama it means filling an empty but crucial position in the female protagonist's relational triad. And while the western's hero must usually leave the community at the film's end, the hero of the family melodrama is integrated into the family and the community.

Carol Gilligan describes caring and responsiveness as feminine characteristics, but – while more common among females than among males – they are not essentially feminine.[18] Indeed, in the female-oriented family melodrama, the 'intruder-redeemer' must provide – or at least promise – nurturance and security for the female protagonist. In this respect, he resembles the male heroes of many romance novels. In *Reading the Romance*, Janice Radway draws on Chodorow to describe 'the ideal male partner' as one 'who is capable of fulfilling both object roles in this woman's triangular inner-object configuration'. Radway describes a particular manifestation of this ideal:

> His spectacular masculinity underscores his status as her heterosexual lover and confirms the completeness of her rejection of her childlike self. At the same time, his extraordinary tenderness and capacity for gentle nurturance means she does not have to give up the physical part of her mother's attentions because his 'soft' sexual attention allows her to return to the passive state of infancy where all of her needs were satisfied and her fears were erased at her mother's breast.[19]

The male 'intruder-redeemer' must, in effect, adopt a triadic relational model, becoming a 'sensitive man', offering the protagonist a relationship in which she can be nurtured.[20] Cary, in *All That Heaven Allows*, clearly longs for such a nurturing relationship, and Ron offers this combination of 'spectacular masculinity' and gentleness, filling the roles of both lover and nurturer. But her children, the members of the local country club and even her best friend intervene; they are opposed to her union with Ron, whom they perceive as a gold-digging hick, feeling that as a mother and a member of an upper socio-economic class she has certain responsibilities to her children and her peers that result in limited power to control her life. So until the end they manipulate Cary, thwarting her efforts at self-fulfilment and limiting her power. The 'fantasy' presented on the screen – that of a female being nurtured rather than providing nurturance – gives expression to human needs that could not be met for females. This particular reading of *All That Heaven Allows* must call attention to the film's conclusion.

In order to provide a 'happy ending', to furnish the female protagonist with a male mate and to reintegrate her into the social order, a fantastic rupture is necessary. Because the major portion of the narrative suggests that a union between the female protagonist and the intruder-redeemer is socially inappropriate, only a dramatic break can enable the reassertion of patriarchal structures through the recreation of the protagonist's triad. To accomplish this, the narrative must be ruptured by a marginally believable accident, an unexpected death, or some equally implausible turn of events. This enables the female to act on her desire for the 'intruder-redeemer', even if her action entails a challenge to prevailing social norms. The rhetoric of the ending contradicts that of the major part of the film. In *All That Heaven Allows*, Ron falls off a cliff, suffering a concussion; his accident enables Cary to act. She rushes to his bedside, where they pledge their love and aim toward social integration (Fig. 7).

Picnic tells a similar story, but inflects it differently. The film begins as a stranger, Hal (William Holden), chances on a self-sufficient community of women comprised of the voluptuous and beautiful Madge (Kim Novak); her tomboyish and bookish younger sister, Millie (Susan Strasberg); their single mother, Mrs Owens (Betty Field); and Rosemary Sidney (Rosalind Russell), an 'old maid schoolteacher' who boards with the Owens. The grandmotherly Mrs Potts completes this female community; she lives next door with *her* mother (whose voice is heard but who remains unseen). Hal immediately identifies the most desirable of the women – Madge, around whom the entire narrative moves – and proceeds to solve her 'problem'. But Madge has a prior attachment to Hal's rich friend Alan (Cliff Robertson), which if formalized would allow Madge to move up the socio-economic ladder.

According to Chodorow, the normal triadic model of relationships formed by females is sometimes altered as a result of trauma. *Picnic* plays out this scenario. Mrs Owens, who wants her daughter to marry Alan, is what Chodorow describes as a 'hypersymbiotic mother', a mother who reacts to a trauma – in this case, having been deserted by her husband, the father of her daughters – by losing sight of the distance between herself and her daughter, considering the daughter an extension of herself. Like Cary's immature (though 'adult') children, Mrs Owens moves to limit Madge's power over her body and her future by blocking her relationship with Hal. Normally fluid ego boundaries seem to disappear as she refuses to allow her daughter to separate from her, to individuate. Mrs Owens quizzes Madge about her relationship with Alan, her rich boyfriend, almost salaciously probing into their sexual activities. The hypersymbiotic mother, Chodorow explains, uses her daughter for her own autoerotic gratification. In *Picnic*, Madge's normal progression into female adulthood (and overlapping triads) is precluded by her mother's hypersymbiosis, and Madge can respond only by breaking away. In order to move into the adult world and toward motherhood, Madge must leave her mother and her primary community to join Hal. This 'happy ending' – attainable for Madge only at great cost –

constitutes a move out of a feminine sphere of connectedness and into the masculine sphere of separateness. Both spheres exist, and we need an expanded theory of psychoanalysis to recognize them. We also need an expanded theory to explain the possibility – and the actuality – of various readings of the same text.

For some readers, the narrative is ruptured in *Picnic* as the jealous Rosemary tries desperately, and unsuccessfully, to attract Hal's attention and the jealous Alan tries, successfully, to run Hal out of town. In the process, Hal displays to Madge a vulnerability and a capacity for tenderness, and the previously timid and passive Madge realizes that she desperately loves Hal and that she has some power over her own life; she follows him on the next bus. *Picnic* and *All That Heaven Allows* each spend over an hour telling us that these unions are, at the least, socially and economically undesirable, and probably impossible. But this view is unravelled in the last few minutes, and the unravelling is so artificial (technically and logically) that, for some readers, it calls attention to itself. In this reading, the artificiality of the 'happy ending' which unifies both the couple and the narrative calls attention to the films' internal contradictions. It further supports the argument that these films recuperate woman for patriarchy by giving her what Chodorow describes as desirable but highly unlikely – a nurturing male lover. According to this reading, the films deny the possibility that a woman can live happily in the company of other women; this possibility poses such a challenge to patriarchy that it necessitates the 'happy ending' to reassert masculine control.

A rather different reading is also possible. Failing or refusing to see the conclusion as artificial can result in the reading that romance can actually prevail, encouraging the attitude that such unions are not only possible but desirable. Assumptions basic to such a reading are the relatively modern belief that romance, rather than property or politics, is the most valid basis for marriage and the even older belief that heterosexual marriage is the norm and any other course deviant. Endings like those of *Picnic* and *All That Heaven Allows* reinforce such beliefs, and the possibility of a 'straight' reading – a reading that takes such endings at face value – indicates the power of such an ideology. Janice Radway calls romance literature 'compensatory literature', arguing that it supplies its readers with 'an important emotional release that is proscribed in daily life because the social role with which they identify themselves leaves little room for guiltless, self-interested pursuit of individual pleasure.'[21] Radway compares romance reading to women's institutionalized networks of support in many pre-industrial societies, observing that in suburbanized America, localized support has been replaced, in the case of romance readers, by 'a huge, ill-defined network

Figure 1 *Mildred Pierce*: 'Back on their knees, keeping the façade clean'
(chapter 1)

Figure 2 *Rear Window*'s commercial re-release (chapter 2)

Figure 3   *Rear Window*: the camera as phallus (chapter 2)

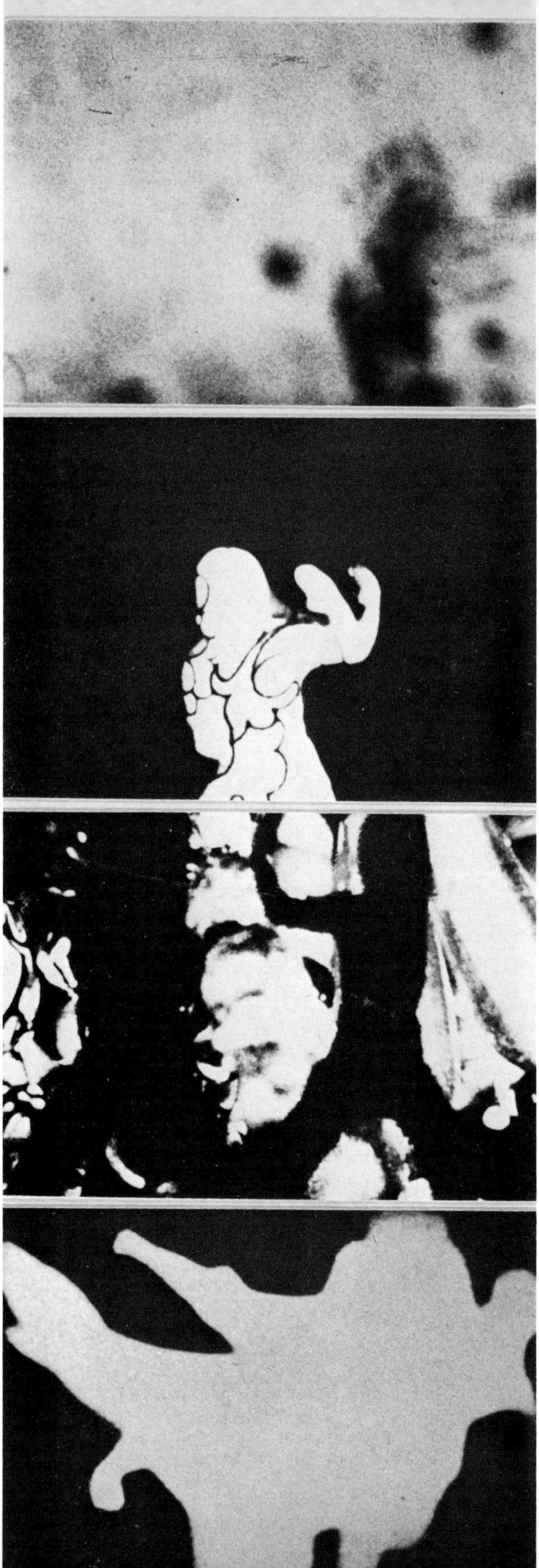

Figure 4 *Self Defense*: The manipulated image (chapter 3)

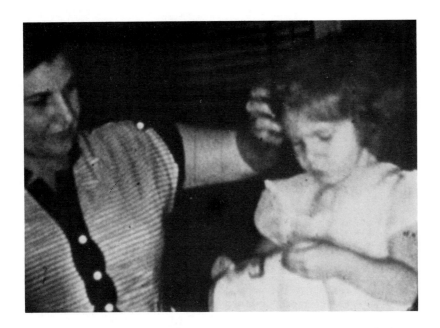

Figure 5 *Daughter Rite*: a play on genres (chapter 3)

Figure 6 *Coma*:
the paternalistic
villain (chapter 4)

Figure 7   The final shot of *All That Heaven Allows*: Ron and Cary pledge
their love in mutual gaze (chapter 6)

Figure 8 Point-of-view in *Picnic* (chapter 6)

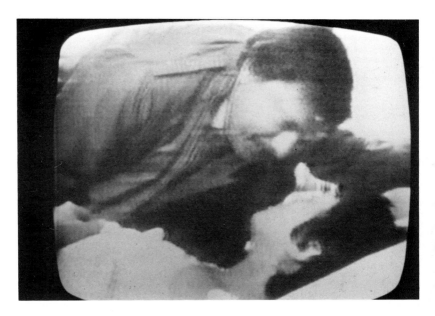

Figure 9 *Cagney and Lacey*: Harvey and Mary Beth in mutual gaze (chapter 6)

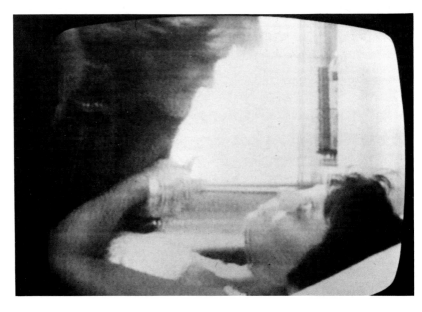

Figure 10 *Cagney and Lacey*: Christine replaces Harvey (chapter 6)

Figure 11 · *Spenser: For Hire*: privileging Sarah's emotions (chapter 6)

Figure 12 Madonna in 'Material Girl': foregrounding desire for the woman ... (chapter 7)

Figure 13 'Material Girl': ... without comment or critique (chapter 7)

Figure 14 *A Different Image*: Alana and Vincent's friendship is destroyed by sexism (chapter 8)

Figure 15 *A Different Image*: female adornment, clothing and body language (chapter 8)

Figure 16 *Born in Flames*: 'Black women, be ready. White women, get ready. Red women, stay ready' (chapter 9)

composed of readers on the one hand and authors on the other. Although it performs some of the same functions carried out by older neighborhood groups, this female community is mediated by the distances of modern mass publishing.'[22]

'Straight' reading of certain kinds of film and television texts operates similarly; Chodorow's and Gilligan's work helps to explain the ways female-oriented texts have resisted explanation by other methods of analysis, as well as the ways they have been read differently by the female communities that have consistently consumed them. The narrative structure of the female-oriented family melodrama indicates the attempt to fill such a compensatory emotional function, the attempt to fulfil needs unmet in daily life. While this would seem to support the view that these are 'politically conservative' texts, it should be noted, following Radway, that they also function to transmit a 'female voice' – a vision of the world based in continuity rather than separation – which could no longer be articulated through local women's networks.

However, arguments like this one, which focus on narrative content, were challenged as feminist film theory became – in common with film theory in general – more concerned with form. Arguments for what Ann Kaplan describes elsewhere in this volume as the 'more or less monolithic (and largely male) gaze' have become central to feminist film theory.[23] Basic to these arguments are the assumptions that, first of all, even though form and content interact, it is form that determines the reading of a given text; secondly, the gazes/looks of both characters and spectators are 'male' or, at best, 'masculine' (this assumption basically gives up *looking* – or voyeurism – to the male); and, thirdly, for any female brazen enough to assume the agency of the gaze, punishment is inevitable. In 'Visual Pleasure and Narrative Cinema', Mulvey observed: 'Traditionally, the woman displayed has functioned on two levels: as erotic object for the characters within the screen story, and as erotic object for the spectator within the auditorium, with a shifting tension between the looks on either side of the screen.'[24] Raymond Bellour concurred, describing American cinema's dependency 'on a system of representations in which the woman occupies a central place only to the extent that it's a place assigned to her by the logic of masculine desire'.[25]

Even now that much feminist film theory has moved beyond the sort of textual analysis which assumes that the text infallibly produces an ideological centring for its spectator, there remains a tendency to assume unsceptically that the narrative and enunciative practices of mainstream cinema operate consistently to maintain a monolithic patriarchal order. For instance, the editors of *Re-vision*, a recently published anthology of feminist film criticism, introduce the volume by noting that the essays included in it 'provide a number of different entries and suggestions for breaking the hold of a monolithic construction of sexual difference'.[26] Kaja Silverman's contribution to the anthology illustrates just how firmly this assumption has taken hold:

> it is by now *axiomatic* [emphasis mine] that the female subject is the object rather than the subject of the gaze in mainstream narrative cinema. She is excluded from the authoritative vision not only at the level of the enunciation, but at that of the fiction.... It is equally *axiomatic* [emphasis mine] that the female subject as she has been constructed by the Hollywood cinema is denied any active role in the discourse.[27]

Silverman argues that the synchronization of sound and image, has operated in conjunction with other mainstream cinematic practices, such as the shot/reverse shot pattern, consistently to silence 'a female voice which has been repressed by patriarchy, but which has nevertheless remained intact for thousands of years at some unconscious level'.[28] While the bulk of her essay analyses feminist films which challenge this repression, the nature of this 'female voice' remains unexplored, as does its capacity to somehow survive the onslaught of consistently repressive mainstream film texts.

A minority voice, a feminine voice, *is* conveyed not only through 'content' but through the basic enunciative practices of film and television. Female-oriented family melodramas do not just tell different stories; they tell them differently. The enunciative practices of mainstream cinema are not – as has often been claimed – inevitably gender-bound, though the dominant pattern does indeed function to place the female as object and to deny her an active role in the production of filmic discourse. This pattern was explicated in Bellour's landmark analysis of the sequence from Hitchcock's *The Birds* in which Melanie crosses Bodega Bay, leaves caged birds in Mitch's house, and then re-crosses the bay. Bellour's reading vividly demonstrates the perverse potential of enunciative conventions. Following Christian Metz, Bellour traces three filmic codes: framing (close/distant), camera movement (still/moving), and point of view (seeing/seen). His analysis of point of view, the most important of the three, traces the movement of its control, showing that when a female character controls the gaze, she will be punished. Point of view is power and, according to Bellour, control of point of view by a female character constitutes sexual aggression. Melanie, initial agent of the gaze, loses control of point of view and is then punished for her aggression by the first attack of the killer birds.

Close analysis of *Not as a Stranger* reveals a similar – though less bloody – punishment for female audacity. The film's first two scenes establish the narrative and enunciative centrality of Luke Marsh. The first scene introduces the character and the situation, and the second focuses on his desirability. It begins with a medium close-up of the pure Kristina (clothed in white, in her operating-room cap, she resembles every Catholic's favourite virgin). Her point of view dominates the first part of this scene and establishes her desire for Luke; he is seen first through her adoring gaze. A conversation ensues – with two-shots and relatively equally shared point-of-view shots – but as she is called away, he assumes control; he remains on screen, not even watching her walk away. The audience has been offered the opportunity to identify with Kristina's point of view, but this opportunity is immediately erased; she does not resume control of point of view again until almost the end of the film. This is Luke's story, and she is merely a player. In both male- and female-oriented family melodramas, the struggle for control of the gaze operates in a manner similar to the struggle for control of the narrative. To prevent the feminine from getting out of control, the film's enunciative structure punishes Kristina for her early and active gaze. She loses not only her husband but the fantasy that he married her for love.

Heidi Hartmann contends that the family is the locus not only of interdependence but of struggle,[29] and this is nowhere more evident than in Hollywood's family melodramas. Here, too, we find a 'feminine voice' and point of view constantly challenging that dominant 'masculine voice', constantly preserving the possibility for change. In both *Picnic* and *All That Heaven Allows*, 'the gaze' remains consistently under female control. *Picnic* moves quickly into an engagement with the major characters as the camera focuses on Hal, establishing his virility and his poverty as he climbs down from a freight train, washes in a nearby river, and approaches a well-kept frame house to ask for work. As Mrs Potts feeds him, attention turns to the house next door, where the female community is established as Madge leans out the window to dry (display) her long blonde hair and Millie, Mrs Owens and Rosemary Sidney all converge on the scene. They notice Hal burning trash next door, displayed semi-nude (Mrs Potts is washing his shirt). Immediately, both Hal and Madge have become the 'objects of desire'. When Hal strides on to the scene, still shirtless, he and Madge become objects of mutual admiration. The collective female voyeuristic pleasure – of the characters and the spectators – is rapidly assumed and organized by one gaze, Madge's, and point of view shots between Hal and Madge build sexual tension, until Mrs Owens interrupts. Cuts between medium close-ups of Mrs Owens and Hal imply her sexuality as well. Embarrassed, he turns to leave as she orders her daughters inside, away from this stranger.

But Madge and Hal will not be separated, and the kindly Mrs Potts calls the two of them to her yard and introduces them. She discreetly retreats, and a series of shot/reverse shots again builds the tension/ attraction between Hal and Madge until, once again, Mrs Owens calls Madge back. Madge dawdles, then gives Hal a desirous look and walks away. He watches her retreat, but Madge is given the final point of view shot. She opens the screen door at the rear of the house and watches as he strides through Mrs Pott's yard (Fig. 8). Finally, she closes the door and ends the scene. Madge and Hal are established as erotic equals, but Madge's control of that final gaze is maintained throughout the film. Quite unlike *The Birds* or even *Not as a Stranger*, *Picnic* maintains Madge as its central focus and as its primary discursive agent. Occasionally, the point of view shots will move away from her control, almost always to make her – or her and Hal together – the centre of attention. Always the point of view shots return to her control. In addition, after it becomes obvious that Madge's hypersymbiotic mother has precluded her normal psychological development, she takes narrative control of the discursive power she has wielded throughout the film; she boards a bus to join Hal, and an aerial shot extricates the viewer from Madge's discursive control.

Ann Kaplan, in her conclusion to *Women and Film*, calls attention to the mutual gazing 'first set in motion in the mother–child relationship', pointing out that this is not the sort of gazing of 'the subject–object kind that reduces one of the parties to the place of submission'. She suggests that 'female sexuality has been taken over by the male gaze, and, in addition, the domination-submission modes may be an inherent component of eroticism for both sexes in western capitalist culture'.[30] I suggest that a tradition of mutual gazing expresses a 'different voice' and a different kind of gaze that we've not heard or seen before because our theories have discouraged such 'hearing' and 'seeing'. At the end of *Picnic*, the female character gives up dominance, and the male character does not assume it. Only through a theory of psychoanalysis that denies connectedness and relies on separation, that denies the feminine and naturalizes the masculine, can we so polarize and simplify the relation between the text and its reader as to assume that all spectator voyeurism is inherently masculine. Enlarging our theories of psychoanalysis to include descriptions of the experiences of more than just the dominant members of our population allows us to perceive challenge and resistance where it exists.

Indeed, challenge and resistance can be discovered where we might least expect it: in American prime-time network television, for example. Prime-time television offers, in its many genres, a diversity even greater than that found in Hollywood at the height of the studio system. Kaplan argues elsewhere in this volume that Music Television offers a 'wide range of gazes with different gender implications' and contends that 'the apparatus itself, in its modes of functioning, is not gender specific', that 'across its "segments" ... we can find a variety of "gazes" that indicate an address to a certain kind of male or female imaginary'.[31] In her work on film, Kaplan does not go far enough. Film, like television, offers a variety of spectatorial positions. Neither film nor television is inevitably male-centred; a strong tradition of resistance is evident in both media.

As in Hollywood film, we find in television series occasional communities of women – *Kate and Allie* (CBS), *The Golden Girls* (NBC), *Cagney and Lacey* (CBS). These series are concerned with the maintenance and development of relationships, not with the acquisition or proving of power. Kate and Allie – divorcees with teenage children – both have occasional flings; their relationship survives, and they work on making sure that it does.[32] The 'golden girls' – Blanche, Dorothy, Rose and Sophia – are another female community, this one formed of 'older' women, divorcees and widows sharing a home in Miami. They bicker and mock each other, but they provide mutual support when it is needed. In fact, the plots of some episodes have focused specifically on their interdependence.

The friendship between New York Police Department detectives Christine Cagney and Mary Beth Lacey is the very basis of *Cagney and Lacey*, and the enunciative strategies of the series call attention to their relationship. The 'Jane scenes', in the women's rest room, are often shot to show the pressures on their relationship; the use of mirrors for the introspection of the characters and for the development of their relationship is sophisticated and noticeable. Occasionally, Christine and Mary Beth engage each other in a mutual gaze that draws attention to their closeness and draws the viewer into the relationship. In a famous two-part episode screened initially in the spring of 1985, Mary Beth discovers a lump in her breast.[33] Her relationship with Christine goes through a rocky period because Christine puts pressure on her to go to a doctor and then to obtain a second opinion. She finds that she does indeed have breast cancer but that there is an alternative to radical mastectomy. As Mary Beth succumbs to a relaxant in preparation for her operation, she speaks enthusiastically to her doctor about Christine. A pleased but embarrassed Christine leaves the hospital to take the New York Police Department's sergeant's examination; a montage sequence flips back and forth between operation and exam – between, for the most part, Mary Beth and Christine. When both are over, Christine visits Mary Beth. In symmetrically organized portions of the final sequence of this episode, Mary Beth and her husband Harvey affirm their closeness and affection, and Mary Beth and Christine affirm their friendship.

The visual conventions normally used to signify heterosexual romance are repeated in the display of the women's friendship, indicating that formal cinematic and televisual conventions are not gender-bound. These conventions can be used to display maternal love as well; they express closeness and affection (Fig. 9). Harvey bends over Mary Beth as he announces Christine's presence. To the sounds of a waltz that punctuates the scene and emphasizes the women's friendship, Christine replaces Harvey, bending over Mary Beth and taking her hand, and, as the sequence ends, Mary Beth and Christine settle into a *mutual gaze*: the frame freezes dramatically, drawing attention to their closeness, as it draws the audience into their relationship (Fig. 10).

Female-oriented television series are in a distinct minority, certainly, but even detective series – that most staunchly masculine of television genres – occasionally show some evidence of a 'feminine voice' in both characters and plots. *Spenser for Hire* (ABC), for instance, indicates that the current stage in the development of the private investigator series has integrated distinctly 'feminine' elements. Private investigators on television have tended to be more 'sensitive' to their friends or clients than their counterparts in police detective series.[34] The title character from *Spenser For Hire*, like his contemporary counterpart on *Magnum, PI*, involves the audience in his thoughts and feelings through voice-overs, and Spenser's voice-overs often concern his friendships. At the beginning of the series, he was involved in a relationship with a strong, independent woman who had a career of her own, and he defined himself (in his regular voice-overs) quite often in terms of their relationship.[35] Like *Cagney and Lacey*, *Spenser for Hire* combines an episodic plot structure with ongoing explorations of its major characters that progress with each episode.[36] *Spenser For Hire* presents and examines a potentially paradoxical character – a man who lives by a strict private moral code but who is also extremely sensitive to the complexities of interpersonal relationships.

An episode entitled 'Children of a Tempest Storm' includes chase scenes through the streets of Boston and enough violence and mayhem to satisfy the most avid detective show fan. But there is something else, too. This episode begins as Spenser is nearly killed by a lunatic on roller skates and, in the process of defending himself, kills the man. When Spenser learns that the man was a father, the only relative and sole support of two children, he takes the children in. Spenser's capacity for nurturing is revealed in his interactions with the children and in the strong-handed manner in which he forces their father's former employer, a Boston crime boss, to provide trust funds for them.

Fictional television occasionally – but only very occasionally – offers explicit commentary on struggles over controversial issues as specific as abortion or as broad as power itself – what it is, how it is negotiated, and what it *means.*[37] Because of the emphasis on Spenser's sensitivity to interpersonal relationships, the series can, in this episode, address abortion. The stance of the series, however, allows for very different readings. In this episode, the issue is power – power over women's (and children's) bodies – and through plot, characters, dialogue, camera work and editing, the series indicates contradictory positions.

In what begins as a subplot, Susan, Spenser's woman friend, finds out that she is pregnant and contemplates an abortion. Both Spenser and Susan are aware of the problems her continued pregnancy would pose. Their relationship is relatively new; Susan is independent for the first time in her life and likes it, but she knows that bearing and caring for a child at this point in her life would end that independence. In one scene, Susan and Spenser address the abortion issue directly without ever actually uttering the word 'abortion'.[38] There is no direct indication that this is the terrain for struggle over control of women's bodies, that words have power. We hear, instead, Susan say things like, 'Saying it out loud makes it seem so selfish, but dammit, this is just the worst time for this to happen.' Spenser refers to 'the baby' and wants to get married: he opposes the abortion. In the best tradition of the nurturing hero, he says to Susan, 'Dammit, Susan, I want to know how you *feel.*' Her response raises the issue of power (personal power) – control over her life, independence. Spenser claims to understand, but abortion complicates the issue for him. He insists that part of the responsibility – and thus part of the decision – is his. Spenser, the protagonist, employs the vocabulary of opponents of abortion, asserting that the 'foetus' is a 'baby' – with rights of its own. He calls attention to *his* feminine emphasis on interpersonal relationships and acknowledges that Susan really is independent, though he wishes it weren't so, 'If it were my decision, I couldn't do it.' Ultimately, however, it isn't his decision; Susan has the abortion. The plot upholds Susan's right to control her body and her future, but women's ultimate authority over their bodies is also subtly denied by Spenser's contradictory position that on the one hand (the 'pro-choice' stance) women do and should have ultimate control over their bodies while on the other (the 'pro-life' stance) they shouldn't, because abortion is wrong.

Formally, the episode is equally inconsistent. Each of the five interchanges between Susan and Spenser ends with a reaction shot of Susan, privileging her point of view, her 'inner thoughts'. Each ends with a close-up or a medium shot of Susan as she cries, hugs Spenser, does both, or watches him walk away. The episode's final shot is a close-up of Susan as she looks down at the flowers Spenser has brought her and then, smiling, looks up at him. The frame freezes on her (Fig. 11). This consistency of point of view privileges her emotions and thoughts, but it is such a subtle consistency that I did not notice it on first viewing; it doesn't stand out. This focus on her reactions allows a reading of Susan as credible and authoritative, as an equal to Spenser, the linchpin of the series.

In this hero, we see further contradiction; Spenser is a man who struggles to reconcile the macho nature of his job – and the aggressive manner with which he pursues it – with his more nurturing, feminine characteristics. In 'Children of a Tempest Storm', Spenser refers quite self-consciously to his macho 'Sam Spade image', as he takes in the two orphaned children and as he holds and comforts Susan. He is so attuned to their relationship that, when Susan becomes pregnant, he guesses. And though he is initially unsure how he would react to the abortion, he comes through for Susan in the end, developing as a character for whom relationships are at least as important as abstract concepts. We see a battle between the different voices Carol Gilligan describes, this time within a single (male) character; that this occurs at all indicates a heightening of the ideological battle over gender construction. That a character can convincingly encompass both voices indicates an ideological shift, in which 'feminine discourse' gains in power – indeed, becomes capable of articulation even within a genre not traditionally considered the province of such feminine matters.

In the final sequence of 'Children of a Tempest Storm', 'hearts and violins' music punctuates the reconciliation of Spenser and Susan, as Spenser's voice-over tells their story: 'Susan and I had gone to war. We came out on opposite sides of an excruciating moral dilemma. To our unyielding sorrow, had found no compromise. Susan and I had gone to war. But we still, unyielding, loved each other. Guess maybe that's the only road to peace.'

Guess maybe that blend of voices indicates not compromise but powerful equals standing together. The stance of the episode remains ambiguous, with the vision of a strong and independent Susan still plagued by occasional insecurity, juxtaposed with that of a caring and responsive Spenser still working in a job dependent for its existence on 'masculine' standards of justice. If the concept 'detective' is central to *Spenser for Hire*, and that concept carries with it an adherence to a strict, abstract, masculine code, it is nevertheless changing, and the character Spenser is a tool in the struggle over its meaning. Not only do we now see strong female detectives (*Cagney and Lacey*), we also begin to see strong male detectives who perceive the limitations of rigidly structured codes. And with the changes in the concept 'detective' come changes in gender definition.

The languages that we speak in turn speak in and through us. A more feminine 'detective' becomes naturalized for television, and the boundaries distinguishing 'male' and 'female' change. A minority discourse – a feminine voice – has been engaged in a long-standing, active, though not always explicit, opposition to the dominant, masculine discourses in popular American film and television. Drawing on and expanding theories that acknowledge a long overshadowed minority discourse allows us to see a tradition of challenge in the contested narrative spaces not only at the margins, but at the very centre, of American culture.

Notes

1. Carol Gilligan, *In a Different Voice*, Cambridge, Massachusetts, and London: Harvard University Press, 1982, p. 1.
2. Deanna L. Hall and Kristin M. Langellier, 'Storytelling Strategies in Mother–Daughter Communication', International Communicaions Association, Chicago, Illinois, May 1986.
3. My study of Hollywood family melodramas of the 1950s culminated first in my PhD dissertation, *Gender Representation in American Family Melodramas of the Nineteen-Fifties*, and later in *Gender, Representation and Power: A Cultural Studies Approach to Reading the Representation of Gender in Hollywood's Family Melodramas of the 1950s*. An article that includes analyses of American network television programming, 'Reading Feminine Discourse in Prime-Time Television in the US', appeared in *Communication*, vol. 9 (1987), pp. 289–303.
4. Laura Mulvey, 'Afterthoughts on "Visual Pleasure and Narrative Cinema" Inspired by *Duel in the Sun* (King Vidor, 1946)', *Framework*, nos. 15/16/17 (Summer 1981), pp. 12–15.
5. Nancy Chodorow, *The Reproduction of Mothering*, Berkeley: University of California Press, 1978.
6. Carol Gilligan, 'The Conquistador and the Dark Continent: Reflections on the Psychology of Love', *Daedalus*, Summer 1984, pp. 75–95 (this reference p. 88).
7. Gilligan, 'The Conquistador', pp. 90–91.
8. Nancy Chodorow, *The Reproduction of Mothering*, p. 218.
9. This strain of psychoanalytic film theory was pursued initially by Christian Metz, Raymond Bellour, Thierry Kuntzel and their colleagues.
10. *Not as a Stranger* (1955), based on Morton Thompson's novel of the same name, was produced and directed by Stanley Kramer and released by United Artists. It was adapted for the screen by Edna and Edward Anhalt and starred Olivia de Havilland, Robert Mitchum, Frank Sinatra and Gloria Grahame.
11. Luke's and Harriet's carrying on is represented in a truly remarkable scene that juxtaposes Luke and a whinnying black stallion with Harriet and a bucking and eager palomino mare.
12. This tendency has resulted in distinctly different camps within American communication studies and in people refusing to talk 'across paradigms'. In what has become mainstream feminist film theory, the 'baby was thrown out with the bathwater' as theorists rejected a sociological approach in favour of a 'formalist' approach.
13. My study of Hollywood family melodramas of the 1950s was limited to those which depicted contemporary families and to films in *Variety*'s annual lists of top twenty money-makers. Of the twenty-five films included in the study, there were two exceptions to this rule, included because they were sequels to films that did make the lists: *Belles on Their Toes* (1952) was a direct sequel to *Cheaper by the Dozen*, a male-oriented film (1950), and *All That Heaven Allows* (1955) was an indirect sequel to *Magnificent Obsession*, intended to capitalize on its success by combining the same cast, director and producer. These

two films and four others comprise a significant sub-category: the female-oriented family melodrama; they are oriented around, through, and toward females. The other four films are *Magnificent Obsession* (1954), *Picnic* (1956), *Peyton Place* (1957) and *Imitation of Life* (1959).

14. Nancy Chodorow, *The Reproduction of Mothering*, p. 200.

15. Steven Neale, *Genre*, London: British Film Institute, 1980, p. 59.

16. They fail to account, for instance, for my own ability to write this article and for my current professional activities.

17. *Picnic*, adapted from a play by William Inge, was directed by Joshua Logan, who also directed the play. It starred Kim Novak, William Holden, Rosalind Russell, Susan Strasberg, Cliff Robertson, Betty Field, Arthur O'Connell and Nick Adams. *All That Heaven Allows* (1955) was produced by Ross Hunter for Universal and directed by Douglas Sirk. It starred Jane Wyman, Rock Hudson, Agnes Moorehead, Conrad Nagel and Virginia Grey.

18. Carol Gilligan, 'The Conquistador and the Dark Continent: Reflections on the Psychology of Love', *Daedalus*, Summer 1984, pp. 75–95 (this reference p. 92).

19. Janice Radway, *Reading the Romance*, London and New York: Verso, 1987, p. 147.

20. Current hopeful and cynical usage of the term 'sensitive man' makes the quotation marks requisite.

21. Janice Radway, *Reading the Romance*, pp. 95–6.

22. Janice Radway, *Reading the Romance*, p. 97.

23. E. Ann Kaplan, 'Whose Imaginary? The Televisual Apparatus, the Female Body and Textual Strategies in Select Rock Videos on MTV', this volume, p. 136.

24. Laura Mulvey, 'Visual Pleasure and Narrative Cinema', *Screen*, vol. 16, no. 3 (1975), p. 7.

25. Janet Bergstrom, 'Alternation, Segmentation, Hypnosis: Interview with Raymond Bellour', *Camera Obscura*, nos. 3/4, p. 93.

26. Mary Ann Doane, Patricia Mellencamp and Linda Williams, 'Feminist Film Criticism: An Introduction', in *Re-vision: Essays in Feminist Film Criticism*, Frederick, Maryland: University Publications of America, in association with the American Film Institute, 1984, p. 14.

27. Kaja Silverman, 'Dis-embodying the Female Voice', in *Re-vision*, pp. 131–49 (this reference pp. 131–2).

28. Kaja Silverman, 'Dis-Embodying the Female Voice', p. 137. While she indicates that the 'female voice' is something more than sound, like the voice Gilligan talks about, her focus in this essay is on sound, and she concentrates on the relationship of this narrower conception of 'voice' to imagery.

29. Heidi Hartmann, 'The Family as Locus of Gender, Class and Political Struggle: The Example of Housework', *Signs*, vol. 6, no. 3 (Spring 1980), pp. 266–94.

30. E. Ann Kaplan, *Women and Film*, New York and London: Methuen, 1983, p. 205.

31. E. Ann Kaplan, 'Whose Imaginary?' p. 136.

32. *Kate and Allie* is a CBS series starring Susan Saint James as Kate and Jane Curtin as Allie. Created by Sherry Coben, its executive producers are Mort Lachman and Merrill Grant; it premièred in March of 1984. Created by Susan Harris, *The Golden Girls* premièred on NBC in the autumn of 1985 and became a surprise hit. It stars Rue MacClanahan (Blanche), Bea Arthur (Dorothy), Betty White (Rose) and Estelle Getty (Sophia, Dorothy's elderly mother).

33. See my 'Reading Feminine Discourse: Prime-Time Television in the US', *Communication*, vol. 9 (1987), pp. 289–303, for an extended analysis of the last scene of this episode. *Cagney and Lacey* is a CBS series and a Mace Neufield/Barney Rosenzweig Production, made for Orion Television. The series' Executive Producer is Barney Rosenzweig, and its creators were Barbara Avedon and Barbara Corday; the regular cast is composed of Sharon Gless (Christine Cagney), Tyne Daley (Mary Beth Lacey), Al Waxman (Lt Samuels), Martin Kove (Victor Izbecki), John Karlen (Harvey Lacey), Harvey Atkin (Sgt Coleman), Tony LaTorre (Harvey Lacey, Jr) and Troy Staten (Michael

Lacey). The episode was written by Patricia Green and directed by Ray Danton. *Cagney and Lacey* premiered in March 1982, and 1987–88 is its last season.

34. For example, the title characters on *Mannix* and *The Rockford Files* were distinctly more concerned with relationships than police detectives like Baretta, whose girlfriends were already dead before the credits rolled, and Columbo, whose wife was only a voice on the telephone. Starring Mike Connors, *Mannix* ran on CBS September 1967 to August 1975, and *The Rockford Files* starred James Garner and ran on NBC from September 1974 to June 1980. *Baretta* ran on ABC from January 1975 to June 1978, originally starring Tony Musante, who was replaced by Robert Blake at the beginning of the show's second season. Baretta was an unorthodox police detective who lived in a seedy hotel with his pet cockatoo. *Columbo* (NBC, September 1971–September 1978) starred Peter Falk as a dishevelled and non-violent police detective whose beguiling manner led his adversaries (usually murderers) to underestimate him.

35. The regular cast of *Spenser For Hire* (ABC) was initially composed of Robert Urich (Spenser), Avery Brooks (Hawk), Barbara Stock (Susan Silverman), Ron McLarty (Sgt Frank Belson) and Richard Jaeckel (Lt Martin Quirk). At the beginning of the 1986–7 season, Silverman's character, Susan, was written out of the series (in a voice-over) and replaced by a female lawyer, Rita Fiore (Carolyn McCormick). Susan returned at the beginning of the 1987–8 season. The characters are based on those created by Robert B. Parker and the series was developed for television by John Wilder. 'Children of a Tempest Storm' was written by Robert Hamilton and directed by William Wiard, with Robert B. Parker serving as a consultant.

36. In '*Magnum*: The Champagne of TV?', *Channels of Communication*, vol. 5, No. 1 (May–June 1985), pp. 23–6, Horace Newcomb coined the term 'cumulative narrative' to explain *Magnum PI*. A cumulative narrative depends on audience familiarity and builds its characters over a period of time, sometimes in flashbacks, sometimes through references to past episodes. Neither *Cagney and Lacey* nor *Spenser For Hire* utilize flashbacks, but they develop primary characters in much the same way, including episodes that vary from the police detective or private investigator programme formulae.

37. In another episode of *Spenser For Hire*, it becomes obvious that a benevolent employer with a record of helping and watching out for his workers has lost his power to do so to an unscrupulous mobster. The employer wants to will his company to its workers, and the mobster wants to assume control before this can occur. Spenser intervenes, and the terms of the will are enforced, distributing power in the business more equitably and putting 'in charge' the employers' protégée, a woman. Something of a hierarchy remains, but as a worker-owned business, it is a hierarchy with a difference. In yet another episode, a lawyer – who had been the first to help Spenser after he quit the Boston police force to go out on his own – has been found guilty of abusing the power of his position and, thus, has lost it. During the course of the episode, we (and he) learn(s) that he can only regain power *for* himself. He acts honorably and does begin the reassumption of power.

38. The only time in this episode that a character actually speaks the word 'abortion' occurs when Susan's doctor – a woman and a friend – informs her that she is pregnant and they discuss her options.

7

Whose Imaginary? The Televisual Apparatus, The Female Body and Textual Strategies in Select Rock Videos on MTV

E. Ann Kaplan

The social Imaginary that I shall explore in Music Television (MTV)[1] has been constructed through the contradictory post-1960s historical moment in which rock videos arise as a mass popular culture form. It is the mapping in the 1980s of the new 1960s discourses about politics, sex and romance on to the increasingly high-tech stage of an already advanced capitalism that partly produces the extraordinary MTV Imaginary.

A symptom of the new high-tech stage of advanced capitalism is the deployment of television as itself a unique kind of apparatus, very different from the filmic one. Since MTV embodies in extreme form the characteristics of this apparatus, it is worth dwelling briefly on it, particularly as it has been described by Jean Baudrillard. Baudrillard points to television's cultural role in developing what he calls the new 'cold' universe of communication.[2] The universe involves marked changes in the relationship of subject to image; for while the movie screen harnesses the subject's desire through appearing momentarily to provide a longed-for plenitude,[3] the television screen keeps the subject in a position of alienation. The television screen's constantly changing 'texts', of whatever kind, provide the constant *promise* of plenitude, but this is for ever *deferred.* Instead of the illusory and temporary plenitude of the cinema, the television screen–spectator relationship mimics the subject's original discovery of split subjectivity before the mirror. The decentred, fragmented self that becomes the subject's human condition (although masked in daily life by the illusory construction of a permanent 'self') is duplicated in the processes of television watching; the crucial difference from daily life is the constant *expectation* of unity, oneness, in the *next* text-segment.

Baudrillard takes things a step further, arguing that the television screen symbolizes a new era in which 'The Faustian, Promethean (perhaps Oedipal) period of production and consumption' has given way to 'the narcissistic and protean era of connections, contact, continuity, feedback and generalized interface that goes with the universe of communication.' By this, Baudrillard means that the whole earlier 'intimate' universe (in his words, 'projective, imaginary and symbolic'), with its domestic scene, interiority, private space–time correlative to a public space, is all disappearing. 'Instead,' he says, 'there is a screen and a network. In place of the reflexive transcendence of mirror and scene, there is the nonreflecting surface, an immanent surface where operations unfold – the smooth operational surface of communication.' He concludes that 'with the television image – the television being the ultimate and perfect object for this era – our own body and the whole surrounding universe become a control screen.' (See Chart 1.)

For Baudillard, this entails a dramatically different relationship of the subject to objects; people, for him, no longer project themselves into their objects in the old ways of getting psychological gratification out of them. If the psychological dimension can still be marked out, one has the sense that this is no longer actually the terrain in which things take place; we have instead usage of things (Baudrillard has the automobile in mind, but what he says applies equally to the television set), and a range of potentialities that we can produce through operating the machine. We are thus in the position of mastery and control, and can play with various possibilities. This is far different from relating to the object (car, television set) as a psychological sanctuary.

Baudillard's ideas are significant enough to warrant examination in relation to MTV, since the phenomena he outlines seem to apply particularly to that channel. How true is it that 'we no longer live in the drama of alienation' (Marx's world) but rather in that of 'the ecstacy of communication'? How true is it that the old 'hot, sexual obscenity' (the

Chart 1: Summary of Baudrillard's Scheme

Old 'hot' universe			*New 'cold' universe*		
Investment	}		Hazard		{ Ecstasy
Desire	} Expression		Chance		{ Obscenity
Passion	} Competition		Vertigo		{ Fascination
Seduction	}				{ Communication
Processes of hysteria (female) and paranoia (male)			Processes of schizophrenia, elimination of boundaries, exteriorization of the interior		

world of Freud) has been succeeded by 'the cold and communicational, contactual and motivational obscenity of today'? Does MTV offer an example of such a universe?

To begin with, it does seem that, in line with Baudrillard's theory, MTV partly exploits the imaginary desires allowed free play through the various 1960s liberation movements, divesting them, for commercial reasons, of their originally revolutionary implications, reducing them to the 'radical chic' and the pornographic. But at the same time its chosen non-stop, twenty-four-hour format of short, four-minute texts inevitably enables expression of positions critical of the status quo not necessarily favoured by the institution. Given Baudrillard's conceptualizations, however, we need to analyse how far these 'alternate' positions in fact have anything behind them – any ongoing alternative politics in the realm of the social formation. How far do the left/humanist positions have referents? How far are they, like much else on MTV, mere simulacra, with nothing behind, mere representations, images?[4]

I am, then, interested in the myths, images and representations evident in the rock videos played on MTV as these might be seen as both reflecting unconscious changes in young people's 'real conditions of existence'[5] and as tapping into the unsatisfied desire remaining in the psyche from the Lacanian mirror-phase, in the manner suggested above. MTV at once embodies and then further develops major cultural changes. I shall extend these arguments by looking at how the televisual apparatus functions, and at the psychic processes it involves. I will then discuss the implications of the televisual imaginary specifically for women before undertaking some textual analyses of female representation in select rock videos by female stars.

By 'televisual apparatus,' I mean the complex of elements including the machine itself – its technological features (the way it produces and presents images); its various 'texts', including ads, commentaries, displays; the central relationship of programming to the sponsors, whose own texts – the ads – are arguably the real television texts;[6] the now various sites of reception from the living-room to the bathroom. Scholars may focus on problems of enunciation, that is of who speaks a text, and to whom it is addressed, which includes looking at the manner in which we watch television, its presence in the home, the so-called 'flow' of the programmes, the fragmentation of the viewing experience even within any one given programme, the unusual phenomenon of endlessly serialized programmes; or they may study the ideology embedded in the forms of production and reception, which are not 'neutral' or 'accidental,' but a crucial result of television's overarching commercial framework.

One of the still unresolved issues that work in this area has to address (whether explicitly or implicitly) is that of the degree to which theories of film are applicable to the very different 'televisual' apparatus. Since feminist film theory evolved very much in relation to the classic Hollywood cinema, it is particularly important for women approaching television to consider how far that theory is relevant to the different apparatus that television is; for example, do theories about the 'male gaze' apply to watching television, when usually there is no darkened room, where there is a small screen, and where viewing is often interrupted by commercials, people coming in, or by the viewer switching channels? To what extent is the television spectator addressed in the same manner as the film spectator? Do the same psychoanalytic processes of subject construction apply? Will semiotics aid in illuminating the processes at work? Is there a different form of interaction between the television text and the female viewer than between the cinema screen and the female spectator? What might that relation then be?

Much recent film theory has argued that one cannot make any distinction between the apparatus and the narrative, since it is the apparatus itself that produces certain inevitable 'narrative' effects (such as, in the film, the forced identification with the look of the camera). Thus, we need to know how the televisual apparatus is used in any one television genre to represent the female body – to see what possibilities there are for different kinds of female representation, and how bound by the limits of the apparatus are images of woman on television.

Let me first say something about the construction of what I have elsewhere called the 'decentred' spectator through the very rapid flow of what are comparatively short segments within a continuous, twenty-four-hour channel.[7] Here MTV carries to an extreme elements present in other TV programmes in the United States, particularly those that are also twenty-four-hour stations like continuous weather and news channels; but also those that are daily 'serials' in some form or another, for instance, game shows, talk shows, the soaps, and also the news (which is regularly slotted and so highly stylized as to be 'drama'[8]).

All of these programmes exist on a kind of horizontal axis that is never ending, rather than consisting of discrete units consumed within a fixed two-hour limit, like the Hollywood movie, or other forms such as the novel, which also have a fixed, and clearly defined 'frame'. Television in a certain sense is not so bounded. Rather television texts resemble an endless film strip, turned on its side, in which the frames are replaced by episodes. Or, as Peggy Phelan has argued, perhaps a better model is that of Foucault's Panopticon, in which the guard surveys a series of prisoners through their windows.[9] Phelan is interested in setting up the television producer as the 'guard' and the individual television viewer as the 'prisoner' who watches in 'a sequestered and observed solitude'. But I think the guard metaphor works well also for the spectator's relationship to the various episodes that represent, in Foucault's words, 'a multiplicity that can be numbered and supervised': in fact, for the television viewer, that desire for plenitude, for complete knowledge is of course forever delayed, forever deferred. The television is seductive precisely because it speaks to a desire that is insatiable – it promises complete knowledge in some far distant and never-to-be-experienced future; its strategy is to keep us endlessly consuming in the hopes of fulfilling our desire; it hypnotizes us through addressing this desire, keeps us returning for more.

This strategy is particularly evident in MTV since the texts here are only four minutes long and so keep us for ever watching, for ever hoping to fulfil our desire with the next one that comes along. The mechanism of 'Coming Up Next ...' that all programmes employ, and that is the staple of the serial, is an intricate aspect of the minute-by-minute watching of MTV. Lured by the seductiveness of the constant promise of immediate plenitude, we endlessly consume.

Now, the question is how does this decentring televisual apparatus position women? Are women necessarily addressed in specific ways by the apparatus, as was argued (at least initially) for the classic Hollywood film? Is there something inherent in the televisual apparatus that addresses woman's social positioning as absence and lack, as again was the case for the Hollywood film?

These questions take me beyond the confines of my topic, but it is possible that what is true for MTV is true also for other television programmes: namely, that instead of a more or less monolithic (and largely male) gaze as was found in the Hollywood film, there is a wide range of gazes with different gender implications. In other words, the apparatus itself, in its modes of functioning, is not gender specific *per se*; but across its 'segments,' be they soap opera segments, crime series segments, news segments, morning show segments, we can find a variety of 'gazes' that indicate an address to a certain kind of male or female Imaginary. If the address in some videos is not exactly genderless, people of both genders are often able to undertake multiple identifications.

What this implies is that the televisual Imaginary is more varied than the cinematic one; it does not involve the same regression to the Lacanian mirror-phase as theorists discovered in the filmic apparatus. In the case of MTV, for example, instead of the channel evoking aspects of the Lacanian mirror-phase Ideal Imago – a process that depends on sustained identification with a central figure in a prolonged narrative – issues to do with split subjectivity, with the alienation that the mirror-

Chart 2: Polarized Filmic Categories in Recent Film Theory

The classic text (Hollywood)	The avant-garde text
Realism/narrative	Non-realism/anti-narrative
History	Discourse
Complicit ideology	Rupture of dominant ideology

image involves, are evoked instead. (See Chart 2.) In other words, filmic processes (at least for the male viewer) heal the painful split in subjectivity instituted during the mirror-phase, while MTV rather reproduces the decentred human condition that is especially obvious to the young adolescent.

MTV thus addresses the desires, fantasies and anxieties of young people growing up in a world in which traditional categories and institutions are apparently being questioned. I have elsewhere argued that there are five main types of video on MTV, and that a whole series of gazes replaces the broadly monolithic Hollywood gaze (See Chart 3 for summary of these types and of how the gaze affects female images). The plethora of gender positions on the channel arguably reflects the heterogeneity of current sex-roles, and the androgynous surface of many star-images indicates the blurring of clear lines between genders characteristic of many rock videos.[10]

Because of both the peculiarities of the televisual apparatus and the new phase of youth culture produced by the 1960s, most of the feminist methodologies that have emerged in television research so far are inappropriate for the rock videos on MTV. This is mainly because of the sophisticated, self-conscious and skewed stance that these television texts take toward their own subject matter. It is often difficult to know precisely what a rock video actually means, because its signifiers are not linked along a coherent, logical chain that produces an unambiguous message. The mode, to use Fredric Jameson's contrast, is that of *pastiche* rather than parody. By this Jameson means that whereas modernist texts often took a particular critical position *vis-à-vis* earlier textual models, ridiculing specific stances or attitudes in them, or offering a sympathetic, comic perspective on them, postmodernist works tend to use *pastiche*, a mode that lacks any clear positioning with regard to what it shows, or toward earlier texts that are used.[11]

This has implications for gender first because the source of address of the rock video text is often so unclear – consequently it is also unclear whether the male or the female discourse dominates; and second because attitudes toward sex and gender are often ambiguous. One finds

Chart 3: Types of Gaze in Music Television

		MODES (All use avant-garde strategies, especially self-reflexivity, play with the image, etc.)				
		Romantic	*Socially conscious*	*Nihilist*	*Classical*	*Postmodernist*
	Style	Narrative	Elements varied	Performance Anti-narrative	Narrative	Pastiche No linear images
Predominant MTV themes	*Love/sex*	Loss and Reunion (Pre-Oedipal)	Struggle for autonomy: Love as problematic	Sadism/ masochism Homo-eroticism Androgyny (Phallic)	The male gaze (Voyeuristic, Fetishistic)	Play with Oedipal positions
	Authority	Parent figures (positive)	Parent and public figures Cultural critique	Nihilism Anarchy Violence	Male as subject Female as object	Neither for nor against authority (ambiguity)

oneself not knowing, for instance, whether or not a video like John Parr's 'Naughty Naughty', or John Cougar Mellencamp's 'Hurts So Good',[12] are virulently sexist or merely pastiching an earlier Hollywood sexism. Even in the category that I call 'classical,' where the gaze is clearly voyeuristic and male, there is a studied self-consciousness that makes the result quite different from that in the dominant commercial cinema.

A different but equally problematic ambiguity is just as prevalent in the videos made from lyrics by female stars as in those of white male stars featured on the channel. But, before going into that, let me note that it is precisely here that the cycling of videos featuring female singers across the twenty-four-hour flow is important for understanding first the broad gender address of MTV and, related to this, the kind of Imaginary that predominates. Both issues are further linked to the overarching commercial framework of MTV, in that only those female representations considered the most 'marketable' are frequently cycled: and what is most marketable is obviously connected with dominant ideology, with the social Imaginary discussed above, and with the organization of the symbolic order around the phallus as signifier.

According to a recent quantifying study of MTV, videos featuring white males take up 83 per cent of the twenty-four-hour flow.[13] Only 12 per cent of MTV videos have central figures who are female: 11 per cent white, 1 per cent Black (the figure is 3 per cent for Black males). Brown and Campbell assert that 'white women are often shown in passive and solitary activity or are shown trying to gain the attention of a man who ignores them' (p. 104). Among the 12 per cent of videos featuring women, the only ones frequently cycled are those in which the female star's position is ambiguous, where what we might call a post-feminist stance is evident.

Before discussing what I mean by this 'post-feminist' stance, I want first to note the other kinds of female representations that do appear on the channel, if only rarely. First, there are videos in the 'socially conscious' category that make the kind of statement one could call 'feminist' (for instance, Pat Benatar's 'Love Is a Battlefield', or her more recent 'Sex as a Weapon'; or Donna Summer's 'She Works Hard for the Money'); these have quite conventional narratives, although they do not adhere strictly to Hollywood codes. Second, there are occasional videos that appear to comment upon the objectifying male gaze (as perhaps does Tina Turner's 'Private Dancer') and whose visual strategies creatively embody those deconstructive aims. Finally, some videos attempt to set up a different gaze altogether, or to play with the male gaze, as arguably happens in the recent Aretha Franklin/Annie Lennox video 'Sisters Are Doin' It for Themselves'. Except for Benatar's 'Love Is a Battlefield', these videos remained in circulation for only a short period of time, and then not at a high density rate.

It is important that the channel's format of short, four-minute texts does permit gaps through which a variety of enunciative positions are made possible. I am thus able to 'stop the flow' as it were, in order to concentrate on constructions of the female body other than the prevailing 'post-feminist' or various 'male gaze' ones. But this is with full awareness that these isolated moments are in fact overridden by the plethora of texts presenting other positions. The various possibilities for 'seeing otherwise' in these different figurations of the female body are worth exploring as part of understanding what popular culture *can* do; but the ordinary MTV spectator will get little opportunity for this kind of 'seeing'. For such female images do not fit into the rich sensation of glossy surfaces, bright colours, rapid action, or the parade of bodies in contemporary clothing that the dominant videos offer.

Take, for example, the video, 'Material Girl', featuring Madonna, the female star who perhaps more than any other embodies the new post-feminist heroine in her odd combination of seductiveness and a gutsy sort of independence. 'Material Girl' is particularly useful as a point of discussion because it exemplifies a common rock-video phenomenon, namely the establishment of a unique kind of intertextual relationship with a specific Hollywood movie. For this reason, and because of difficulty of ensuring the text's stance toward what it shows and the blurring of many conventional boundaries, I would put the video in the 'postmodern' category in my chart, despite its containing more narrative than is usual in this type.

As is well known, 'Material Girl' takes off from the famous Marilyn Monroe dance/song sequence in *Gentlemen Prefer Blondes* (1953), 'Diamonds Are a Girl's Best Friend'. The sequence occurs towards the end of the film when Esmond's father has severed Lorelei (Monroe) financially from Esmond, her fiancé, forcing her to earn her living by performing. In this sequence, having finally found Lorelei, Esmond is sitting in the audience watching the show. We thus have the familiar Hollywood situation in which the woman's performance permits her double articulation as spectacle for the male gaze (that is, she is object of desire for both the male spectator in the diegetic audience and for the spectator in the cinema watching the film). The strategy formalizes the mirror-phase situation by framing the female body within both the stage proscenium arch and the cinema screen.

During this sequence, which starts with Esmond's astonished gaze at Monroe from the theatre seat (presumably he is surprised anew by Monroe's sexiness), Monroe directs her gaze toward the camera that is situated in Esmond's place. The space relations are thus quite simple, there being merely the two spaces of the stage and of the theatre audience. We know that the film is being made under the authorial label 'Howard Hawks', and that within the diegesis, the stars – Monroe and Jane Russell – are setting up the action. But we also know that, despite a certain control of the narrative, the patriarchal world in which they move constrains them: that is, their very activity (namely the pursuit of the rich husband) is shaped by their positioning as sexual objects in a patriarchal world. Within 1950s Hollywood codes, narratives rarely made other objectives possible for female figures.

When we turn to the video inspired by the Monroe dance sequence, we see that the situation is far more complicated. (See Chart 4.) First, it is unclear who is 'speaking' this video, even on the remote 'authorial label' level, since credits are normally not provided. Is it perhaps Madonna, as historical star subject? Or is it one of the two narrative figures, Madonna I and Madonna II? (Madonna I is the movie-star protagonist within the diegesis that 'frames' the stage-performance plot about the 'material girl'; Madonna II is the figure within that dance

Chart 4: Summary Analysis of Madonna's 'Material Girl'

Level I: Madonna as historical subject, as star in consumerist circulation; this
subject should be seen as multi-determined.
This level superimposes itself as a discourse on the discourse of the fictional
world of the video.

Level II: Narrative strategies within the video:
a) Use of diegatic 'spaces' pastiches classic realist codes:
   Spaces overlap, boundaries are not clearly marked
   Unclear whose gaze structures many shots; unorthodoz editing;
   Shifting enunciative strategies: who is speaking this text?

Spaces and discourses that struggle for dominance:
1) The director's discourse and gaze;
   Spaces: Screening-room, dressing-room, outside studio;
2) Madonna I, protagonist/film star in love story (director wins her love).
   Spaces: Same as for director.
3) Madonna II, character within the performance of 'Material Girl' (presumably
   being filmed).
   Madonna II appears to assert her own desires, and, as the 'material girl',
   controls the discourse.
   Spaces: The studio stage-set.
b) *Soundtrack:* primarily the song, 'Material Girl'.
   The studio-set story of the 'Material Girl' dominates the soundtrack,
   imposing itself even over the spaces for the director's and Madonna I's
   love story. Their story is only given two short pieces of dialogue.

The various diegetic spaces, thus, are not hierarchically ordered as in the usual
classic text, where main story and framing story would be clearly marked. There
is rather a conflation of narrative lines, or their flattening out on a single plane.
Sound-image relations are not necessarily synchronized diegetically.

---

performance, the 'material girl' of the video – and song's – title.) Is it the
director who has fallen in love with her image and desires to possess
her? Focusing first on the visual strategies and then on the soundtrack,
different and still more confusing answers emerge.

Visually, the director's gaze seems to structure some of the shots, but
this is not consistent as it is in the Monroe sequence. And shots possibly
structured by him (or in which he is later discovered to have been
present) only occur at irregular intervals. The video begins by foregrounding the classic Hollywood male gaze: there is a close-up of the
director, played by Keith Carradine (the video thus bows again to the
classic film), whom we soon realize is watching rushes of a film starring
'Madonna I'. With an obsessed, glazed look on his face, he says, 'I want

her, George.' George promises to deliver, as we cut to a two-shot of the men, behind whom we see the cinema screen and Madonna I's image, but as yet hear no sound from the performance (Fig. 12). The camera closes in on her face, and on her seductive look first out to the camera then sideways to the men around her (Fig. 13). As the camera now moves into the screen, blurring the boundaries between screening-room, screen and film set (the space of the performance that involves the story of the material girl, Madonna II), the 'rehearsal' (if that is what it was) ends and a rich lover comes on to the set with a large present for Madonna I.

This then is desire for the woman given birth through the cinematic apparatus, in classical manner; and yet, while the sequence seems to *foreground* those mechanisms, it does not appear to critique or in any way comment upon them. In Jameson's terms, the process is pastiche rather than parody, which puts it in the postmodernist mode. Considering the visual track alone, the blurring of the diegetic spaces further suggests postmodernism, as does the ensuing confusion of enunciative stances. For while the director's gaze clearly constructed the first shot-series, it is not clear that his gaze structures the shot in which Madonna I receives the present. We still hear the whirring sound of a projector, as if this were still the screening-room space; and yet we are *inside* that screen – we no longer see the space around the frame, thus disorienting the viewer.

We cut to a close-up of a white phone ringing and a hand picking it up, and are again confused spatially. Where are we? Whose look is this? There has been no narrative preparation for the new space or for the spectator address: the phone monologue by Madonna I (the only time in the entire video that she speaks) establishes the space as her dressing-room. As she speaks, the camera behaves oddly (at least by standard Hollywood conventions), dollying back slowly to the door of her room, to reveal the director standing there. Was it then his gaze that structured the shot? At the moment of reaching him, the gaze certainly becomes his, and Madonna I is seen to be its object. The phone monologue that he overhears, as does the viewer, establishes that Madonna I has just received a diamond necklace. This causes the director to throw his present into the waste-paper basket that a janitor happens to be carrying out at that moment. It also establishes that Madonna I is *not* the 'material girl' of her stage role, since she offers the necklace to her (presumed) girlfriend on the phone.

We now cut back to the stage space that we assume to be the film set; it is not clear, because the diegesis does not foreground the processes of filming, and yet there is no audience space. Rather, Madonna II sets up a direct rapport with the camera filming the rock video and therefore with the television spectator, deliberately playing for her/him rather than for the man in the frame. But the spatial disorientation continues: there is a sudden cut to the rear of a flashy red car driving into the studio, followed by shots of Madonna I's elegant body in matching red dress (knees carefully visible), of her rich lover bending over her, and of her face and apparently dismissive reply. Whose gaze is this? Who is enunciating here? As Madonna I leaves her car, we discover the director again, but this series of shots could not have been structured by his gaze.

We cut back to the stage/film set for the most extended sequence of the performance in the video. This sequence follows the Monroe 'Diamonds' dance closely, and stands in the strange intertextual relationship already mentioned: we cannot tell whether or not the Monroe sequence is being commented upon, simply used, or ridiculed by exaggeration (which sometimes seems to be happening). Things are further complicated by the fact that *Gentlemen Prefer Blondes* is itself a comedy, mocking and exaggerating certain patriarchal gender roles. The situation is confused even more by occasional technical play with the image, destroying even the illusion of the stability of the stage/set space: at least once, a two-shot of Madonna II and one of the lovers is simply flipped over, in standard rock-video style but in total violation of classic codes that seek to secure illusionism.

Since there is no diegetic audience, the spectator is now in direct rapport with Madonna I's body, as she performs for the television spectator. There is again no diegetic source of enunciation, which continues to be the case until the end of the video, when the director and Madonna I finally are firmly situated in the same space: boy wins girl in a pastiche (perhaps) of the classical 'happy ending'. The spectator either remains disoriented, or secures a position through the body of the historical star, Madonna, implied as 'producing' the video or simply fixed on as a centring force.

This brief analysis of the main shots and use of diegetic spaces in 'Material Girl' demonstrates the ways in which conventions of the classic Hollywood film, which paradoxically provided the inspiration for the video, are routinely violated. The purpose here was to show how even in a video that at first appears precisely to remain within those conventions – unlike many other videos whose extraordinary and avant-garde techniques are immediately obvious – regular narrative devices are not adhered to. But the video violates classic traditions even more with its sound–image relations.

This raises the question of the rock video's uniqueness as an artistic form, namely as a form in which the sound of the song and the 'content' of its lyric exist prior to the creation of images which accompany music and words. While there are analogies with both opera and the Hollywood musical, neither prepares us for the rock video with its unique song-image relationship. The uniqueness has to do with a certain arbitrariness of the images used with any particular song, with the lack of conventional spatial limits, and with the frequent, extremely rapid, montage editing not found generally (if at all) in Hollywood musical song/dance sequences. It also has to do with the precise relationship of sound – both musical and vocal – to image. This latter relationship involves first the links between musical rhythms and significations of instrumental sounds and the images provided for them; and second links between the meanings of the song's actual *words* and the images conjured up to convey that 'content'.

This is obviously a very complex topic – which I can only touch on here – but I shall demonstrate some of the issues in relation to 'Material Girl', where again things are far simpler than in many other videos. We have seen that on the visual track there are two distinct but linked discourses, that involving the director's desire for Madonna I (his determined pursuit and eventual 'winning' of her), and that of Madonna I's performance, where she plays Madonna II, the 'material girl'. These discourses are not hierarchically arranged as in the Hollywood film, but rather exist on a horizontal axis, neither one being subordinated to the other. In terms of screen time, however, the performance is privileged.

When we turn to the soundtrack we find that, after the brief intro-ductory scene in the screening-room (a scene, by the way, often excised from broadcasts of the video), the soundtrack consists entirely of the lyric for the song 'Material Girl'. This song deals with the girl who will only date boys who 'give her proper credit', and for whom love is reduced to money. Thus, none of the visuals pertaining to the director–Madonna I love story have any correlate on the soundtrack. We merely have two short verbal sequences (in the screening-room and the dressing-room) to carry the entire other story: in other words, sound-track and image track are not linked in those shots. An obvious example of this discrepancy is in the shot of Madonna I (arriving at the studio in the flashy car) rejecting her rich lover: Madonna lip-synchs 'That's right', from the 'Material Girl' song – a phrase that refers there to her only loving boys who give her money – in a situation where the opposite is happening: she *refuses* to love the man who is wealthy!

In other words, the video's soundtrack refers only to the stage performance and yet dominates the visuals depicting the framing story about Madonna I. The common device in the Hollywood musical of having the dance interlude simply as an episode in the main story seems here to be reversed: the performance is central while the love story is reduced to the status merely of a framing narrative. Significant here also is the disjunction between the two stories, the framing story being about a 'nice' girl, and the performance being about a 'bad' girl: but even these terms are blurred by the obvious seductiveness of the 'nice' girl, particularly as she walks toward the car at the end in a very 'knowing' manner.

Thus the usual hierarchical arrangement of discourses in the classic realist text is totally violated in 'Material Girl'. While Madonna I is certainly set up as object of the director's desire, in quite classical manner, the text refuses to let her be controlled by that desire. This is achieved by unbalancing the relations between framing story and performance story so that Madonna I is overridden by her stage figure, Madonna II, the brash, gutsy 'material girl'. The line between 'fiction' and 'reality' within the narrative is therefore blurred: this has severe consequences just because the two women are polar opposites.

In *Gentlemen Prefer Blondes*, on the other hand, no such confusion or discrepancy exists. From the start, the Monroe character's single-minded aim is to catch a rich man, and she remains fixed on that throughout. The function of her 'Diamonds Are a Girl's Best Friend' performance is to express what has been obvious to the spectator, if not to Esmond, all along, and to let Esmond get the idea, were he smart enough. Monroe sings a song that expresses her philosophy of life, but we are clear about the lines between the stage fiction and the context of its presentation on the one hand, and Monroe as a character in the narrative on the other. Part of the confusion in the Madonna video comes about precisely because the scene of the performance is not made clear and because the lines between the different spaces of the text are blurred.

The situation in 'Material Girl' is even more problematic because of the way that Madonna, as historical star subject, breaks through her narrative positions via her strong personality, her love of performing for the camera, her inherent energy and vitality. Madonna searches for the camera's gaze and for the television spectator's gaze that follows it because she relishes being desired. The 'roles' melt away through her unique presence and the logical narrative incoherence discussed above seems resolved in our understanding that Madonna herself, as historical subject, is really the 'material girl'!

It is perhaps Madonna's success in articulating and parading the desire to be desired in an unabashed, aggressive, gutsy manner (as against the self-abnegating urge to lose oneself in the male evident in the classic Hollywood film) that attracts the hordes of twelve-year-old fans who idolize her and crowd her concerts. The amazing 'look-alike' Madonna contests (for example, a recent Macy's campaign in New York) and the successful exploitation of the weird Madonna style of dress by clothing companies attests to this idolatry. It is significant that Madonna's style is a far cry from the conventional patriarchal feminine of the women's magazines – it is a cross between a bordello queen and a bag lady: young teenagers may use her as a protest against their mothers and the normal 'feminine' while still remaining very much within those modes (in the sense of spending a lot of money, time and energy on their 'look'; the 'look' being still crucial to their identities, still designed to attract attention, even if provocatively).

In some sense, then, Madonna represents the post-feminist heroine in that she combines unabashed seductiveness with a gutsy kind of independence. She is neither particularly male nor female identified, and seems mainly to be out for herself. This post-femininism is part of a larger postmodernist phenomenon which her video also embodies in its blurring of hitherto sacrosanct boundaries and polarities of the various kinds discussed. The usual bi-polar categories – male/female, high art/ pop art, film/television, fiction/reality, private/public, interior/exterior – no longer apply to many rock videos, including 'Material Girl'.[14]

This analysis of 'Material Girl' has shown the ambiguity of enunciative positions within the video, which is in turn responsible for the ambiguous representation of the female image. The positioning of a video like 'Material Girl', moreover, within the twenty-four-hour flow on the commercial MTV channel, lets us see that it is precisely *this* sort of ambiguous image that appears frequently, as against other possible female images, in videos which are only rarely shown. The post-feminist ambiguous images are clearly the ones sponsors consider 'marketable', since they are those most often cycled and also propagated in the ad texts interspersed among the video texts.

But let me, as suggested earlier, 'stop the flow' and look briefly at other female representations with their different kinds of gaze and enunciative stances. It is significant that some of the female rock stars just preceding Madonna, such as Cyndi Lauper, Donna Summer and Pat Benatar, came in on the coat-tails of the 1970s feminist movement. Interestingly enough, however, in the early 1980s they reflected different aspects of the 'new' woman, Lauper often taking a woman-identified stance, Summer at times an apparently 'feminist' one, and Benatar embodying the 'tough-woman' image.

In accord with a dominant strand of 1970s American feminism, all three stars attempted to 'give woman a voice'. The videos made from their lyrics fall broadly into the 'socially conscious' category in Chart 3, and are most often made in comparatively conventional narrative/realist style. The exception of Lauper's first video, 'Girls Just Want to Have Fun', which comments playfully on young women's resistance to the confining traditional roles that their parents still demand and employs all kinds of deconstructive technical devices (including the scrunching up of women's images into balls that are then circled in space) to make its point. Part of the video's humour comes from the contrast between the extremely banal but tuneful pop music track and the imaginative visual devices.

This video embodies a common theme, namely a strong anti-parental sentiment, often expressed through deliberate ridicule of adults. (Lauper's 'Girls' in fact features her own mother, filmed in Lauper's home, evidently agreeing to be stereotyped.) Lauper's next, and highly successful video, 'Time After Time', which belongs in the romantic category, has a vague feminist angle in the heroine's decision to leave her boyfriend, evidently inspired by Marlene Dietrich's (first) refusal of her lover in *Morocco*. But more obviously feminist is the (in its time unusual) representation of a close mother–daughter bonding. The video intermingles the heroine's love for the man with her love for her mother, suggesting a pre-Oedipal quality to the love-affair. When her boyfriend rejects her, the girl conjures up an image of her mother comforting her, which in turn evokes memories of earlier closeness with her mother (there is a shot of the two hugging in an obviously working-class kitchen). Insisting on leaving her lover, despite his pleas, the heroine stops to hug her mother once more on her way to the station and the mournful parting.

The problem with this sort of representation of the mother is that while it may be gratifying to see close mother–daughter bonding in a video (there are increasingly fewer videos that deal with parents at all, let alone in any positive manner), the mother is presented in realist codes that cannot conceal her powerlessness. She comes across as an oppressed figure, pathetic, even weak. Peripheral to the narrative as usual, she cannot help her daughter, merely commiserating rather than taking control or bringing about change. (I have elsewhere[15] argued that, paradoxically, some of the videos in the romantic category by male stars, such as Paul Young's 'Every Time You Go Away', may open up new space precisely through avoiding any literal representation of the mother. Addressed as an absent figure, the mother-surrogate's gaze is nevertheless inscribed in such videos in a way that makes itself more powerfully experienced than in literal images.)

Similar problems beset the more explicitly feminist video by Donna Summer, 'She Works Hard for the Money', shown in 1982–3. This hard-hitting video makes explicit its political message about woman's oppression. It focuses on a working-class woman's double jeopardy as single working parent, oppressed both within the home and on the job. The video's textual strategies are largely realist, except that the story is narrated rather untraditionally by Summer herself, in the position of 'host', conducting the viewer through the heroine's daily life. Summer 'shows' us how she has to work two jobs, do all the housework and put up in addition with two quarrelling, ungrateful kids. The images reveal the heroine in one appalling situation after another, there being no respite, while 'Summer' provides as it were a didactic 'reading' of the images as exemplifying woman's lot. The only mitigating aspects to the misery are our host's personal solidarity with the heroine (but, as host, she is outside the diegesis and cannot help her); and the final scene in which all kind of women, from different professions, gather together on the street to dance. It is a nice but utopian moment, resolving in a fantasied solidarity of what in fact requires concrete *social* change.

Pat Benatar's far more successful and frequently cycled 'Love Is a Battlefield' embodies Benatar's tough-woman stance. (Benatar in an interview criticised most female stars for their self-denigrating romantic preoccupations, the 'If you leave me, I'll die' syndrome; she herself prefers the 'If you leave me, I'll kick your ass' stance. This explained, she noted, why she finds male stars far more interesting than female ones!) Benatar's early video exposes the limitations of the nuclear family – the heroine is thrown out of her home at the start – and reveals women's vulnerabilities in the big city. Ending up as a prostitute, the heroine nevertheless takes action against the male oppressing her friend; once again, the women side with one another, marching bravely out of the brothel to engage in a warlike, threatening dance on the street before going their separate ways.

The difference between these two 'feminist' videos – Summer's and Benatar's – explains the relative success of the latter, as against the short cycling of the first. For the female representations in Benatar's video almost belie the strong woman-identified theme in their reliance on the standard 'look' of the patriarchal feminine: the heroine, played by Benatar herself, is particularly glamorous, and the prostitutes' clothes, while somewhat unconventional, are colourful and attractive.

All these videos are important in offering alternate female narrative/thematic positions, if not alternate images. This distinction is significant, since it reveals the limitation of a traditional liberal-humanist feminist politics expressed through fairly conventional filmic codes. Perhaps because of their kind of feminist politics, these female stars have been far less ready to experiment with form than have average male stars. (It is significant that most of the highly touted, and prize-winning experimental videos have been produced by male video directors for male stars or groups such as the Cars, Dire Straits, Simple Minds, Phil Collins, David Bowie, Mick Jagger, Michael Jackson, Rush, the Power Station, A-Ha. The list at once reflects the dominance of white male figures in the rock-video phenomenon and also perhaps addresses basic issues having to do with 1970s feminist aesthetic and political strategies.

It is precisely these strategies that Tina Turner's 'Private Dancer' effectively questions. This video, instead of presenting an explicit feminist message in the manner of Benatar's and Summer's, attempts to expose woman's position in the dominant male Imaginary. It analyses the structure of a male unconscious that reduces women to mere cyphers, signs in a male discourse, or instruments of pleasure shaped to satisfy male fantasies.

The video's enunciative strategies work to deconstruct the male Imaginary: the heroine, played by Turner herself, is first seen in realist images entering the high-class bordello where she tells us, through the song lyric, that she works as a 'Private Dancer'. Turner continues to speak this video as she moves from being a realistic character to a kind of female *metteur-en-scène*, or a magician, conjuring up different aspects of the male erotic unconscious. Dressed now in elegant evening-gown, Turner addresses the camera directly, in close-up or medium-shot, but the angles chosen diminish fetishization of her form. Her words here speak to the performer's own life and hopes – the need for money that brings her here; the wish for a family, home and fun – the video aiming to construct a disjunction between 'woman' and 'male fantasy'.

From this position, the heroine creates for the television viewer the dream world of her clients, but in such a way as to highlight the oppressiveness of the fantasies imposed on the women in the bordello. The actresses and dancers participating in the fantasies are made to perform like robots or mannequins, reduced as they are to mere mechanical embodiments of what men desire. Sometimes, the figures are seen to be operated, like puppets, by ribbons tied to their limbs. They are revealed to be at the command of the male customer, producing the required image as would a machine.

The video's visual techniques produce the effect of a dream-space: one male fantasy, performed by the robot-like, mechanical figures, is made to merge into the next, the camera often floating in on a scene, watching it for a while until the image dissolves into another, when the camera will float out again. The effect is that of swooning, or of a dream-world in which anything can happen and in which one is not in control. The *mise-en-scène* adds further to the dream-like quality through the veils and netting that is draped across the image and through the claustrophobic sense of being in an enclosed, artificial space.

Some of the fantasies conjured up involve the heroine herself, so that we get the double articulation of her narration outside of the male fantasies she conducts us through and her positioning within those fantasies. The result is our understanding her physical/bodily ensnarement within the male Imaginary but her psychic detachment from it. It is this representation of a psychic detachment that permits the exposing of the male erotic unconscious. The video constructs a kind of meta-language within which to let us see *how* the heroine's body is (ab)used, *how* women are mere passive objects of male desire, entrapped within a male fantasy world from which there is no escape. The blocking of woman's subjectivity and of her own desires is graphically depicted.

The video ends as it began with a realist image of the dance-hall where clients and customers first meet. We have seen that this is a space controlled by the ever-watching madame, making sure that her 'dancers' are doing their job of pleasing the clients. The heroine is shot in close-up with her client, and then, suddenly, seen to push him away and walk off the floor, as the video ends. This moment of negation of her role exposes the pathetic degree of resistance available to the woman. She cannot *change* anything, or free herself of the male constructions; she can only walk away from the scene, temporarily take herself out of the role.[16]

This video is quite different from others produced for Turner, and its Turner-image is unusual. As should be obvious, I am not imputing any authorial control to the historical star-subject being discussed here, since it is unclear how much control a star has, and in any case my focus is on *text* rather than stars. Videos produced for stars in no way attempt to construct an image consistent from one text to another; a star's image will depend on what seems most marketable at the particular moment, and on the general style tone/image of the single, or of the record from which the single comes. Since selling the record is the base-line, it is this that will control the 'look' of the video being made for the sale of the song and its record. In Turner's case, a number of videos were made from her very successful and remarkable staged London performance, where she unabashedly promoted her body as a sexual commodity. One can argue that in a video like 'What's Love Got to Do with It' Turner attempts to gain control over her own sexuality through deliberately enticing male desire. Her short, tight leather skirt with the slit up the side, her bestockinged legs and high-heeled shoes are in this case used simply to assert control over the males by refusing them what her dress seems to offer. Turner here comes close to Benatar's 'tough-woman' image, seeming to ask women to band together rather than giving in to male desire. But this is again a position taken up only in the one lyric from which this video was made.

The last variation from the prevalent 'post-feminist' female representation I shall deal with in my stopping of the twenty-four-hour MTV flow is evident in the recent Aretha Franklin/Annie Lennox 'Sisters Are Doin' It for Themselves' video. The female images here are arguably different from those in either the feminist-message video or the deconstructive Turner video. At first glance, the Franklin/Lennox video looks like the feminist-message type, but on a closer examination the video seems to attempt to move beyond the mere, often romantic, celebration of women's achievements that it does also include.

First there is the amazing contrast between the images of the two star-subjects themselves, seen in performance on a huge outdoor stage before crowds of ethnically mixed female fans: Franklin's image is embedded in discourses of the historically 'strong', Black, female blues singer, as well as those of the Black, no-nonsense matriarch. Her image is now frequent on MTV, as she appears in her own successful videos, or in this 'Sisters' video; or as an homage-image, as she is in Whitney Houston's 'How Will I Know'. Lennox, meanwhile, typifies the new androgynous rock-video discourses which are largely, however, a male phenomenon. Here she is resplendent in white male-style jacket, black leather pants, heavy boots and short cropped blonde hair. Franklin, by contrast, performs in a simple red gown. There is thus a bringing together of powerful, current alternative female images with the past strength of Black female discourses.

This is an aspect of the video developed in the cutaways from the two women performing to montage sequences of shots of women spliced together. These intercut shots are of three main kinds: those showing women in non-traditional jobs, from Presidents to construction workers; those showing women in the old patriarchal 'feminine' rituals such as the traditional Indian marriage, or the cheerleader; and, finally, clips from films like Schlesinger's *A Kind of Loving* (1962) or Vidor's *Our Daily Bread* (1934), which show women as classic sex-objects or idealized mother-figures.

This montage sequence reminds the female viewer of where women have been and of where they have gotten to, but the intermixing of the various sets of images suggests the continuity of the old positions along with the new. There is thus an attempt to avoid the utopian element of the feminist-message video by showing the series on a continuum rather than in a clear past versus present hierarchical ordering.

Most interesting perhaps is what the video does with the images of Dave Stewart (Annie Lennox's co-performer and co-writer for the 'Eurythmics'), played upon a huge screen that appears between the images of Lennox and Franklin on stage towards the end of the video. At first, one is perturbed at his presence at all in such a celebration of women's achievements; but it soon becomes clear that the video is using his image to say something about the processes of image-making already raised in the montage clips from male films. Here it appears that instead of the usual control of the female image by the male gaze, Stewart's image is being controlled by Lennox and Franklin as they stand on either side of the screen which depicts his image. It is almost as if they are pulling strings to make the image move in certain ways, much as the women in Turner's video were 'operated' by the male unconscious. Stewart's figure is very much positioned as the object of the women's gazes and, further, is reduced to a kind of mechanical object as the image bounces about, apparently uncontrollably, within the screen.

Finally, there is an interesting attempt in the video to avoid making Franklin and Lennox direct objects of the camera's gaze. While there are inevitably some close-ups of their faces, for much of the time the camera catches them at oblique angles, so that their gazes do not directly meet the camera's. At times, this creates an unfortunate sense of their not relating to each other, but this is in the service of avoiding, as much as possible, an objectifying camera gaze.

'Sisters Are Doin' It for Themselves' then, appears to comment upon the problems of image-making and to foreground the notion that images are constructed rather than 'natural'. It processes old and new female constructions as if to warn us against too readily assuming that old images have been abandoned; it questions the extent to which women have been newly constructed as 'liberated'. Meanwhile, the 'present tense' of the video, that of the concert in which Franklin and Lennox are performing, conveys a sense of female solidarity and celebration in the old utopian mode; but there is a self-consciousness here as well, in that this is presented as yet one more 'image', as the montage sequences and the concert footage are projected on the huge screen. The final shot consists of a huge four-sided box containing images from the video, suggesting the possibility of multiple representations from no central position.

'Sisters' received short play on MTV, seemingly having gotten on to the channel in the first place only because it was top of the British charts. And as we resume the twenty-four-hour flow, such alternative female images once again recede into the background, and the post-feminist image reappears. I shall conclude by outlining how it is that the post-feminist is the dominant image, focusing on both the cultural ideology involved in its production and on the specific involvement of the televisual apparatus.

The televisual apparatus as a whole contributes to the prevalence of the ambiguous female image. To summarize: first, the main force of MTV as a cable channel is consumption on a variety of levels, ranging from the literal (selling the sponsors' goods, the rock stars' records, and MTV itself) to the psychological (selling the image, the 'look,' the style). MTV is more obviously than other channels one nearly continuous advertisement, the flow being broken down merely into different *kinds* of advertisements. More than other channels, then, MTV positions the spectator in the mode of constantly hoping that the next ad segment (of whatever kind) will satisfy the desire for plenitude: the channel keeps the spectator in the consuming mode more intensely because its items are all so short.

Since the mode of address throughout is that of the advertisement, then like the advertisement the channel relies on engaging the spectator on the level of unsatisfied desire; this remains in the psyche from the moment of entry into the Lacanian symbolic, and is available for channelling in various directions. Given the organization of the Lacanian symbolic around the phallus as signifier, it is not surprising that MTV basically addresses the desire for the phallus remaining in the psyche of both genders. This partly accounts for the dominance on the channel of videos featuring white male stars.

Nevertheless, as Chart 3 shows, the male gaze is not monolithic on the channel: here again, the television apparatus enables the production of a variety of different gazes due to the arrangement of a series of short, constantly changing segments which replace the closure of the two-hour film, the classical novel and the theatrical play. There is no possibility within the four-minute segment for regression to the Freudian Oedipal conflicts in the manner of the classical narrative. What we have rather is a semi-comical play with Oedipal positions, as in the postmodern video, or a focus on one particular mode in the Oedipal complex in some of the other video-types outlined in the chart.

The implications of all this for a feminist perspective need close analysis. Feminism, particularly in America, has traditionally relied on a liberal- or left-humanist position. It is these ideologies that provided the stance from which feminists have been able to critique dominant practices and call them 'sexist' or 'patriarchal'. Humanist values, applied specifically to those humans called 'women' who often were not included in humanist cultural projections, formed the basis for arguments to improve women's conditions of existence. If Baudrillard is correct in seeing the television screen and the entire televisual apparatus as symbolizing a new era in which left/liberal humanism no longer has a place, then feminism needs to address the changed situation. Gender has been one of the central organizing categories of what Baudrillard calls the old 'hot' (as against the new 'cold') universe, but this category itself may be in the process of elimination, with unclear (and not necessarily progressive) results. It could be that women will no longer have the humanist position from which to critique what is going on; the new postmodern universe arguably makes impossible the critical position itself, making then irrelevant any 'feminist' stance.

Feminists then, in particular, need to explore television's part in the changed, and still changing, relationship of self to image. This change began at the turn of the century with the development of advertising and of the department-store window; it was then further affected by the invention of the cinematic apparatus, and television has, in its turn, produced more changes. The television screen now replaces the cinema

screen as the central controlling cultural mode, setting up a new spectator–screen relationship which I have here begun to analyse in relation
to MTV. For MTV constantly comments upon the self in relation to
image (especially the television image), to such an extent that this may
be seen as its main 'content'. The blurring of distinctions between a
'subject' and an 'image' – or the reduction of the old notion of 'self' to
'image' – is something for feminists to explore, even as we fear the
coming of Baudrillard's universe of 'simulacra'.[17]

The reduction of the female body to an 'image' is something that
women have long endured: the phenomenon has been extensively
studied by feminist film critics, who were able to assume a humanist
position from which to critique film constructions. From that position
the possibility of constructing other representations always existed. The
new postmodern universe, however, with its celebration of the look,
surfaces, textures, the self-as-commodity, produces an array of images/
representations/simulacra that co-opts any possible critical position by
the very incorporation of what were previously 'dissenting' images; this
makes difficult the processes of foregrounding or exposing gender issues
that feminist film-makers have used. As a cultural mode, postmodernism
would eliminate gender difference as a significant category, just as it
sweeps aside other polarities. Television, as a postmodernist apparatus –
with its decentred address, its flattening out of things into a network or
system that is endless, unbounded, unframed and whose parts all rely on
each other – urgently requires more thorough examination, particularly
in relation to its impact on women.

Notes

1. The term 'social Imaginary' brings together concepts developed by Jacques Lacan,
Louis Althusser, Roland Barthes, and others. In particular, it combines Lacan's notions of
the subject split at the moment of entry into the Symbolic with Althusser's conception of
Ideological State Apparatuses. The two most relevant texts here are Lacan's 'The Mirror
Stage as Formative of the I', reprinted in *Ecrits: A Selection*, Alan Sheridan (trans.),
London and New York: W.W. Norton and Co., 1979, pp. 1–7; and Louis Althusser,
'Ideology and Ideological State Apparatuses (Notes Towards an Investigation)', in *Lenin
and Philosophy and Other Essays*, Ben Brewster (trans.), New York and London: Monthly
Review Press, 1971, pp. 127–86.

MTV – Music Television – is a twenty-four-hour, non-stop cable station for which
subscribers do not pay an extra fee. It is made up of rock video, VJs' ('video jockeys')
comments, music news, interviews with rock stars, advertisements by sponsors and
advertisements for MTV itself. MTV is beamed across America wherever cable service
exists, and latest audience figures are 28 million, ranging in age from twelve to thirty-four.

2. Jean Baudrillard, 'The Ecstasy of Communication', in *The Anti-Aesthetic: Essays
in Postmodern Culture*, Hal Foster (ed.), Port Townsend: Washington Bay Press, 1983,
pp. 125–38.

3. For more discussion of these differences generally, see Sandy Flitterman, 'Fascina-

tion in Fragments: Psychoanalysis in Film and Television', in *Channels of Discourse: Television Criticism in the 80's*, Robert Allen (ed.), Chapel Hill: North Carolina University Press, 1987. An expanded version of the present essay, particularly in relation to differences between movie and television screens, can be found in E. Ann Kaplan, *Rocking Around the Clock: Music Television, Postmodernism and Consumer Culture*, London and New York: Methuen, 1987.

4. By 'simulacra' Baudrillard means a world in which all we have are simulations, there being no 'real' external to them, no 'original' that is being copied. It is as if all were reduced merely to exteriors, there no longer being any 'interiors'. For full development of the notion of 'simulacra' see Jean Baudrillard, *Simulations*, Paul Foss, Paul Patton and Philip Beitchman (trans.), New York: Semiotext(e), 1983.

5. Althusser, 'Ideology and Ideological State Apparatuses (Notes Towards an Investigation)'; p. 162.

6. Sandy Flitterman, 'The Real Soap Operas: TV Commercials', in *Regarding Television: A Critical Anthology*, E. Ann Kaplan (ed.), Los Angeles: American Film Institute, 1983, pp. 84–96. See also my article in *Channels of Discourse*.

7. For details of these arguments, see Kaplan, *Rocking Around the Clock*.

8. Robert Stam, 'Television News and Its Spectator', in *Regarding Television*, pp. 23–44.

9. Peggy Phelan, 'Panopticism and the Uncanny: Notes Toward Television's Visual Time', unpublished paper, 1986.

10. For further discussion of the classic avant-garde film polarity and of Chart 3, see Kaplan, *Rocking Around the Clock*.

11. Fredric Jameson, 'Postmodernism and Consumer Society', in *The Anti-Aesthetic*, p. 113.

12. For details of videos referred to in this essay, see the Videography below.

13. Jane Brown and Kenneth C. Campbell, 'The Same Beat But a Different Drummer: Race and Gender in Music Videos', *Journal of Communication*, vol. 36, no. 1 (1986), pp. 94–106. That the video is directed by a woman, Mary Lambert, does not alter my assessment of the video as post-feminist. I would not want to collapse biological gender with ideological stance.

14. Madonna has recently offered a dramatically changed image in her new 'Papa Don't Preach' video. While abandoning her trashy bag lady image for a new svelte, gamine-style modern teenager, Madonna nevertheless still combines traditional images (in this case the 'little girl' and the 'whore'). For more discussion of this change see Kaplan *Rocking Around the Clock*.

15. E. Ann Kaplan, 'Sexual Difference, Pleasure and the Construction of the Spectator in Music Television', *Oxford Literary Review*, vol. 8, nos. 1–2 (1986), pp. 113–22.

16. While race is absent as any overt part of the narrative in 'Private Dancer' it perhaps accounts for the video's uncanny ability to present what may be a predominantly white male Imaginary. But this is a very complex terrain, far beyond my topic here. For more discussion of possible differences in Black and white sexuality, see Jacqueline Bobo and Alile Larkin's essays in this volume.

17. Baudrillard, *Simulations*.

Videography

John Parr, 'Naughty Naughty', *John Parr*, Atlantic Records, 1984.
John Cougar Mellencamp, 'Hurts So Good', *American Fool*, Riva/Polygram Records, 1982.
Pat Benatar, 'Love Is a Battlefield', *Get Nervous*, Chrysalis Records, 1983.
Pat Benatar, 'Sex as a Weapon', *Seven the Hard Way*, Chrysalis Records, 1986.
Donna Summer, 'She Works Hard for the Money', *She Works Hard for the Money*, Mercury/Polygram Records, 1983.
Tina Turner, 'Private Dancer', *Private Dancer*, Capitol Records, 1984.

Aretha Franklin and Annie Lennox, 'Sisters Are Doin' It for Themselves', *Be Yourself Tonight*, RCA Records, 1986.

Madonna, 'Material Girl', *Madonna*, Sire/Warner Brothers Records, 1985.

Cyndi Lauper, 'Girls Just Want to Have Fun', *She's So Unusual*, Portrait Records, 1983.

Cyndi Lauper, 'Time After Time', *She's So Unusual*, Portrait Records, 1983.

Paul Young, 'Every Time You Go Away', *The Secret of Association*, Columbia CBS Records, 1985.

Tina Turner, 'What's Love Got to Do With It?', *Private Dancer*, Capitol Records, 1984.

Whitney Houston, 'How Will I Know', *Whitney Houston*, Arista Records, 1985.

Madonna, 'Papa Don't Preach', *True Blue*, Sire/Warner Brothers Record, 1986.

8

Black Women Film-makers Defining Ourselves: Feminism in Our Own Voice

Alile Sharon Larkin

From the moment that Africans were brought to the Americas and made slaves, we lost much more than our freedom. We lost control of our image. Film and television have been crucial in this legacy of loss, our loss of name and culture, for Hollywood has the power to rewrite, redefine and recreate history, culture, religion and politics. Hollywood has the power of the spoken word and the visual image and all sounds and dreams.

Ousmane Sembene, a Senegalese film-maker, has a very important scene in his film *Ceddo* (1977) which documents the use of Islam and Christianity to colonize African people. Sembene shows an Imam, the Islamic spiritual leader, coming to power in a community, replacing the traditional African ruler. Sembene highlights his first act as Imam: he assembles the entire village. Every man, woman and child – even the babies – are brought before him, one by one, and renamed. Their own culture is prohibited and they must now practice Islamic culture, synonymous with the Islamic faith. The film shows the Christian missionary waiting his turn, for he will perform the same trick: teaching the people that his religion is superior, a religion synonymous with Western culture. Once a person of colour is converted to this Europeanized Christianity[1] she/he too changes her/his name to a so-called Christian name, in reality a European name, and begins to practise Western culture, begins to laugh at her/his own gods and herself or himself.

The poet Henry Dumas speaks of our transformation:

Oh these cold white hands
manipulating
they broke us like limbs from trees

> and carved Europe upon our African masks
> and made puppets[2]

The communications media's racist representations of Black people helps to maintain an oppressive society. Early cinema reflected and promoted values and concepts of oppression, and today the film industry continues to popularize these concepts. Thus, the communications media, by affirming already existing social patterns, has both perpetuated and fostered racism and sexism to new generations.

As a Black woman film-maker, my objective is to contribute to the development of our own definitions. My objectives are ultimately no different from that of many Black male film-makers. Yet I find that my 'gender-consciousness' is being defined by feminists within Western culture in the same way that my Blackness has been defined by that dominant culture.

I believe that many contemporary Black women artists have been compelled to speak in a voice that is not really our own. As a Black woman film-maker it is important that I address this in order to deal with the issue of Black women film-makers defining ourselves.

An ideology or belief which attempts to compartmentalize the nature and form of the oppression of African people solely into gender and/or class, is ultimately destructive to our achieving genuine equality and liberation in Western society and in the world. To do so is to redefine the history and experiences of African people in the interests of white supremacy. As a Black woman I experience all areas of oppression – economic, racial, and sexual. I cannot 'pick and choose' a single area of struggle. I believe it is in this way that feminists and other progressive whites pursue their own interests at the expense of those of us subjected to racism. They do not have to deal with the totality of oppression, and instead may conform to, or accept the policies of, institutional racism, as defined by Louis Knowles and Kenneth Prewitt in their book, *Institutional Racism in America*.[3] Knowles and Prewitt state that

> maintenance of basic racial controls is now less dependent upon specific discriminatory decisions. Such behavior has become so well institutionalized that generally the individual does not have to exercise choices to operate in a racist manner. The rules and procedures of the large organizations have already pre-structured the choice. The individual only has to conform to the operating norms of the organization and the institution will do the discriminating for him.[4]

Feminism succumbs to racism when it segregates Black women from Black men and dismisses our history. The assumption that Black women and white women share identical or similar histories and experiences presents an important problem. Historically, white women have also been our oppressors. Historically, Black men have abused us, but they have never held the kind of power that white women hold in this culture. Both historically and currently, white women participate in and reap the benefits of white supremacy. Feminism must address these issues, otherwise its ahistorical approach towards Black women can and does maintain institutional racism.

The prevalent media images of Blacks have their foundation in vaudeville and in the minstrel shows. The same basic stereotypes were later carried over to film and television. Initially Black roles were performed by whites in blackface in both the minstrel shows and in early films. Any actual Black person on stage performed only the roles of 'comic stooge' or 'faithful servant'.[5] Today the essence of these stereotypes remains in the American media. The following is an outline of the most common stereotypes or role-image possibilities for Blacks in film and television, from an article by Sedeka and Alhamisi Wadinasi.[6] Although several of the names for these stereotypes come from slavery culture, the Wadinasis reapply them to contemporary Black characters.

The *Contented Slave* loves her/his station in life and only occasionally prays for things to get better. Her/his predicament is understood as God's will. (This stereotype includes the many portrayals of mammy characters in American films, such as *Gone with the Wind* (1939). (On US network television, Fred Sanford, for instance, the father and junkyard owner of the American situation comedy *Sanford and Son* is a peculiar mixture of Local Colour Negro, Wretched Freedman and Contented Slave. In that he is happy with his lot, does not evolve as a character – psychologically, intellectually or politically – and does not try to improve himself except in the service of a buffoon-like comedy, Fred Sanford exhibits aspects of the Contented Slave.)

The *Wretched Freedman* is the type of Black who cannot hold down a job for very long, is not successful as the head of the family and invariably looks for answers in the bottle. (James Evans of the situation comedy *Good Times*, now seen in re-runs, played a Wretched Freedman, unemployed more often than he was employed.)

The *Brute Negro* is the militant black who is excessively anti-white, anti-society and pro-Black. (Michael Evans, the youngest son on *Good Times*, fits this description.) While most of the examples here are limited to fictional film and television characters, the stereotypes also apply to other media representations of Blacks, for instance, the network news presentation of Blacks struggling for improved rights and living conditions.

The *Comic Negro* is the Black who does not have a serious or intellectual aspect and whose mission in life is to be funny and stupid –

nothing more. (Film characters Steppin Fetchit, and Prissy in *Gone with the Wind*, as well as radio and television characters Amos and Andy are historical examples which apply here. More currently – and more subversively – Eddie Murphy embodies traits of the Comic Negro.)

The *Local Colour Negro* is a combination of all the primary black stereotypes that one supposedly encounters in the black community; the preacher and gospel singer (the new television comedy series *Amen* with Sherman Hemsley), the wino, hustler, dope pusher, prostitute and/or street gang member (the 'bad guy' on any number of police and adventure shows like *Miami Vice*, for instance), the matriarch, and also the deserted or divorced wife replete with eight children and on welfare.

The *Exotic Primitive* is the unusual Black with 'white' talent (usually referring to intelligence, education, creativity), a token Black, or preferably a Black who just jumped off the boat from Africa. (Roger, the son on television's *What's Happenin'* is an Exotic Primitive because he is very intelligent, does well in school and aspires to be a writer; Webster, the little boy on *Webster*, is a precocious Black child adopted by a white family and therefore a token Black in a white world, as is Diahann Carroll in *Dynasty* and *The Colbys*.)

The *Tragic Mulatto* is the Black who is constantly told she/he is neither Black nor white but a hybrid. Seeking her/his identity becomes the primary preoccupation. Currently the trend for the hybrid is to rejoice in being a hybrid and to function more comfortably in the white world as an exotic personality. (Jennifer Beales is the embodiment of the Tragic Mulatto or hybrid in any of her films – *Flashdance* (1983) being a good example.)

I supplement the Wadinasis' definitions with additional categories reflecting the current trend of racism in the media. The *Disembodied Fantasy* has generally replaced the Tragic Mulatto, producing another hybrid. This hybrid is not necessarily a biological mulatto. It includes Blacks who are adopted by white families or communities – such as in the American TV shows *Gimme a Break, Webster, Different Strokes*. Nell, the singing live-in maid of *Gimme a Break*, has evolved from 'faithful servant' to member of a white family, affectionately called Aunt Nell by the children. In both *Webster* and *Different Strokes*, white families adopt Black children. These characters then become mulattos through relationship. They become part of white families with no serious connection to the Black world, thus leading to both the disembodiment and the fantasy. The fantasy is the image promoted on American national television, while the reality is that the United States remains an institutionally racist society. New generations reflect this. In December 1986 white youths in Howard Beach, New York, attacked three young Black men because they 'intruded' into their (white) community. This resulted in the death of one of the Black men. In January 1987, in all-white Forsyth County, Georgia, Ku Klux Klan members and their supporters hurled rocks and bottles at participants in a civil rights march in honour of the anniversary of Martin Luther King's birthday.

Television, by constantly placing Blacks in unreal family situations within the white world, encourages Blacks not to direct anger at whites. On a weekly basis, viewers see white families raising and nurturing their Black wards. These programmes are fantasies in which the extended Black family, as well as the Black community, is non-existent. Viewers see Black children being raised in a non-oppressive environment. Black servants become beloved members of the family. This culture, unable to stand accountable for past and present racism, creates contemporary fantasies reminiscent of the American myth of benevolent slave masters who took better care of their slaves than they did of themselves.

Lastly, I add the stereotype of the *Lone Ranger,* as a contemporary manifestation of the Exotic Primitive. This is a Black character who supports the white leading character. This Black person once again has little or no connection with the Black community (Tubbs in *Miami Vice,* Hawk in *Spenser: For Hire*).

Besides the stereotypical images of Black people in television situation comedies and dramas, there are the patronizing and often blatantly racist characterizations of real Blacks in documentaries such as *The Vanishing Family: Crisis in Black America,* made by Bill Moyers and shown on the CBS network in 1986: it also won the 1986 Golden Baton Award, described as broadcast journalism's highest accolade. This documentary voices concern about single Black mothers, focusing on teenagers receiving welfare. The documentary implies that these single mothers do not constitute a real family (hence the programme's title with its unstated implication that the family in the process of vanishing is nuclear); that the young fathers are irresponsible and immoral; and that the young mothers, by having children outside of marriage coupled with receiving welfare payments, displayed traits such as promiscuity, laziness, and so on.

I found several major problems with this documentary. In the first place, the single parent family is also rising in the white community. Young white women are having babies outside of marriage more frequently, and the high divorce rate in the United States makes single-headed households increasingly commonplace. White women and children (as well as white men) live in poverty and receive welfare. So why not deal with the 'Vanishing Family, Crisis in White America'? I would question Mr Moyer's motives for making his documentary on Blacks without delving into the factors in American society which have ensured the destruction he describes. For at the beginning of American history is the kidnapping and enslavement of Africans: children were sold away from their mothers and Black people were bred like animals in order to produce more slaves. Black men were taught to be studs for the slave-master and Black women to bear future slaves as well as to submit sexually to white men.

Moyers's ahistorical approach to the subject conveniently omits all of this data. Rather, the introduction makes clear the programme's intention specifically *not* to deal with racism, or to take any sort of historical perspective whatsoever. A Black spokeswoman (identified only at the programme's end as Caroline Wallace, head of a community organization) says, 'It's not racism, it's lack of motivation. I'm not even talking about racism.... We're destroying ourselves.' She is followed by Moyers himself who informs us, 'But for the majority of white children family still means a mother and a father. This is not true for most Black children. For them things are getting worse. Today Black teenagers have the highest pregnancy rate in the industrial world, and in the Black inner-city practically no Black teenager gets married. This is not a racist comment. What's happening goes far beyond race.'

The introduction, then, serves not only to sidestep the issues of race and history, but sets up a structure in which Blacks, as individuals, can be blamed for their own problems, rather than addressing those problems in the context of an oppressive society. The documentary's tactic is to 'blame the victim'. Moreover, it does so by presenting 'Black agents' such as Caroline Wallace to spout racist viewpoints. (This tactic is used often in the media. The oppressive institution uses a member of the oppressed group as its spokesperson. Another example was Reagan's selection of a Black ambassador to South Africa to represent a national policy of support for apartheid.)

Later in the programme Moyers tells us, 'You won't find in these neighbourhoods the prime-time family of Bill Cosby. There are success-ful, strong Black families in America, families with parental authority and the values of work, discipline and achievement. But you won't find many around here [the inner-city ghetto].'

The Black community protested against the documentary, saying it was out of perspective because of its ahistorical approach to our problems and its dismissal of racism as a root cause of our condition. As a result there was a round-table discussion following the broadcast in which members of the Black community attempted to put the issues into their proper context. However, this proved to be much less powerful than the programme itself: a half-hour of talking heads could not compete with the images and attitudes reflected in a full-length docu-mentary.

Most of the criticism of the show during the round-table discussion dealt with the negative presentation of young Black males, but the documentary was equally abusive of Black females. One young mother referred to herself as 'lazy' because she was on welfare. This woman was a single parent, rearing several children. The fact that she saw herself as 'lazy' and that viewers could accept this as such is indicative of a society that places little value on child-rearing and home-making and, once again, has the victim blaming herself.

Black people are also present on television commercials and as news personalities, but our presence here is equally problematic. For instance, we could pose the following questions: Why do Blacks on news programmes sound exactly like white people? Why have they altered their appearance to look as white as possible? The answer is that Blacks have come to understand that in order to get a job you must talk as 'white' as possible. You must alter your physical appearance. The degree of respect, credibility and employment you get depends on how well you conform to the white status quo.

Referring back to the Wadinasi's popular stereotypes, Blacks in commercials and on news programmes may be perceived as Exotic Primitives, blacks with 'white' talents. They are non-threatening to the white community while providing assimilationist role models to the Black community. They have successfully conformed, in the eyes of a white culture.

In a further development of their analysis of media representation of Blacks, Sedeka and Alhamisi Wadinasi find there are a series of well-defined stages through which Blacks pass in order to develop a healthy and positive self-image within a racist society.[7] As a result of this process, a Black person comes to define him or herself as a Black, adequate and non-inferior person. The stages have been designated as follows: (a) *Pre-encounter,* in which Blacks are programmed to view and think of the world as being non-Black, anti-Black, or the opposite of Black, and that behaviour and basic attitudes toward self are determined by 'white' logic; (b) *Encounter,* during which Blacks begin to feel that they are somebody, and develop a Black perspective on life; (c) *Immersion,* in which everything of value must be relevant to Blackness; (d) *Internalization,* when, finally, Blacks develop a secure self-concept and Black perspective, work for Black community control and identify with all oppressed peoples.

The Wadinasis conclude that Black situation comedies almost invariably cast Blacks in a state of constant confused identity, and of latent self-hatred, with the result being that characters never advance beyond the Pre-encounter stage. They analyse James Evans, the husband and father on the series *Good Times,* as an example of a character in the Pre-encounter stage.

He, too, felt inadequate because of his lack of education, which, he claimed, precluded his competition for better jobs, and prevents him from 'escaping' the ghetto. In short, the Pre-encounter stage constituted the parameter of his philosophy, and epitomized his understanding and acceptance of the vicious cycle syndrome. To be sure, he possessed feelings of inferiority, humility, or submission, in which his life was bombarded with negative emotional states about his self-concept. Too often, he felt inadequate, anxious and self-depreciated.[8]

Michael Evans, the youngest son on the same series, is one of the few Black situation comedy characters who reaches the Encounter stage in the Wadinasi's analysis. But, by reaching this stage he becomes a Brute Negro. 'He is ridiculed because of his urgent desire to learn about and to glorify his heritage, which his relatives are obviously ashamed of.'[9]

Limited media images result in presenting television and movie audiences with restricted definitions of, and possibilities for, Blacks. In general, we are not presented as developing spiritually, emotionally or intellectually beyond the pre-encounter stage as defined by the Wadinasis.

These limitations of the Black image continue to thrive simply because racism is alive and well in the United States in this decade. Joel Kovel in his book, *White Racism – a Psychohistory*, states:

> The general direction of American reform has been to paint over an old symptom with a newer one in order to protect the underlying disease. Thus did slavery yield to late 19th century racism ... now in modern times, racial distinctions themselves are anachronistic, and culture must choose a different structure to preserve its inner plague.... Metaracism is a distinct and very peculiar modern phenomena [*sic*]. Racial degradation continues on a different plane and through a different agency; those who participate in it are not racists – that is, they are not racially prejudiced – but metaracists, because they acquiesce in the larger cultural order which continues the work of racism.[10]

The concerns and directions of feminism and progressive politics prove to be limited because they too often exclude the implications of racism with regard to sex and class. As long as both feminism and progressive politics do not deal with the totality of oppression, they too conform to institutional racism. For feminists in particular, this is evident in scholarly works, creative works and all forms of struggle which impose white women's historical, cultural and societal experiences and definitions on women of colour. Many feminist historians and editors have omitted the contributions of Black women to world culture in the same way that white male historians have omitted Black people's contributions in their works. Dr Bell Hooks gives us insight into the historical reality of this problem in the women's movement in her book, *Ain't I a Woman: Black Women and Feminism*:

When the women's movement began in the late 1960s, it was evident that the white women who dominate the movement felt it was 'their' movement, that is the medium through which a white woman would voice her grievance to society.... Their racism did not assume the overt expressions of hatred; it was far more subtle. It took the form of simply ignoring the existence of black women or writing about them using common sexist and racist stereotypes. From Betty Friedan's *The Feminine Mystique* to Barbara Berg's *The Remembered Gate* and on to more recent publications like *Capitalist Patriarchy and the Case for Socialist Feminism*, edited by Zillah Eisenstein, most white female writers who considered themselves feminist revealed in their writing that they had been socialized to accept and perpetuate racist ideology.[11]

Thus feminism must address the fact that many Black women see feminism as a 'white woman's movement', not at all separate from the rest of white society. Even in media representations white women seem to have fared better than either Black men or Black women. One increasingly sees white women portrayed as lawyers, doctors, builders of corporate empires, and even President of the United States, both in situation comedies and in television drama series.

White feminists' insistence that Black women condemn Black men is seen by many of us as a tactic once again to divide and conquer us as a people. The poet Lucille Clifton captures the distrust many Black women feel towards white feminists in her poem, 'To Ms Ann':

> i will have to forget
> your face
> when you watched me breaking
> in the fields,
> missing my children
>
> i will have to forget
> your face
> when you watched me carry
> your husband's
> stagnant water.
>
> i will have to forget
> your face
> when you handed me
> your house
> to make a home,
>
> and you never called me sister
> then, you never called me sister

and it has only been forever and
i will have to forget your face.[12]

Yes, Black women must express their oppression at the hands of Black men, but what about the historical oppression of Black women and men, at the hands of white women? Dr Hooks argues that 'even though white men institutionalized slavery, white women were its most immediate beneficiaries. Slavery in no way altered the hierarchical social status of the white male but it created a new status for the white female.' Black female slaves now did the housework, cooking, served as wet nurses to white children at the expense of her own, as well as providing child-care. Black women also worked in the fields beside Black male slaves and were used as breeders to produce more slaves. Dr Hooks maintains that,

> the only way her [the white woman's] new status could be maintained was through the constant assertion of her superiority over the black woman and man. All too often colonial white women, particularily those who were slave mistresses, chose to differentiate their status from the slave's by treating the slave in a brutal and cruel manner. It was in her relationship to the black female slave that the white woman could best assert her power.... Severe beatings were the method most white women used to punish Black female slaves.... Such treatment naturally caused hostility between white women and enslaved black women.[13]

Susan B. Anthony wrote to Frederick Douglass in 1869:

> The old antislavery school says that [white] women must stand back, that they must wait until male Negroes are voters. But we say, if you will not give the whole loaf of justice to an entire people, give it to the most intelligent first. If intelligence, justice and morality are to be placed in the government, then let the question of [white] women be brought up first and that of the Negro last.[14]

Alice Walker poetically captures the historical and contemporary reality of Black women in this society, as well as the dilemma of a limited feminism in her essay, *One Child of One's Own*:

> It took viewing 'The Dinner Party', a feminist statement in art by Judy Chicago, to illuminate – as art always will – the problem. In 1975 when her book, *Through the Flower* (Anchor), was published, I was astonished, after reading it, to realize she knew nothing of Black women painters. Not even that they exist. I was gratified therefore to learn that in 'The Dinner Party' there was a place 'set,' as it were, for Black women. The illumination came when I stood in front of it.
> All the other places are creatively imagined vaginas (even the one that looks

like a piano and the one that bears a striking resemblance to a head of lettuce: and of course the museum guide flutters about talking of 'Butterflies'!). The Sojourner Truth plate is the only one in the collection that shows – instead of a vagina – a face....

It occurred to me that perhaps white women feminists, no less than white women generally, cannot imagine Black women have vaginas. Or, if they can, where imagination leads them is too far to go....

Perhaps it is the Black woman's children, whom the white woman – having more to offer her own children, and certainly not having to offer them slavery or a slave heritage or poverty or hatred, generally speaking: segregated schools, slum neighborhoods, the worst of everything – resents. For they must always make her feel guilty. She fears knowing that Black women want the best for their children just as she does. But she also knows Black women are to have less in this world so that her children, white children, will have more (in some countries, all).[15]

For Black people – black men and black women – sexism and racism have always gone hand in hand. The two are inseparable. Western society has created a definition of manhood and then created a societal structure which excludes the vast majority of Black men in American society and in the world from realizing that definition. The Western world defines manhood as money and power based on knowledge and technology. He who has such power is the Man in the Western world and the world in general. This Man creates deities in his image and controls religion, as well as governments, institutions, natural and material resources, life and death. The Black man has no such power. He has historically been viewed as less than a man in the Western world and, as Alice Walker previously stated, Black women have been viewed as less than women. The sexism/racism connection has meant rape for Black women and it has meant lynchings and castration for Black men.

Thus, until feminists and other progressive whites consider the total picture, it remains possible to be feminist and racist. In a feminist art project dealing with heroines at the Women's Building in Los Angeles, a white woman chose the prehistoric 'Lucy' as her heroine. 'Lucy is a tiny lady three feet tall, sixty pounds light and 3.5 million years old. Lucy is the oldest, most complete skeleton of any erect walking human ancestor ever found.'[16] I pose the following questions: Why is it that the remains of a prehistoric Ethiopian woman are called 'Lucy'? Did it ever occur to the white world that Lucy is not an African name? The Ethiopians do not call her Lucy. We deal here with the issues of defining and renaming which I spoke of earlier. Something so simple is so important.

With regard to 'Lucy' we are talking about humanity's origins, but we are also talking about a Black woman. As we succumb to institutional racism, things are automatically whitewashed. The Public Broadcasting

System screened a documentary on the discovery of 'Lucy'. The audience was introduced to the anthropologists at the site in Africa. The programme included an animated segment which brought the ancient people to life. They were not Black people; the artist had whitened them. They did not look like the Ethiopians at the site; they looked like the white anthropologist.

As a Black woman film-maker I would have featured visuals of contemporary Ethiopian women as part of the documentary. I would have let Ethiopian men and women talk about 'Lucy'. Most importantly, I would not have called her, as did the documentary, by the name that the Western anthropologist, Donald Johanson, gave her from a pop song out of his culture: 'Lucy in the Sky with Diamonds' by the Beatles. I would have mentioned this, but I would have called her what her Ethiopian children call her: 'Wonderful'.

As Black women film-makers, I and my sisters come with a different vision. Perhaps in the future we will retell this African woman's story. We have many, many stories to retell. We have the seemingly never-ending task of countering the negative images, the subliminally racist images that continue to flow from the commercial industry. Our films are often called feminist, because we deal with issues important to women. The Black women film-makers that I speak of make films about incest, male–female relationships, and other subjects considered women's issues. We strive to tackle these sensitive issues with an historical approach. We strive to present the total picture in an effort to heal and unite our community.

We are part of an international movement. Within this movement are film critics and film historians, as well as film archives, film societies, festivals, symposiums and exhibitions. Every film genre is represented – documentary, dramatic feature, comedy, short, animation and experimental.

Our films were first seen in Europe. They are now shown on a limited basis throughout the world. By limited I mean they are seen primarily at film festivals, on university campuses, at cultural centres and at museums. Yet the audience is varied, consisting of film buffs, college students, intellectuals, young people, old people, Black and white.

I have often heard it said that our films are not 'universal'. The terminology is very important, because in a racist system universal has come to mean 'white', commercially viable, and therefore what one strives to achieve. Anything else is defined as limited and for this reason undesirable. The fact that our audiences are composed of a wide range of people disproves notions of 'universal' and 'commercial'.

As we travel with our work and interact with audiences, our presence also destroys stereotypes. Audiences are shocked, amazed and pleasantly surprised to learn that young Black women and men are producers and directors. Suddenly, new and exciting possibilities are open to them. They discover that you do not have to be white, male, middle-aged or rich to make films. Our presence gives them hope and empowerment because they realize that if we can do it, so can they.

As more and more Black women enter the field of film-making, many do so with a commitment to deal with the totality of our Black female experience. Because of the limitations of 'feminism' many of them shun this label. For instance, independent film-maker Kathleen Collins (*The Cruz brothers and Mrs Malloy* (1980), *Losing Ground* (1982)) sees 'black women filmmakers as part of a larger redemptive process that black women have to achieve'. She says,

> The only residual softness that's possible in this culture, as far as I am concerned, is in the hands of black women.... They must have the capacity to forgive black men. White women don't necessarily have to forgive white men, because white men had real power. So whatever power they exercised, they have exercised it out of an intense and godawful, nightmarish relationship to the culture.
>
> We absolutely must forgive them. It is the only possibility of love left in this culture. The stronger person is only as strong as his or her capacity to forgive the weaker person. And to separate oneself from black men is to allow America the final triumph of division. If they can actually succeed in dividing black men and women, then there is no emotional victory left in this culture.[17]

Film-maker Ayoka Chenzira, whose works include *Secret Sounds Screaming: The Sexual Abuse of Children* (1986), *Syvilla: They Dance to her Drum* (1979) and *Hairpiece – a Film for Nappy Headed People* (1982), also stresses the issue of forgiveness in her films and videos. In an interview about her work on the sexual abuse of children, Chenzira says:

> We live in a society where living is very difficult for a lot of people and par-ticularly difficult for people of color. Anger gets expressed in a number of ways. The first thing we need to do is recognize the problems, then find solutions. Part of finding solutions is educating everybody in the process. And you don't educate people by making them feel bad about themselves.
>
> The women and men in the sex-abuse piece had been made to feel bad about themselves. So it would almost defeat my purpose to attack men to make them feel bad about themselves. That's not going to stop them from raping women. I think women who feel empowered have the responsibility to share that with everybody. That means men, older people, and children. And if you don't share this empowerment, you continue to set up this vicious cycle of hateful relationships.[18]

Illusions (1982), a dramatic film by Julie Dash, is a testament to the essence of Black women who were exploited in Hollywood films but never acknowledged. Millions of people looking at the glamorous blondes and brunettes singing and dancing in Hollywood musicals never imagined that these women were often lip-synching to the voices of Black women. Through the words of her character, Esther Jeter, Dash speaks for those women who 'closed their eyes and imagined that they were up on that screen singing their songs'.

In *Illusions*, Dash redefines the role of the 'mulatto'. The Tragic Mulatto is not tragic anymore. Mignon Dupree is a film producer. Mignon is very light and passing as white in Hollywood. It is the only way to get work in Hollywood where she breaks ground as a white female producer but would be totally barred from such a position as a Black person. Mignon Dupree is no victim but a proud Black person who passes not out of shame but to help her people. Mignon has evolved beyond the Pre-encounter stage which traps most Black characters in Hollywood films and television series. She may be classified as a character in the Internalization stage. In this stage, 'Blacks develop a secure Black self-concept and Black perspective, work for Black community control, and identify with all oppressed peoples.'[19]

Kathleen Collins's *Losing Ground* is a humorous look at a Black woman intellectual's quest for a more complete sense of identity. She is a philosophy professor, her husband a free-spirited artist. Collins expands American society's definitions of Black womanhood because Black women are not thought of as intellectuals married to artists. The film challenges the assumption that these activities and lifestyles are solely white, middle-class aspirations. The professor has a young Black male student in one of her classes, who is majoring in film. He convinces the professor to be in his film, an enactment of the song, 'Frankie and Johnny'. Through his film-making within the film, Collins mirrors the marital conflict the professor is experiencing with her husband, while also poking fun at the Tragic Mulatto stereotype.

Collins's expansion of the roles of Black women in American society has met with some resistance. When Dr Phyliss Klotman, Director of Indiana University's Black Film Center Archives, screened *Losing Ground* before a European audience, the audience rejected it saying it was not real, that Black Americans lived in ghettos. They could not imagine a Black woman as a philosophy professor. According to racist stereotypes and notions, such a career is the domain of the white and middle class, and Black film-makers who create Black characters with these goals, dreams or aspirations are imitating 'white middle-class values'. Again, our reality as a people is very narrowly defined when the pursuit of higher education, appreciation of fine arts and hard work are considered to be foreign to the Black experience.

Black women film-makers continuously face audiences and critics who challenge our definitions of ourselves because the stereotyped images continue to flow through movie screens and television sets, both in the United States and elsewhere. Audiences throughout the world strongly believe in the stereotypes they so frequently view.

My narrative film, *A Different Image* (1982), dramatizes the implications of sexism on a young Black woman and a young Black man. *A Different Image* offers a new perspective on sexism, reflecting how Black men are also victims of Western sexism. The friendship between the two main characters, Alana and Vincent, is eventually destroyed when sexism serves as a destructive force on their relationship (Fig. 14). Alana is never 'really' seen as a person in her own right by the men in the film, because Western society dictates that men view women as sex objects. The film shows three generations of Black men relating to Alana in this way. It also presents the male side of the conflict as Vincent is pressured to see his female friend as a sex object. Peer pressure insists that he is not a 'man' unless he behaves in a sexist way. Although most responses to *A Different Image* have been favourable, some negative criticism has come from 'radical' feminists and Marxists. Criticism has revolved around the following issues: their definitions of sexism versus my own – it would be their demand that I condemn Black men and align myself with white women against the patriarchy. Other feminists have problems with female adornment, clothing and body language in the film. My character, though modestly dressed within the Western world, wore bright colours, bangles, make-up and was very sensual (Fig. 15): I assume my critics would have preferred a more androgynous look. Some viewers did not approve of the friendship between the young woman and the young man; or of the film's point of view, which vacillated between the effect of sexism on the young man and its effect on the young woman. Finally, a few white progressives believed that my Pan-Africanism is a naive and incorrect solution for the problems of Black people.

I believe such criticism often comes from the limited frame of reference previously discussed. Such criticism may stem from a lack of awareness of the history, traditions and culture of Black people. We need and have critics who can analyse our work on a comprehensive level: visually, historically, politically and culturally.

One such critic, Clyde Taylor, speaks of Black women film-makers and their contribution to the field:

> The black women directors who emerged at UCLA in the late 1970s extended the aesthetic tendencies of the movement, grounding perceptions of black

culture in African sources, exploring vehicles of symbol, icon, and ritual beyond normative practice, and explicating concerns for social justice. Their particular contribution came in presenting self-defining black women on the screen, an effort that represents a more drastic departure in cinema history than comparable portraits of black male figures. What is remarkable and remarkably fresh about the films of Julie Dash, Alile Sharon Larkin, and Barbara McCullough is their portrayal for nearly the first time of black women with an existence for themselves.[20]

Our problems are vast. We have the skills, talent and energy to create films and video in our own voice. What we lack is cash and access. We lack access to movie houses, public broadcasting stations, cable stations and major funding sources. We are told films must be feature length, colour and 35 millimetre; yet independently produced films meeting these criteria are still excluded from distribution venues. Public broadcasting stations show a variety of British programmes while Black American independent film is virtually non-existent on these stations. Major funding agencies not only practice tokenism when it comes to funding us, but refuse to consider projects that do not put whites in a positive light.

Black women film-makers bring forth new dimensions in dealing with the issues of sexism, because they deal with the totality of our experience. This is feminism in our own voice. In order to understand our voice, white feminists must move beyond the 'blindness' described by Alice Walker; they must see us as women who give birth to sons as well as daughters; women who have fathers, brothers, husbands, lovers and friends crushed and devastated by the racism/sexism connection. Our stance at this point is a very idealistic one. Film-maker Kathleen Collins is correct: it requires much strength. To repeat, we are not saying we excuse men who rape, murder and abuse women and children from responsibility or punishment for their crimes. And yet, in Collins's words: 'we must not allow America that final triumph of division'.

As independent Black women film-makers, we actively create new definitions of ourselves within every genre, redefining damaging stereotypes. As we examine the films of Black women we find rooted and aware characters who live in the real world. We create with the understanding that our humanity is not a given in this society. A primary struggle in our work is to recapture our humanity.

And so it is a vicious circle. We hope that with our films we can help create a new world, by speaking in our own voice and defining ourselves. We hope to do this, one film at a time, one screening at a time, to change minds, widen perspectives and destroy the fear of difference.

CHRISTINE GLEDHILL job-shares the post of Editor, Study Materials, in BFI Education, is a freelance writer, lecturer and mother of two sons. She has contributed to *Women in Film Noir, Re-vision: Essays in Feminist Film Criticism* and has edited *Home Is Where the Heart Is: Studies in Melodrama and the Woman's Film*. She has taught in the United States at the University of California at Los Angeles and Temple University.

E. ANN KAPLAN is Director of the Humanities Institute at the State University of New York at Stony Brook. Her books on feminist and psychoanalytic theory and popular culture inside *Women and Film: Both Sides of the Camera* and *Rocking Around the Clock: Music Television, Postmodernism and Consumer Culture*. She is currently working on *Motherhood and Representation: 1830–1960*.

ALILE SHARON LARKIN is an independent film- and video-maker whose work includes *Your Children Come Back to You, A Different Image* and *Miss Fluci Moses*. She lives in Los Angeles and travels throughout the United States giving workshops on the work and experiences of Black women film-makers.

E. DEIDRE PRIBRAM (Editor) is an independent film- and video-maker based in Philadelphia. Her work includes *Axis 1 Diagnosis, Just The Facts Ma'am, Single Parent Families* and *Aladar*.

LINDA WILLIAMS is an Associate Professor of English at the University of Illinois at Chicago where she teaches film and literature. Her publications include *Figures of Desire: A Theory and Analysis of Surrealist Film* and the co-edited volume *Re-Vision: Essays in Feminist Film Criticism*. She is currently completing a book on film pornography entitled *Hard Core: Power, Pleasure and the Frenzy of the Visible*.